D1614614

CASE STUDIES IN
Emotion-Focused Treatment of Depression

A COMPARISON OF GOOD AND POOR OUTCOME

JEANNE C. WATSON

RHONDA N. GOLDMAN

LESLIE S. GREENBERG

AMERICAN PSYCHOLOGICAL ASSOCIATION
WASHINGTON, DC

Published by
American Psychological Association
750 First Street, NE
Washington, DC 20002
www.apa.org

To order
APA Order Department
P.O. Box 92984
Washington, DC 20090-2984
Tel: (800) 374-2721; Direct: (202) 336-5510
Fax: (202) 336-5502; TDD/TTY: (202) 336-6123
Online: www.apa.org/books/
E-mail: order@apa.org

In the U.K., Europe, Africa, and the Middle East, copies may be ordered from
American Psychological Association
3 Henrietta Street
Covent Garden, London
WC2E 8LU England

Typeset in Goudy by Stephen McDougal, Mechanicsville, MD

Printer: United Book Press, Inc., Baltimore, MD
Cover Designer: Berg Design, Albany, NY
Technical/Production Editor: Devon Bourexis

The opinions and statements published are the responsibility of the authors, and such opinions and statements do not necessarily represent the policies of the American Psychological Association.

Library of Congress Cataloging-in-Publication Data

Watson, Jeanne C.
    Case studies in emotion-focused treatment of depression : a comparison of good and poor outcome / by Jeanne C. Watson, Rhonda N. Goldman, and Leslie S. Greenberg.
        p. cm.
    Includes bibliographical references and index.
    ISBN-13: 978-1-59147-929-1
    ISBN-10: 1-59147-929-0
    1. Depression, Mental—Treatment—Case studies. 2. Emotion-focused therapy—Case studies. I. Goldman, Rhonda N. II. Greenberg, Leslie S. III. American Psychological Association. IV. Title.
    [DNLM: 1. Depressive Disorder—therapy—Case Reports. 2. Psychotherapy, Brief—methods—Case Reports. 3. Treatment Outcome—Case Reports. WM 171 W339c 2007]
    RC537.W288 2007
    616.85'2706—dc22   2006100457

British Library Cataloguing-in-Publication Data
A CIP record is available from the British Library.

Printed in the United States of America
First Edition

To our clients' courage, patience, and trust, in the hope that we may grow and develop as therapists.

CONTENTS

PREFACE

This collection of case studies was designed as a companion volume to an earlier book, *Emotion-Focused Therapy for Depression*, by Greenberg and Watson (2005). In the first book, the authors outlined the theory and practice of emotion-focused therapy (EFT) for the treatment of depression. The etiological factors that contribute to depression as well as the specific mechanisms of change were highlighted, and specific ways of treating depression using EFT interventions were presented. This book was designed to exemplify and highlight the application of the EFT treatment protocol to different clients to provide a fuller, richer overview of how a brief therapy for depression using emotion-focused techniques unfolds over the course of treatment.

This book draws from three different research studies that investigated whether a brief EFT treatment protocol (16–20 sessions) would be effective in treating depression as compared with client-centered and cognitive–behavioral treatments. The case studies in this book represent the culmination of a number of process and outcome studies over the past 15 years that have investigated such factors as the role of the working alliance, clients' emotional processing, therapeutic empathy, clients' and therapists' interpersonal processes, and clients' cognitive processing as well as the specific changes that clients make during the session that are related to positive therapeutic outcomes. By bringing some of this work together in one volume, we hope that the practice, theory, and research of EFT will be enriched, supported, and challenged to become even more effective for clients with depression.

We would like to acknowledge the numerous individuals who contributed to the successful completion of this work. First, we thank the staff at the American Psychological Association, especially Susan Reynolds, Linda McCarter, Ron Teeter, and Devon Bourexis for believing in the project and contributing their expertise to enhance the final product, as well as the many others along the way who helped to bring the work to completion. Second, we would like to express our gratitude to the clients and therapists who participated in the research studies and gave of themselves and their time to further the study of EFT. Finally, the support of our family and friends is invaluable as we continue to try to improve treatment outcomes.

I

INTRODUCTION

1

INTRODUCTION: OVERVIEW OF THE TREATMENT PROTOCOL

Research studies have shown that emotion-focused therapy for depression works as well or better in some ways than other empirically validated treatments (Elliott, Watson, Goldman, & Greenberg, 2003; Greenberg & Watson, 1998; Watson, Gordon, Stermac, Kalogerakos, & Steckley, 2003). Although emotion-focused therapy (EFT) is effective with many clients, some clients do not improve after a 16- to 20-week treatment. To improve the clinical practice, teaching, and understanding of the change factors in psychotherapy, psychologists need to understand the differences between those clients who are able to benefit from a short-term treatment and those who are not. The emphasis on randomized clinical trials to establish the efficacy of different treatments has impeded the search to understand which people benefit from different treatments, the times when treatment would be most useful for different clients, and the identification of other moderating variables that affect treatment outcome. Because of their overall effectiveness, it is often assumed that brief treatments can be applied universally without a comprehensive understanding of which clients might benefit from short-term interventions and which would not.

3

Psychotherapy is a private exchange that occurs behind closed doors. One can learn about it thirdhand through the lenses of either therapists or clients or more personally and experientially as one of the participants. Theoretical writings and manuals provide a framework and a guide to therapists on how to conduct therapy, but they do not provide an adequate sense of the process and structure of an entire course of therapy or how the procedures outlined in treatment manuals are customized to fit specific clients. Since Freud (1901/1977), research clinicians have tried to illuminate the opaque nature of the therapeutic exchange by providing case histories of specific treatments (Stricker & Gold, 2006; Yalom, 1989). In this book we present six case histories of clients who completed a brief emotion-focused treatment for depression. The clients were drawn from three different randomized clinical trials that compared EFT, client-centered, and cognitive–behavioral therapy in the treatment of depression (Goldman, Greenberg, & Angus, 2005; Greenberg & Watson, 1998; Watson et al., 2003).

Our objectives in presenting the case histories were threefold. The first objective was to provide a more thorough overview of how different tasks and client objectives can be woven together for successful treatment outcomes to complement the earlier treatment manual, *Emotion-Focused Therapy for Depression,* by Greenberg and Watson (2005). Although the interventions used across different cases were similar, it can be useful to see how these were tailored to fit individual clients and to show how similar interventions and ways of conceptualizing clients' problems can be relevant to a variety of different client experiences and narratives. To this end we have highlighted the case formulations and ways of thinking about each client at the beginning of therapy and over the course of treatment. This is followed by an overview of the three treatment phases outlined by Greenberg and Watson (2005). The case history chapters end with a brief summation of the case and an overview of the client's outcome on a number of different postsession and treatment outcome measures. These measures provide the client's perspective on the therapeutic relationship and the types of changes the client has made over the course of therapy.

The second objective was not only to look at what happens when therapy is going well but to examine cases in which therapy is not successful to try to better understand the factors that inhibit the successful resolution of clients' presenting problems in short-term therapy. Many of the therapeutic interventions that are used in EFT have been modeled on successful events and cases using task analysis. Rice and Greenberg (1984) developed task analysis as a method for developing models of change events to better understand what steps clients and therapists need to perform to ensure the successful resolution of specific cognitive–affective tasks in therapy. Research clinicians identified moments or periods of time in therapy when clients seemed to resolve important issues or make significant shifts in perspective and subjected these moments to intense process and discourse analysis to describe the process of change to replicate it with other clients.

As a result of the earlier focus on successful cases, we do not have a clear understanding of what goes wrong or does not work for those people who do not successfully resolve either specific tasks or their depression in a brief treatment. In this book we wanted to shift some attention from good outcome cases to poor outcome cases to try to explicate the factors that contribute to poor outcome as compared with good outcome. It is important if we are to improve treatment outcomes that we develop ways of identifying when clients are having difficulty and develop ways of working with them to overcome these problems to try to ensure successful resolution of the problems that brought them into therapy.

The third objective, following from the second, was to identify client factors that might contribute to successful outcome in brief emotion-focused treatments for depression. It is clear that not all clients benefit from short-term treatments. To improve our clinical practice, teaching, and understanding of the change factors in psychotherapy, we need to try to understand the differences between those clients who are able to benefit from a short-term treatment of EFT and those who are not. By identifying client and treatment variables that contribute to good and poor outcome, we hope to contribute to an overall understanding of the theory and practice of EFT and to improve treatment outcomes and delivery for our clients.

EMOTION-FOCUSED THERAPY FOR DEPRESSION

The theory underlying EFT is that depression arises from problems in affect regulation and results from maladaptive, blocked, and unprocessed emotional experience (Greenberg, Elliott, & Foerster, 1990; Greenberg & Watson, 2005). In this view people are seen as active processors involved in constructing their own experience from their automatic reactions (Greenberg & Pascual-Leone, 1995, 2001; Watson & Greenberg, 1996). An important goal in EFT is to help clients access and process their emotions to change problematic emotion schemes and construct new meaning. Emotion schemes are defined as ways of organizing experience that encompass clients' perceptual, situational, bodily, symbolic, and motivational processes about themselves and their environments. In EFT, changes in clients' problematic emotion schemes, seen to be at the root of depression, occur through the deepening of clients' experiencing, which leads to more effective emotional processing. Emotion-focused interventions work to help clients become more aware of, tolerate, regulate, transform, and accept their feelings. One of the challenges for EFT psychotherapists is to help clients regulate their levels of emotional arousal and develop alternative ways of behaving that promote the experience of more positive emotions and the appropriate expression of feelings.

A number of important steps in the processing of emotional experience (Foa & Kozak, 1986; Greenberg & Paivio, 1997; Greenberg & Watson, 2005; Kennedy-Moore & Watson, 1999; Lane & Schwartz, 1992; Salovey, Hsee, & Mayer, 1993) have been identified, including the awareness of bodily sensations, the labeling of bodily sensations and affective experience, the accessing of new emotions, the reflection on affective experience, and the modulation of affect to promote appropriate emotional expression. This model of emotional processing sees these activities on a continuum beginning with awareness and concluding with considered, appropriate expression; however, these activities need not occur in a linear fashion. For example, emotional expression may occur prior to labeling or reflection and modulation. However, adequate modulation and regulation of emotion require that clients engage in becoming aware of their experiences and in labeling them to understand and clarify their emotional states to increase resilience and problem solving and to develop alternative ways of behaving.

One way that EFT therapists enhance clients' emotional processing is by providing clients with therapeutic relationships in which therapists are attuned to clients' emotional states to validate their affective experiences and bring them into conscious awareness using empathic responses. Awareness and the processing of bodily felt experience is a central focus of EFT in the treatment of depression. One premise of EFT is that clients need to spend time in an empathic relationship to become aware of, label, and understand their emotional experience before they can begin to modulate it. Clients are encouraged to become aware of, label, and explore their sensorimotor experience so that the unassimilated sensory and affective information can be verbalized and recoded in linguistic memory. As they process their experiences in this way, clients come to modulate them and learn new ways of regulating their experiences and of accessing new experiences. A number of research studies have found that deeper client experiencing and enhanced emotional processing are significantly related to good outcome in both the resolution of depression and trauma (Greenberg & Foerster, 1996; Greenberg & Malcolm, 2002; Paivio & Greenberg, 1995; Pos, Greenberg, Goldman, & Korman, 2003; Samilov & Goldfried, 2000; Watson & Bedard, 2006).

The Principles of Emotion-Focused Therapy

As outlined by Greenberg and Watson (2005) in their book *Emotion-Focused Therapy for Depression*, a manual for the treatment of depression, the two basic principles of EFT are establishing an empathic healing relationship and facilitating the resolution of tasks. Therapists who practice EFT use specific tasks to work with clients' emotional processing to facilitate changes in clients' emotion schemes, how they treat themselves, and how they interact with others.

Relationship Components

The development and maintenance of an empathic relationship has three foci, which include therapists' empathic moment-to-moment attunement; communication to clients of empathic understanding, acceptance, and genuineness; and facilitating collaboration on the tasks and goals of therapy. First, EFT therapists attend to clients' style of speech, vocal quality, body language, and emotional processing style to guide their moment-to-moment interventions. They are particularly attuned to clients' emotional experience and work to track and respond empathically to their clients' inner subjective experience. This requires that therapists be present and highly focused on their clients' experiences as they attend to the nuances of clients' narratives and integrate this with information from other nonverbal sources. A core assumption of therapy is that although therapists may develop tentative conceptualizations and formulations of clients' problems, these always take second place to clients' flow of experiencing, and therapists try to stay responsive to new and emergent experiences in their clients and shifts in clients' perspectives and understandings.

Second, therapists create a safe environment in which their clients feel genuinely accepted and understood as they track and follow or try to amplify their clients' emotional experiences. Communicating empathy, acceptance, and genuineness allows clients the freedom to explore their experience and confront their wounds, fears, anxieties, pain, and parts of their experience that they might view as shameful. It is not enough that therapists feel or think they understand their clients' experiences or what they are feeling, their understanding has to be communicated and received by the client to have therapeutic impact. The provision of a safe environment facilitates a number of important processes in EFT. First, it helps clients to feel bonded with their therapists and to believe that somebody is on their side, which provides hope and encouragement at times when clients may feel quite discouraged, hopeless, and demoralized. Second, feeling safe allows clients the freedom to focus intently on their own experiences to reflect on them deeply, to explore themselves and acquire self-knowledge, and to devise new ways of behaving. This type of concentration and focus is facilitated in a safe environment in which clients do not have to be concerned with being judged, criticized, or attacked by others.

The third important aspect of forging a therapeutic relationship is establishing agreement and collaboration on the tasks and goals of therapy. Initially therapists need to listen to clients' narratives to identify problematic aspects of clients' experiences. Together they need to come to a shared understanding of what clients are doing and experiencing that may be contributing to their depression. Often this requires a subtle reframing of clients' experiences to ensure a fit with therapists' conceptualizations and ways of working. For example, clients may need to agree that their habit of invalidating their feelings is contributing to their depression or that their criticisms and attacks on themselves lead to depressed moods. If clients are to benefit from EFT, it is important that they agree that talking about their feelings and their personal experiences can be productive. Clients need to feel that the ways in which their therapists are thinking about their problems and the suggestions they make to try to resolve their problems make sense and fit with clients' expected goals and outcomes.

Although establishing a productive therapeutic relationship is the primary concern early in therapy, it continues to be important throughout therapy as clients and therapists engage in the exploration and resolution of problematic issues and renegotiate their relationship when necessary. Therapists who practice EFT need to be extremely sensitive to signs of rupture, disagreement, or moments when their clients express perplexity and doubt so that they can intervene appropriately. At any signs of rupture it is important that EFT therapists acknowledge and attend to these events and talk about them with their clients in a way that is nonblaming and uncritical to try to resolve them and repair the alliance to further the goals of treatment.

Task Components

A number of tasks have been identified in EFT to resolve particular cognitive–affective problems that clients bring up over the course of therapy. These include *empty-chair* tasks for unfinished business, *two-chair* tasks to change critical and punishing ways of treating the self or to resolve ambivalence, *systematic evocative unfolding* to resolve reactions that clients find problematic, *focusing* to facilitate the representation and awareness of inner experience, and the *creation of meaning* to resolve disillusionment at challenges to cherished beliefs as well as a number of different types of empathic interventions (Elliott et al., 2003; Gendlin, 1996; Greenberg & Foerster, 1996; Leijssen, 1998; Rogers, 1965; Watson, 2006).

Empty-chair work is indicated when a client expresses or acknowledges negative feelings for a significant other, for example, unresolved anger, grief, or disappointment. The empty-chair task requires that clients imagine the significant other for whom they have these lingering bad feelings in an empty chair to evoke the feelings and perceptions that are associated with the other. Clients are then encouraged to express their feelings and resentments to the imagined other and to articulate their needs. The process facilitates the expression of unmet needs and helps clients define and differentiate from significant others. In this process of differentiation, clients often come to see the other in a new light by either feeling more compassion for the limitations of the other or getting sufficient distance so that the other no longer feels so powerful. In the latter case, clients are usually better able to hold the other accountable for any wrongdoing or neglect that they may have suffered as a result of contact with them.

Two-chair work is indicated when clients are experiencing conflict about different courses of action or when they criticize, blame, attack, and frighten themselves. The two-chair task requires clients to act out two different aspects of themselves: for example, to voice criticisms while sitting in one chair and then to move to the other chair to respond to the criticisms. In this way clients are encouraged to isolate their self-criticisms in one chair and to experience the impact of those criticisms in another chair. In a similar fashion, clients can act out the different sides of a conflict in two different chairs. The objective of isolating the criticisms in separate chairs is to make clients more aware of how they are treating themselves and how these behaviors may be contributing to their moods. Once the critical voice has been isolated and its impact acknowledged, clients are encouraged to develop alternative responses to counteract the criticisms and treat themselves with compassion, acceptance, care, and support.

Systematic evocative unfolding is indicated when clients are confused or puzzled by a reaction or response they had to a specific event or when therapists feel that clients want to get more in touch with their emotions or experience around specific events. The task of systematic evocative unfolding requires therapists and clients working together to build vivid, detailed images of specific situations or events to evoke clients' episodic memories with their attendant sights, sounds, and feelings. The objective is to bring a situation or memory sufficiently alive in a session so that clients can pinpoint moments when specific reactions occurred to identify the triggers for particular reactions, feelings, or behaviors. Once the triggers have been identified, therapists and clients are in a position to understand how clients may have construed certain events, for example, a person's tone of voice that the client experienced as intrusive or critical. Once clients have identified their construals, they are in a position to reflect on their construals to see whether they fit with the particular situations at hand or whether they need to be reprocessed so that clients are not ambushed by their reactions in similar situations in the future.

Focusing is indicated when clients do not have a clear sense of what is troubling them. The focusing task requires clients to clear a space to attend to their bodies and especially the parts of their bodies where they experience feelings; often this is the diaphragm, but it may be other parts of the body such as legs, feet, neck, or back. Clients are asked to attend to the sensations and feelings in their bodies and to try to allow words or images to form that might describe or represent the sensations or experiences in some way. As clients are able to become aware of and label their experiences, they are in a better position to identify their needs and wants and to understand how events and other people are impacting them. The capacity to focus and attend to inner experience is essential to the successful outcome of EFT.

Creation-of-meaning work is indicated when clients express disillusionment or distress that a cherished belief has been shattered. This is commonly experienced after a traumatic event when clients no longer see the world as safe or themselves as inviolable. The creation-of-meaning task requires therapists to empathically help clients to reprocess events so that they can identify their cherished beliefs and reflect on them in the light of the recent trauma. Together, clients and therapists work to reconstruct new worldviews that can integrate new realities with old perspectives.

In addition to these longer and more complicated tasks, EFT therapists have identified a number of different types of empathic responses that can be used at different times to facilitate different client processes. The empathic responses include empathic affirmation, empathic understanding, empathic exploration, empathic evocation, empathic conjecture, and empathic refocusing.

- *Empathic affirmation* is indicated when clients are expressing vulnerable and painful feelings. At these times EFT therapists endeavor to validate their clients' experiences and provide a supportive and soothing acknowledgment of the pain.
- *Empathic understanding* responses convey that therapists have a general overview of what their clients are sharing at any given moment.
- *Empathic exploration* responses are used to focus clients on their feelings, evaluations, or assumptions. They are tentative and probing responses to help clients unfold and examine the hidden corners of their experience.
- *Empathic evocation* is used to heighten or illuminate how clients are feeling about specific events at different points in time. Here EFT therapists use evocative language that is vivid, specific, and idiosyncratic to capture their clients' sense of what is happening inside.
- *Empathic conjecture* is used when therapists are trying to help clients differentiate and articulate their core experiencing or emotion schemes. Here EFT therapists tentatively offer ways of describing clients' inner states to help clients label their inner experiences and represent them in new ways.
- *Empathic refocusing* responses are used to highlight aspects of a situation or experience that clients may not have attended to previously while remaining within clients' frames of reference (Elliott et al., 2003; Greenberg, Rice, & Elliott, 1993; Greenberg & Watson, 2005; Watson, 2001).

These tasks are implemented at different times in therapy with clients' agreement and full participation to help them overcome the difficulties that they bring to therapy. Although all the tasks may be useful in the treatment of depression, we have observed that some tasks are more salient than others in helping clients overcome depression (Greenberg & Watson, 2005). Three foci have been identified as integral to the task component of EFT: facilitating clients' differential processing, growth and choice, and task completion (Elliott et al., 2003).

The first focus of the task component is on facilitating differential processes in clients during the session. There are two aspects to differential processing. One refers to the practice of facilitating different client processes at different times, for example, attending to various emotional states, actively expressing emotional experience, or reflecting on the meaning or nature of a reaction or behavior. The second aspect refers to the introduction of specific tasks to help clients resolve particular cognitive–affective problems such as unfinished business, conflict splits, or problematic reactions.

The second focus of the task component of EFT is on growth and choice. Therapists who practice EFT foster growth and choice in their clients. This is done by fostering self-determination and in-session decisions as clients focus on and become aware of their feelings and needs. Clients are encouraged to reflect on their needs and find ways of realizing them in their current life situations. Therapists also focus on their clients' strengths to help them change.

The third focus is task completion. Therapists who practice EFT try to facilitate resolution of the cognitive–affective difficulties that clients have brought into treatment. This requires that therapists balance in-the-moment responsiveness with active stimulation. Therapists have to continually monitor their clients' reactions to determine whether they require empathic validation and exploration around a particular issue or a more active collaborative stance to resolve unfinished business or to find a new way of treating themselves, for example, becoming less self-critical.

The Phases of Treatment

Greenberg and Watson (2005) have identified three different phases over the course of an emotion-focused treatment for depression. These include the *bonding and awareness* phase, the *evoking and exploring* phase, and the *transformation* phase. Although these three phases are presented sequentially, they recur over the course of treatment and feed into each other to form a recursive pattern. The other important component of providing brief EFT is *case formulation*. Prior to reviewing the three phases of treatment it is important to provide an overview of case formulation in EFT.

Case Formulation

Case formulation in EFT for depression is process oriented and tentative (Elliott et al., 2003; Greenberg & Watson, 2005). The primary objective is to help tailor the specific interventions to clients' presenting problems and issues. Therapists who practice EFT use case formulation to sensitize themselves to what is poignant and salient in clients' lives and relevant for exploration and to help them identify specific tasks during the session that fit with their clients' needs and objectives. Case formulation adjusts moment to moment as new information is revealed and clients' processing changes or deepens in the session. Therapists listen to clients' vocal quality, the quality of their emotional processing, and the content of clients' narratives to understand and focus on what is alive and immediate in clients' experiences during the session. As they attend to clients' narratives and descriptions of their presenting problems and concerns, EFT therapists attend to a number of different client markers including *markers of characteristic style, mode of engagement markers, task markers,* and *micromarkers*. These markers guide EFT therapists in their interventions and responses and help them remain responsive to their clients' goals and directions in the session.

Markers of characteristic style refer to those statements that clients make that indicate how they treat themselves and others. These statements inform therapists about whether their clients are self-critical and punishing of themselves and others or whether they are compassionate, accepting, protective, and nurturing of themselves. Through observation of clients' characteristic styles, EFT therapists begin to formulate a sense of clients' behaviors that might be contributing to their depression. For example, they may become aware that clients are highly self-critical or silence themselves and their needs, thereby making themselves feel depressed and hopeless. By identifying the characteristic ways that clients treat themselves, EFT therapists can begin to formulate which interventions and tasks might be particularly relevant to help alleviate their clients' depressions. These markers help therapists remain attuned and responsive to those client statements that indicate that clients are treating themselves negatively so that they can suggest relevant tasks such as two-chair work or empty-chair work at appropriate times in the session. Clients' early attachment histories and in-session narratives provide windows into their characteristic styles of being in the world and the dominant emotion schemes that they use to interpret, view, and act in the world.

Therapists who practice EFT attend to clients' modes of engagement markers to understand how they are processing their emotional experiences. Some clients can be swamped by their emotional experiences and feel overwhelmed and out of control, whereas others can be distant from their experiences and unable to process them actively in the session. Therapists listen to whether their clients are aware of their emotional experiences, and can label, modulate, reflect on, and express them in ways that are self-enhancing and promote the realization of their goals and objectives. The manner in which clients process their emotional experiences guides EFT therapists to intervene differentially, for example, being empathic when clients are trying to label their experiences or using more evocative interventions to bring clients' experiences into awareness.

The most important markers that EFT therapists use to guide their practice are task markers. These are client statements in the session that indicate that clients have particular cognitive–affective problems that require attention; for example, clients may be conflicted about engaging in treatment or about how to respond to a colleague at work. Alternatively, they may be focused on trying to process lingering bad feelings toward a significant other or trying to understand a puzzling reaction to a recent event. These client statements can guide EFT therapists to suggest tasks such as two-chair work or empty-chair work to help clients resolve specific issues. It is important that clients want to work on the particular tasks suggested to them by their therapists and that they see the tasks as relevant to their goals and objectives.

Moment to moment, EFT therapists listen to client micromarkers to help identify what is alive for clients at any particular moment in the session. Therapists listen and attend to verbal and nonverbal markers to have a sense of when clients are in touch with their emotional experiences, processing events or experiences in new ways, or distancing from their emotional experience. To do this, therapists attend to the poignancy of clients' narratives and the quality of clients' descriptions. They listen to the quality of their clients' language, specifically, whether it is idiosyncratic, specific, and vivid or whether it is abstract, intellectual, and without detail. In addition, they attend to the synchrony between themselves and their clients. They attend to whether their clients are receptive to their interventions; whether their interventions seem to fit with how clients are thinking about their problems; or whether there is hesitation, doubt, and a sense of disrupted flow during the sessions. Clients' vocal quality is also a good indicator of when clients are processing their experiences in new ways and are in touch with their emotional experiences or more distant and removed from them. Therapists gather this information as they engage in the different phases of treatment and reformulate and revise their formulations in the light of new information. Case formulation begins early in treatment and continues through the different phases to ensure a good fit between therapists' and clients' goals and objectives.

Bonding and Awareness

The bonding and awareness phase is the first stage of treatment, during which clients and therapists establish therapeutic relationships and begin to develop a focus for therapy. Therapists who practice EFT focus first on helping their clients to feel supported, accepted, and understood, and bonded with their therapists. As they begin to develop a therapeutic bond, EFT therapists attend to clients' emotional experience and work to make clients more aware of their emotional experience as they share the details of their lives and their reasons for coming into therapy. This initial stage of therapy is very important as clients begin to become more aware of how events affect them and their unique ways of responding.

As therapists begin to develop a sense of clients' responses to events and an awareness of clients' major life events and ways of coping, therapists can often begin to see why clients respond as they do to specific events. This insight allows therapists to identify clients' problematic emotion schemes and begin tailoring their treatments for each client so that the interventions are relevant and meaningful. For example, a therapist might observe that a client is quite harsh with him- or herself, expecting him- or herself to assume total responsibility for his or her own and others' well-being. Listening to the client's life story, the therapist may learn that the client's parents were alcoholics and emotionally unavailable, so at a young age the client developed the expectation that he or she was responsible for him- or herself and his or her siblings and carried this expectation over into other areas of adult life. At the same time, the therapist may be aware that the client learned to invalidate his or her feelings so that he or she is tuned out of his or her moment-to-moment experiencing, trying to push on regardless of the cost to him- or herself. As therapists and clients become aware of the salient and significant events in clients' lives they can turn their attention to evoking and exploring their clients' experiences in the session. The goal is to access the client's core emotion scheme in order to help the client process and transform it by generating new adaptive emotions and creating new meaning.

Evoking and Exploring

During the evoking and exploring phase, therapists try to promote clients' experiencing in the session. Therapists who practice EFT help clients explore their experiences to evoke their emotional reactions to events so that these can be processed in conscious awareness. Clients are encouraged to experience their emotions and become aware of their bodily sense of events, which they may have disowned or denied previously. As clients explore and become aware of their emotional experiences during the sessions, they are able to articulate and identify the emotion schemes that underlie their reactions and ways of being in the world. Often maladaptive emotion schemes based on fear and shame are accessed. These are then transformed by accessing other, more adaptive emotions and by examining and reflecting on experience to potentiate changes in clients' behavior. To evoke clients' experiences, EFT therapists listen for moment-to-moment markers to help them identify live moments in clients' experiencing during sessions that may need to be processed. In addition, they attend to specific task markers to help identify particular cognitive–affective tasks that may be problematic for clients. Therapists attend to clients' expressions of problematic reactions, expressions of intense emotion, self-critical comments, or exchanges with significant others that leave clients with negative feelings. It is important to help clients become aware of their emotional experience so that they can explore and symbolize it in words and have the opportunity to understand their experience in new ways. This process illuminates clients' core maladaptive emotion schemes and can help generate new ways of feeling that can transform more maladaptive emotions. Once clients begin to understand their needs, they can begin to work out new ways of behaving to satisfy their needs and goals.

Transformation

The final phase, transformation, is concerned with constructing alternative ways of responding and constructing new meaning. Here EFT therapists help clients develop new ways of viewing their experiences and focus on constructing new ways of treating themselves and of being with others. Once clients have processed their emotional experience, have come to see its import, and have identified the triggers for their reactions and their characteristic ways of responding, they are able to develop alternative responses. Therapists help clients develop alternative ways of responding to others and of treating themselves; for example, therapists may encourage their clients to access self-protective anger, be more self-assertive, grieve for past losses, or develop self-soothing behaviors, or they may help their clients to express their feelings and needs to others in ways that can be heard and responded to positively. During this final phase, clients have the opportunity to access new adaptive emotional experiences that transform old maladaptive ways of responding and reflect on their experiences so they can come to see them in new ways. They are often able to construct new meaning so that they interpret the behavior of others in a new light. They may realize that a parent was indeed benevolent and loved them despite being unavailable, or they may realize that a cruel, attacking parent is weak and vulnerable and feel more empowered in their dealings with that person.

THE CASE STUDIES

Our objective in the following chapters is to analyze three good outcome cases and three poor outcome cases to illustrate the process and structure of an emotionally focused treatment for depression. We selected the cases from two different randomized clinical trials in the treatment of depression using EFT and analyzed the cases from a variety of different perspectives to try to illuminate the underlying processes specific to each.[1] We used a number of different process measures to help illuminate clients' and therapists' interactions. These include the Experiencing Scale (Klein, Mathieu, Gendlin, & Kiesler, 1969), Levels of Client Perceptual Processing (Toukmanian, 1986), and the Structural Analysis of Social Behavior (Benjamin, 1974). In addition, we used self-report measures including the Working Alliance Inventory (Horvath & Greenberg, 1989), the Client Task Specific Change Measure—Revised (Watson, Greenberg, Rice, & Gordon, 1996), the Beck Depression Inventory (Beck, Ward, Mendelson, Mock, & Erbaugh, 1961), the Rosenberg Self-Esteem Inventory (Rosenberg, 1965), the Inventory of Interpersonal Problems (Horowitz, Rosenberg, Baer, Ureno, &

---

[1] All client identifying information was changed to protect confidentiality.

Villasenor, 1988), the Symptom Checklist—90—Revised (*SCL–90–R*; Derogatis, 1983), and the Dysfunctional Attitudes Scale (Weissman & Beck, 1978). We describe each of these briefly next.

Process Measures

Process measures are used by third-party raters to identify different client processes over the course of treatment using transcripts of therapy sessions or videotaped recordings. Four process measures were used in the case histories that follow to identify the ways in which clients were processing their experiences emotionally and cognitively, interacting with their therapists, and treating themselves. These observations help to explicate the therapeutic process and provide markers of shifts in the ways in which clients process information, undergo emotional experiences, and treat themselves and others. As such, they add weight to therapists' observations and clients' self-report measures of outcome and define the types of changes that clients make during the course of therapy.

The Experiencing Scale

The Experiencing Scale (Klein et al., 1969) describes the quality of clients' emotional processing during the therapy hour. The scale consists of seven stages that identify the extent to which clients are processing their emotional experience from *not at all* at the low end of the scale to processing it *in greater depth* at the higher end. The scale evaluates the extent to which clients explore and integrate their inner experiences to achieve self-understanding and problem resolution (Pos et al., 2003; Watson & Bedard, 2006; Watson & Greenberg, 1996). The stages of the scale are as follows:

- At Stage 1 clients discuss events, ideas, and interactions with no reference to their own feelings.
- At Stage 2 clients refer to others and make reference to the self without expressing emotions.
- At Stage 3 clients begin to pepper their narratives with some reference to how they are feeling or reacting.
- At Stage 4 clients have shifted from an external frame of reference to an internal one; they are revealing their own subjective worldviews with their feelings, perceptions, and experiences clearly expressed.
- At Stage 5 clients have begun to examine and explore in a purposeful way their experiences and reflect on their emotional reactions and behavior to try to understand them better.
- At Stage 6 clients have come to new perspectives about themselves or how they feel about themselves. This stage is charac-

terized by a shift that indicates that clients are able to reframe their problems or to see themselves or others in new ways.

- At Stage 7 clients continually refer to their inner worlds and experiences to process events. This stage reveals an ongoing process of in-depth self-understanding that provides new perspectives for solving significant problems (Klein et al., 1969).

The Experiencing Scale is a useful guide to how aware clients are of their emotional experience and an indicator of whether they are working productively in experiential therapy. It is also an indicator of when clients have resolved problems or shifted their understandings so that they are looking at their experiences in new ways. Although shifts can be indicators of dramatic change, sometimes they are also indicators of different ways of conceptualizing a problem, for example, when clients shift from viewing themselves as victims of their moods to seeing that it is their self-critical behavior that may be contributing to their feelings of depression and become committed to changing this way of treating themselves.

Levels of Client Perceptual Processing

The Levels of Client Perceptual Processing (LCPP; Toukmanian, 1986) is used to categorize different patterns of clients' cognitive processing in psychotherapy in terms of the diversity of information that clients attend to and the kinds of mental operations they use to process information. The LCPP is useful to understand whether clients are analyzing their experiences, differentiating their internal feelings and subjective awareness, and using rules and external standards to judge their behavior or acquiring new perspectives that shift their understanding of themselves and others and integrating this information in new ways.

The measure consists of seven mutually exclusive levels, including undifferentiated statements, elaboration, externally focused differentiation, analytic differentiation, internally focused differentiation, reevaluation, and integration, described as follows:

- Level 1 refers to undifferentiated statements that convey a packaged, condensed view of events. They have a glib, pat quality that lacks a sense of reflection or analysis.
- Level 2 elaborations describe those utterances that are descriptive and add information; however, they are tight, unreflective descriptions of events.
- Level 3 identifies differentiation with an external focus and refers to those observations that are made using an external frame of reference. The client uses external rules and standards to make sense of his or her experience.

- Level 4 identifies analytic differentiation or those statements that are objective and intellectual. The clients' statements reflect the ability to make distinctions, but these are made using systematic logic instead of from an internal perspective.
- Level 5 refers to differentiation with an internal focus and describes statements that are made form an internal perspective. They are uniquely personal and convey the speaker's idiosyncratic view of events.
- Level 6 comprises reevaluation and refers to those statements that reflect the speaker considering alternative ways of viewing experience. These are propositional in nature and reflect a tentative shift in perspective.
- Level 7 identifies integration and refers to those comments that show that the speaker has integrated information from a variety of sources to capture a common meaning or infer a relationship or the speaker has adopted a new perspective.

Structural Analysis of Social Behavior

The Structural Analysis of Social Behavior (SASB; Benjamin, 1974; Benjamin, Foster, Roberto, & Estroff, 1986) measures the quality of interpersonal process in dyadic relationships. It is based on a circumplex model of social behavior with two orthogonal axes related to the interpersonal dimensions of affiliation and control. There are three surfaces, each representing a particular focus of interpersonal behavior. Surface 1 depicts interpersonal process in which the focus is on the other; Surface 2 depicts interpersonal behavior in which the focus is on the self; and Surface 3 depicts intrapsychic behavior or how the person treats him- or herself. Each surface contains 36 interpersonal behaviors that represent unique combinations of affiliation and control. The 36 behaviors on each surface may be collapsed into eight clusters and four quadrants. Quadrant 1 represents accepting, validating behaviors; Quadrant 2, neglectful, withdrawn behaviors; Quadrant 3, coercive, punishing behaviors; and Quadrant 4, nurturing, guiding behaviors. The surface and cluster is noted in parentheses, for example (SASB 3-6) indicates Surface 3, Cluster 6 for the scoring of specific parts of the clients' dialogues.

The SASB is a useful measure to help examine how clients and therapists are interacting and treating each other in the session. As such, it provides a good window into the therapeutic alliance and how it is unfolding over the course of therapy. In addition, SASB ratings highlight how clients treat themselves. The ratings illuminate moments when clients are being self-critical, oppressive, neglectful, self-accepting, or nurturing. By tracking these behaviors over the course of therapy, therapists are able to identify problematic issues for clients and observe how these change over the course of treatment.

Self-Report Measures

Self-report measures provide the changes that clients identified after every session, and their working alliance scores provide an overview of the progress of therapy for each client.

Postsession Measures

Some measures were administered at the end of every session to assess the working alliance and the changes that occurred for clients during the session. The working alliance was completed by all clients, and the client task specific measure, by four of the six clients.

Client Task Specific Change Measure—Revised. The Client Task Specific Change Measure (Watson et al., 1996) is a postsession measure that consists of 16 questions that ask clients to identify specific changes they experienced in the session on a 7-point scale. For example, clients are asked whether they resolved lingering bad feelings toward a significant other or whether they better understand how their thoughts affect their feelings and behavior as a result of the activities they performed during the session. A total mean score comprising all the items provides an index of client change during the session. The items are relevant to both EFT and cognitive–behavioral therapy. Clients with scores of 5 or higher are reporting moderate to high amounts of change in terms of their understanding of their problems, how they are treating themselves, and how they are feeling about themselves and others.

Working Alliance Inventory. The Working Alliance Inventory (Horvath & Greenberg, 1989) is a 36-item self-report questionnaire to assess the working alliance on the dimensions of tasks, goals, and bonds. Clients rate the extent to which there is agreement with their therapists on the tasks and goals of therapy and whether they feel liked by their therapists on a 7-point scale. The measure has been found to have good interitem reliability (Horvath & Greenberg, 1989). Clients with scores of 5 or higher are reporting good to excellent working alliances with their therapists.

Outcome Measures

Clients' scores on five outcome measures were obtained to provide an index of whether clients benefited from treatment.

Beck Depression Inventory. The Beck Depression Inventory (BDI; Beck et al., 1961) is a 21-item questionnaire that measures the various aspects of depression, including affect, cognition, motivation, behavior, and somatic symptomology. This instrument has been found to be a reliable and valid measure of depression and to be sensitive to clinical changes in the depth of depression. Scores of 1–10 indicate no depression; scores of 10–15 indicate mild depression; and scores of 15 or higher indicate severe depression. Test–retest reliability ranges from .6 to .9 (Beck et al., 1961). Beck, Steer, and

Garbin (1988) reported validity coefficients ranging from .66 to .86 and internal consistency coefficients ranging from .73 to .93. Internal reliability tests have yielded results ranging from .82 to .93 (Beck et al., 1961).

Rosenberg Self-Esteem Inventory. A 10-item version of the Rosenberg Self-Esteem Inventory (Rosenberg, 1965), the Rosenberg Self-Esteem Scale (Bachman & O'Malley, 1977), was used to assess clients' levels of self-esteem. This instrument has shown good internal consistency and validity. Excellent internal reliability (.89–.94), test–retest reliability (.80–.90), and adequate sensitivity to change have been reported.

Symptom Checklist—90—Revised. The Symptom Checklist—90—Revised (SCL–90–R; Derogatis, 1983) is a widely used 90-item self-report inventory that measures general symptom distress and common psychiatric symptoms. Participants respond to the amount of distress they experience on a 5-point Likert-type scale ranging from 0 (*not at all*) to 4 (*extremely*). Internal consistency estimates for all 9 subscales range from .77 to .90, with test–retest reliability for a 1-week interval ranging from .80 to .90 (Derogatis, Rickels, & Roch, 1976). Concurrent and discriminative validity for the SCL–90–R (Schmitz, Kruse, Heckrath, Alberti, & Tress, 1999) and the SCL–90–R depression subscale have also been established (McGough & Curry, 1992).

Inventory of Interpersonal Problems. The Inventory of Interpersonal Problems (IIP; Horowitz et al., 1988) is a self-report instrument consisting of 127 items. Responses are scored using a 5-point Likert-type scale with responses ranging from 0 to 4. It is used to measure the severity of distress arising from interpersonal sources. Respondents rate the degree to which each situation is experienced as being problematic, for example, "I am too needy." The authors report overall test–retest reliability between .89 and .98 and internal consistency ranging from .89 to .94 (Horowitz et al., 1988). The IIP has been shown to be sensitive to clinical change and has correlated well with alternative measures of clinical improvement, including the SCL–90–R (Horowitz et al., 1988).

Dysfunctional Attitude Scale. The Dysfunctional Attitude Scale (DAS; Weissman & Beck, 1978) is a measure of personal beliefs and is used to measure dysfunctional thinking. The DAS consists of 40 items that assess dysfunctional thoughts, beliefs, and attitudes such as "I should be upset if I make a mistake" and "I am nothing if a person I love doesn't love me." Clients who have dysfunctional thoughts are thought to be more vulnerable to depression. Responses are scored on a 7-point scale (1 = *not at all agree*; 7 = *totally agree*), and the overall scores are obtained by summing across the 40 items, yielding scores that range from a minimum of 40 to a maximum of 280. Sample means range from 115 to 125 (Kuiper & Olinger, 1989). Higher scores indicate a greater susceptibility for a belief in "depressotypic" attitudes (Beck, Rush, Shaw, & Emery, 1979). The DAS has high internal consistency coefficients that range from .79 to .93 and test–retest reliability coefficients that range from .79 to .81 (Kuiper & Olinger, 1989).

Case Summaries

By triangulating information from clients, therapists, and third-party observers, we have attempted to present an in-depth picture of what occurs in a single session and over the course of a 16- to 20-week treatment of depression using EFT. The presentation of six case histories supplements the Greenberg and Watson (2005) text that outlined the treatment of depression using an emotionally focused approach but also serves to focus attention on those cases in which clients do not immediately respond to brief treatment to better understand the needs of these individuals and to better tailor treatments for their benefit.

Good Outcome Cases

Part II presents the three good outcome cases. We chose the good outcome cases to illustrate different types of changes as a function of 16 to 20 weeks of EFT. All three clients improved dramatically on the BDI so that their scores at the end of treatment were 0, indicating that they were no longer depressed. There was more variation on the other measures, with some clients, such as Anna, reporting fewer problems on some measures and other clients, such as David and Gayle, reporting significant improvement in terms of their self-esteem and interpersonal difficulties.

Each case is unique. David was dealing with unresolved grief and problems in his career; Gayle had multiple problems, including needing to differentiate from her mother and set limits on her mother's abusive behavior; and Anna was learning to validate and express her feelings. As they wrestled with their depressed feelings, all three clients moved quickly to sharing deeply painful experiences about significant others with their therapists, including the death of a parent, rejection and exploitation by an ex-boyfriend, and a mother's unpredictable angry outbursts. The good outcome cases show how easily these clients engaged in therapy. None of the three needed to be convinced of the merits of participating. They quickly formed positive alliances with their therapists from the beginning to the end of treatment.

In chapter 2 we see that David quickly responds to his therapist's interventions, and they are able to come to an agreement on the focus of treatment and the major issues that David wants to work on in therapy (p. 31). His therapist is able to facilitate partial and full resolutions early in therapy (p. 39) to help David generate new responses and better ways of treating himself. There is an easy fit between the specific tasks and the formulation of the problem proposed by his therapist and the client's view of his difficulties. Two-chair work is effective in helping David become more aware of and combat his inner critic and empty-chair work helps him to resolve his grief about his mother's death so as to move forward into the present in a more self-affirming and optimistic manner.

In chapter 3 Gayle is in touch with and able to express her feelings (p. 60). She is a good example of a client who is able to use the therapeutic relationship to consciously and deliberately generate new responses. Her therapist helps her to become more empathic toward herself and to stand up for herself when she is criticized and put down. With the therapist's encouragement Gayle is able to imagine her mother in an empty chair, which helps to make her feelings more accessible and enables her therapist to empathize more easily with her difficulties. By helping her to express her feelings appropriately, the therapist is able to move Gayle from a stance of blame and complaint to one of actively protecting herself and setting limits with others (p. 77). Gayle entered treatment with multiple difficulties, including disturbances of mood, some personality issues, health concerns, and work-related difficulties. Many of these are resolved over the course of a brief treatment of EFT.

In chapter 4 Anna's therapist helps her develop her inner voice by focusing on her feelings and encouraging her to express them to others. When necessary, Anna and her therapist are able to negotiate the two-chair task so that it fits more with Anna's aims and objectives. The therapist encourages Anna to pay attention to her body so that she is more aware of her feelings in the moment and can use this knowledge to develop a stronger sense of self (p. 86). As Anna becomes more aware of and learns to express her feelings, her therapist teaches her to soothe herself and develop ways of calming herself when she feels overwhelmed by her feelings. Anna found all these suggestions so useful that at a follow-up interview 6 months after treatment ended she observed to her therapist that the chair work had become an invaluable tool that she was able to use by herself whenever she felt distressed or unhappy.

Poor Outcome Cases

Part III presents the three poor outcome cases. We chose the poor outcome cases to illustrate specific difficulties with different phases of the treatment model for depression as well as different profiles of poor outcome. One client reported feeling more depressed at the end of treatment according to his score on the BDI; the second reported feeling better immediately following the last session but relapsed 10 days following treatment; and the third did not change significantly on the BDI at the end of treatment. In two cases difficulties in the alliance prevented clients from benefiting from a short-term treatment. The therapists of these two clients had difficulty convincing them that looking at feelings would be useful because both clients felt overwhelmed and terrified of examining their painful experiences. The client who improved temporarily was initially skeptical of processing his feelings but by midtreatment was in agreement that it would be productive and likely to assist him with overcoming his depression. It was not easy for all of these clients to express their feelings, and the details of their lives were so sparse that it was difficult to get a clear inside view of the traumatic and problematic events that they encountered growing up. This was in marked contrast to the good outcome cases. All three clients expressed a deep sense of shame that made it difficult for them to open up and share their experiences with their therapists.

In chapter 5 Richard's therapist tries to frame his depression in terms of how he overburdens himself. Although Richard agrees that he is exhausted and unable to say no, he has difficulty being empathic with himself. It is hard for Richard to identify or show concern for his weak side. He says to his therapist that he is scared of the weak side and more identified with the strong, critical, demanding side (p. 106). Richard speaks of how ashamed he is and how difficult it is for him to be in therapy and reveal himself (p. 107). His therapist tries to forge a positive working alliance but does not adequately deal with Richard's ambivalence about being in therapy. The therapist tries to implement the treatment protocol for depression rather than focusing on Richard's sense of shame and reluctance to explore his feelings.

In chapter 6 Sean comes to see the benefit of exploring and expressing his feelings by the middle of therapy. His therapist consistently tells him that the only way to overcome his feelings of anger is to process his emotions. Sean's motivation to manage his anger more effectively helps him to heed his therapist's suggestion and try an empty-chair task to see if that will help him. His therapist tries to support him by empathizing with and acknowledging his pain (p. 148) as he engages in empty-chair work. It is likely this makes it easier for him to express his pain because he feels that he has an ally against his mother. Unlike the other two clients in the poor outcome cases, Sean is able to relate the experiences of his youth to his behavior in the present. He is determined to overcome his difficulties in spite of feeling overwhelmed and disappointed in himself.

In chapter 7 Hilary is trying to come to terms with parental rejection and neglect. Like Richard she feels very ashamed of her feelings and does not trust that therapy can help her overcome her feelings of depression. Notice how, unlike Gayle in chapter 3, she is not able to move from a position of blame and complaint to one in which she is able to make changes within herself to help her feel better about her situation. There are tentative signs of her beginning to do this toward the end of therapy when she becomes more accepting of having been written out of her father's will and writes her mother to reconnect and to enlighten her about her current difficulties. Hilary does not see the relevance of doing empty-chair or two-chair work to help resolve her feelings (p. 166). Hilary still feels at the mercy of other people and unconvinced that she could do anything to improve her situation even though she is able to let go some of her anger toward her father for disinheriting her (p. 175).

Overall, we hope that this in-depth exploration of six case histories in EFT for depression illuminates aspects of the therapeutic process not usually visible with treatment manuals. These six histories provide a close-up view of what occurs between clients and therapists behind the closed door of a psychotherapy session and subjects the interactions to intense scrutiny to increase understanding and provide direction in terms of the theory, practice, and research of EFT for depression.

CONCLUSION

Finally, Part IV examines the similarities and differences between the good and poor outcome cases. The authors have identified those variables that were common to the good outcome cases and those that were common to the poor outcome cases in an attempt to understand the factors that facilitate positive outcomes in brief therapy. Both client and therapist factors associated with good and poor outcome are identified and ways of working to improve clinical practice are presented.

We hope that the comparison between good and poor outcome clients will increase our understanding of not only the factors that contribute to successful outcomes but also those that inhibit them. The identification of factors that impede treatment success is necessary to help develop interventions that might be more effective and to provide a framework for thinking about different types of clients and how to match them to different treatment options.

II

CASES WITH GOOD OUTCOME

2

EVOKING AND EXPLORING EMOTION

David was a man in his 50s when he came for therapy for his depression. He was married with one adult son. He had experienced depression since the age of 10 when his mother became bedridden and unable to function around the house. David had first sought help for his depression 10 years prior to his current episode. During that time he separated from his wife, and he recalled that his depression lifted and he began to enjoy life more, making friends and attending social functions. However, he reconciled with his wife a few months later because his wife was very distressed by the separation. Some time after the reconciliation, his depression recurred, and it became worse for 2 years before he entered therapy for the second time.

David had had a postgraduate education and a professional degree. He identified difficulties in three main areas including his career, interpersonal relationships, and his marriage. With respect to his career, David noted that he had lost his ambition and that he had difficulty setting goals and starting and completing projects. He expressed concern that he had made the wrong career choice to comply with his mother's expectations. He expressed a desire to switch careers because he felt that the work that he was doing was too detail oriented and did not suit him. He expressed a preference for teaching and interacting with people. When he began therapy he was working out of his home, which he found very isolating. Interpersonally, David described himself as fearful of people, especially authority figures. He had little contact with his family of origin, felt emotionally cut off from his siblings, and had a conflicted relationship with his daughter-in-law. In addition to his dissatisfaction with his career and interpersonal difficulties, David expressed dissatisfaction with his marital relationship. He was concerned about the conflict in his marriage and his wife's critical attitude toward him and her frequent verbal abuse. David observed that he had become more and more withdrawn from his wife so that by the time that he sought treatment they were hardly speaking to each other. He blamed himself for the difficulties in his marriage saying he was lazy and depressed and expressed a longing for a warmer, kinder, more loving relationship.

David was diagnosed pretherapy with major depressive disorder on Axis I; no diagnosis on Axes II and III; problems with primary support group and discord with spouse, siblings, and daughter-in-law on Axis IV; and occupational problems characterized by job dissatisfaction on Axis V. He had a Global Assessment Functioning Scale (GAF) score of 58, indicating moderate difficulty in social and occupational functioning.

CASE FORMULATION

David described a lonely, chaotic childhood. As a child he felt mistreated, ignored, and neglected. He recalled that the dominant emotions expressed at home when he was a child were fear and anger. There was conflict between his mother and grandmother, who lived with them. He recalled an incident when, after an argument with his mother, his grandmother smashed a window in rage. He described his mother as critical and withdrawn. At age 10 his life became bleak and empty after his mother became ill and bedridden; she died when he was 13. After his mother's death, David's father became alcoholic and virtually abandoned the children to the care of neighbors. David assumed responsibility for his siblings until he left to attend university when he was 18.

David's core emotion scheme was that he was unloved, unsupported, and neglected. He was very self-critical and blamed himself for things that went wrong. He felt ashamed and tended to silence his feelings and needs in his interactions with others, particularly his wife. In terms of his emotional processing, David showed characteristics of being both overaroused and underaroused. At times he was quite intellectual and very analytical when presenting his experience; at other times, particularly when recounting painful events, he was reactive and unreflective about his feelings. David cried easily in therapy sessions. Although he was aware of and able to label his feelings, it was hard for him to modulate and reflect on them. Consistent with his emotional processing, his nonverbal behavior, specifically his descriptions, was poignant, congruent, and coherent, and his vocal quality was predominantly externalizing and emotional, indicating that he moved in and out of analyzing his experience and expressing his feelings. His body language was relaxed, and he seemed to bond easily with his therapist. The three primary tasks that were identified as possible ways of intervening to help David resolve his depression were two-chair work to tackle his self-criticism, empty-chair work to resolve his feelings of grief about his mother's death, and empathic affirmation to process his feelings of intense vulnerability.

BONDING AND AWARENESS

During Sessions 1 through 3, the therapist focused on forging a good working alliance and began to highlight how David treated himself to increase his awareness of how he might be contributing to his feelings of depression. From Session 1 it was evident that David was very self-critical. He had high expectations and was very unforgiving of himself. He recalled that he had lost his mother when he was 13 after she had been sick for 2.5 years. He did not attend her funeral, which he subsequently regretted, because he did not have the opportunity to say goodbye. He recalled that no one ever told him why she had died or explained what had happened. He just knew his mother would not be coming home the day his neighbor returned in tears from a visit to his mother in the hospital. After his mother's death, David assumed the responsibility of caring for his father and siblings. He recalled that his mother had been the mainstay of the family but that she was critical, cold, and withdrawn. Toward the end of Session 1, David's therapist suggested that the main themes that seemed important to work on in therapy were his dissatisfaction with his work and his marriage and for him to try to become a little less self-critical because this was contributing to his depression. David agreed and confirmed an appointment for the following week.

In Session 2 David reported that he felt a little better after Session 1. He restated his desire to work on changing how self-critical he was and began to acknowledge how much his wife's anger hurt him. In this session he was able to acknowledge his accomplishments and realized that he had had to "struggle alone for his education." He noted that there had been very little support and that his Dad had died while he was pursuing his graduate degree. Nonetheless, during the previous week he recalled a number of people who had assisted him along the way. He recalled how a neighbor had taken him in and treated him like a son and how one of his teachers had helped him apply for funding to go to university. However, he was concerned that he had pursued his education to please his mother and had not had the chance to find and develop his own interests and passions.

David recalled that his family of origin was fractured. He was the oldest of four children and felt that his siblings envied him; he was seen as the favorite because he had frequently been ill as a child and had required additional care. He did not have a sense of family. David said that his father did not contribute much leadership to the family; instead he behaved more like a brother. The environment in which he grew up was one of uncertainty and fear. As a child he was petrified of his mother and grandmother because of their frequent and intense expressions of anger. He recalled that there was a lot of tension at home because his grandmother was constantly angry with his father, and there was a lot of conflict between his mother and oldest brother.

EVOKING AND EXPLORING FEELINGS

In the next sessions, David's therapist began to suggest more tasks to evoke David's feelings so that they could be expressed and reprocessed and so that David could access alternative feelings and synthesize alternative ways of being. At Session 3 David reported that he had had a difficult week. His computer had crashed, making it difficult for him to meet a deadline. He felt trapped and as if everything was going against him. He wished that he could "roll with the punches" and take things more in his stride. Instead, after he encountered problems he berated himself for doing things that might have contributed to the problems or for not asking the right questions when he was trying to fix them. His therapist observed that David had presented with a clear marker of self-criticism and saw this as an opportunity to see whether David was willing to engage in a two-chair dialogue to try to counteract his self-critical internal dialogue.

David: Yeah, but I still, you know, I still say, I still get angry, like, when I look back at that. You know, maybe I am kicking myself too, like maybe I should have asked about that board, you know, the sound card board, you know, maybe I should have asked, been asking questions too. So in a sense maybe I am kicking myself also.

Therapist: So you kind of say to yourself, "Why didn't I think of this?"

David: Yeah, exactly, why didn't I think about asking the question? You know, and then I sort of assumed that it would work in any type of computer. I didn't know that it had to be a Pentium computer.

Therapist: Right.

David: By the board, to use the board, but it turned out that it did. But I mean, then I sort of say to myself, "Why didn't I check that? Why did I accept?" Like I basically accepted what he told me, and that was it. But I never asked any questions to find out if it works in Pentium or a 46, which I have. Again, partially I was at fault too, and I blame myself for that. I said, "You know, I am in computers. I should know better. I should know to ask these questions, but I didn't."

Therapist: So you have been down on yourself?

David: So I'm down on myself in that respect. Then again, I guess maybe I was confident to do it when you think about it [*laughs*]. Even when I'm down on myself for screwing up the, whatever happened in the systems, screwing it up so that it wouldn't recognize the hard disk drives.

Therapist: So you are cross with yourself or what?

David: Yeah, like I am blaming myself for that.

Therapist: Uh-huh. How do you feel about trying an exercise right now?

David: OK. I would. I think so, yeah.

Therapist: We have talked about the fact that you are very self-critical.

David: Yeah.

Therapist: And you just raised two examples of where you kind of beat up on yourself. Sometimes a really good way of working with that is to try to separate out the critical side of yourself.

David: Uh-huh.

Therapist: And what we usually do is try to physically separate out the different sides of ourselves. We have to put the critical part of you in one chair, and for you to be critical, and then come and have you sit over here and respond to the critic. How does that sound to you? . . . A bit hokey?

David: Well, just a little [*both laugh*]. You hit it on the head.

Therapist: It does sound a bit odd, but it can be very helpful. It helps to keep it clear.

David: Yeah.

Therapist: Would you be willing to try that?

David: Yeah, I would be willing, sure, no problem.

In the preceding dialogue, the therapist has explicitly sought David's agreement to engage in the task. Because it was the first time they were doing a two-chair task, the therapist acknowledged that it might sound weird to physically separate the two sides and speak from two different chairs. David acknowledged this but agreed to go along anyway. David was freely disclosing (SASB [Structural Analysis of Social Behavior] 2-2) and trusting and relying on his therapist (SASB 2-4) as he agreed to do the task and cooperate with her suggestions. In terms of his level of cognitive processing, he presented his behavior and judged it in terms of external standards and rules (LCPP [Levels of Client Perceptual Processing] Level 3). In terms of his affective processing, David was internally focused as he tried to describe his internal world and how he treated himself (EXP [The Experiencing Scale] Stage 4). However, David was very harsh and punitive with himself (SASB 3-6) and tried to restrain and monitor his behavior (SASB 3-5). In the following dialogue, the therapist asked David to enact his critic to increase his awareness of his self-critical statements, to evoke the feelings that the statements generate, and to try to facilitate alternative emotional responses and ways of treating himself.

Therapist: Could you kind of be critical of yourself; what are some of the things you say? Some of the things you just said to me now were "Gee, I was so stupid. Why didn't I think of asking about that sound card?"

David: Yeah.

Therapist: What else do you say to yourself?

David: Well, I just say, I was saying, why did I move the boards? Why did I take the boards out and put them back in again? In other words, assuming that whatever I did with those boards affected the disk drive.

Therapist: So, "You should leave things alone. Why did you interfere?"

David: Yeah, exactly.

Therapist: "Why did you interfere?" What else do you say?

David: Well, like on the, the other thing I said to myself too is maybe I should have fixed the problem. It didn't recognize our disk drive before I started upgrading and taking it over there to upgrade it and put new boards in—you know that was another thing I was saying to myself too. In other words, to solve the first problem, which was the fact that whatever I did affected the hard disk drive. That should have been solved first instead of assuming that it was going to be an easy problem—take it over there and upgrade it and put the problem on their shoulders to do this. Again, I thought it would be an easy problem, but it wasn't—they're still working on the thing.

Therapist: So were you criticizing yourself for taking it to them?

David: Well no, what I'm saying is that I should have solved that hard disk problem, found out why or took it to somebody else to find out why that problem existed before I took it over to the computer people to upgrade my system. How should I say that?

Therapist:	So you didn't handle it well.
David:	Yeah, exactly. I didn't handle, like when I look back, now again, this is looking back . . .
Therapist:	Yes, yes.
David:	I never thought that this would happen. I thought they were trying to fix it, that they were hardware specialists. They employ specialists; they should know how to fix these problems right away.
Therapist:	OK, so what you are saying is, "I was," what is this, too harsh like, "Oh you dummy, like why didn't you do it this way first?"
David:	Yeah.
Therapist:	"Why didn't you think this thing through?"
David:	Yeah, think it better. Yeah, think it through better.
Therapist:	"You should have known better." Is that what you are saying?
David:	Yeah, I should have known better about that, yeah.
Therapist:	Uh-huh.
David:	Well, but again I'm looking, I'm looking at it from, you know, now. But when I initially thought about it, you know, I said, "These people are hardware people. They are going to upgrade my boards so they'll run faster." So I said, "You know, they should be able to fix that without any trouble."
Therapist:	OK.
David:	I did initially, but then after it didn't, then I started blaming myself. Then I started saying, you know, then I should have got that problem fixed first, found out why the hard disk drive didn't work. Then if I solved that problem, then I should have went to them.
Therapist:	OK, so this is how you kick yourself, "You should have known better; you should have done it differently; why did you do that way?" You start questioning yourself.
David:	Yeah, exactly. Well, that would really be the hardest part, just sitting over here [*laughs*].
Therapist:	Is it hard for you to?
David:	No, no I'm just joking [*laughs*]. No, it's hard like to not be critical—that's what I'm saying to you.
Therapist:	So how do you feel over here when this side says, "Why didn't you handle this differently? You should have known better. Why

didn't you fix this first before you take the other one? You should have asked. You should have known."

The therapist has been working to help David articulate his negative self-criticisms. We see that David was engaged in differentiating his experience from an external frame of reference as he applied standards and rules to his behavior to make sense of it (LCPP Level 3). He described his situation from an external perspective and judged it without any reference to his feelings (EXP Stage 2). In terms of the working alliance, he was freely disclosing to his therapist and trusting and relying on her suggestions (SASB 2-2, 2-4). However, he was controlling and managing his own behavior and blaming and belittling himself when things went wrong (SASB 3-5, 3-6). The therapist was trying to heighten and increase David's awareness of these inner processes to facilitate higher levels of emotional processing.

Therapist: How do you feel when you hear that side criticizing you?

David: You know, I mean, I say to myself, like, it's hard to say, but I was pretty stupid over there, that's all. I mean, it was stupid for what I was saying about myself, that's what I think.

Therapist: That is an evaluation. How do you feel when you hear that side criticize?

Here the therapist was trying to teach David the difference between an evaluation and a statement about how he feels. The therapist was trying to help him shift from analyzing and judging his experience to attending to its emotional impact so that he could become aware of the impact of how he treats himself.

David: Well, I don't feel too good.

Therapist: You don't feel too good; what do you feel?

David: I feel depressed, more anxiety. I feel more negativism.

Therapist: So when this side is critical, this side does begin to feel kind of depressed and anxious.

David: Yes, anxious.

Therapist: Worried?

David: Yeah, more worried.

Therapist: What is the anxiety about? Tell this side about the anxiety.

David: I don't know. I guess maybe I sort of believe that I, you try to make me believe that there is something, I'm stupid or . . .

Therapist: So there is a sense that "maybe I did screw up?"

David: Yeah, exactly.

Therapist: And that makes you feel anxious?

David: Yeah, I more or less, you know, feel that there is no worth, you know, it's . . .

Therapist: So it makes you feel worthless?

David: Yeah, worthless, yeah, exactly.

Here David began to focus on his feelings (EXP Stage 4). He focused internally and differentiated his experience in an idiosyncratic manner (LCPP Level 4). As he began to explore his inner experience, he was more self-accepting (SASB 3-2), and as he tried to figure out what was going on, he was more self-protective (SASB 3-4). In terms of the working alliance, he was trusting his therapist and relying on her as he accepted her direction and tried to articulate how he felt in response to the criticism (SASB 2-4, 2-2). In the dialogue that follows, the therapist actively tries to get David to generate new behavior by expressing to the critic the impact of his critical behavior.

Therapist: Can you tell that side, "When you criticize me I kind of feel worthless"?

David: Well, when you criticize me, you make me feel worthless; I become more anxious, more negative.

Therapist: What happens when you get anxious?

David: My mind gets a bit fuzzy.

Therapist: So you can't think?

David: Yeah, I can't think clearly—that's true.

Therapist: What else happens when you get anxious?

David was learning to look out for his own interests as he told the critic how painful it felt when he was criticized (SASB 3-4). However, he did it in a somewhat blaming way because he used *you* statements. Nonetheless, he was differentiating his inner experience in a highly personal and idiosyncratic manner (EXP Stage 4; LCPP Level 5). In the following dialogue the blaming stance is more overt as David recognizes that he is angry with himself. The therapist tries to explore his anger more fully.

David: Well, I feel a bit of anger too, you know, anger against myself, I guess. You know, I sort of get angry, like I think that is part of the problem, like I also get angry at myself.

Therapist: What is the anger?

David: Mostly, you know, the fact that I should be better; I should be smarter.

Therapist:	Can you come over here [*indicating the other chair*]? So that's how you make yourself feel more anxious, right, and more different?
David:	Yeah.
Therapist:	Is it hard moving around, because you know we could try a different . . .
David:	No, it's fine [*laughs*]. I just have injured my foot, but it's . . .
Therapist:	All right, because you could just tell me; we could try a different way of working . . .
David:	Oh no, don't worry about that, I appreciate your worry but . . .

Here the therapist expressed concern that David might have difficulty shifting from chair to chair because he had hurt his foot playing tennis. However, David said he was fine, so they carried on with the task of activating the critical voice to try to facilitate the development of a more self-protective one.

Therapist:	So say this again, "You should do better." What else?
David:	Yeah.
Therapist:	What is the anger?
David:	Well, you shouldn't be stupid; you're stupid; and you're . . .
Therapist:	Stupid?
David:	Yes.
Therapist:	"And you're no good; you're useless; you know all of these . . ."
David:	So you're stupid; you're useless.
Therapist:	Come over here . . . [*indicating the experiencing chair*]. I mean, those are really core, those things that he is saying to you. How do you feel when that side says you're stupid and useless?

David has once again accessed his core criticisms. He was self-indicting and harsh with himself (SASB 3-6). His perceptual and emotional processing shifted down as he once again applied rigid rules and standards to his behavior (EXP Stage 2; LCPP Level 3). Subsequently the therapist focused him on his feelings in response to the criticism. The primary aim here was to make David aware of what he was feeling and to help him express it so that it became known and acknowledged and more revealing of his needs. Then he could renegotiate the balance between his two sides.

David:	Well, I don't feel good, that is for sure; like it makes me, like you say, depressed.
Therapist:	It depresses you?

David: Yes.

Therapist: So you really feel pushed down.

David: Exactly, pushed down and more frustrated and more everything.

Therapist: It frustrates you.

David: You know, more anxiety.

Therapist: Tell the side about the depression. Tell him about this feeling of being pushed down . . .

David: Pushed down, feeling of pushed down is this feeling like you're nothing—that's what it feels like.

Therapist: "So when you criticize me like that—I just kind of feel like I'm nothing—like I am blocked out."

David: I'm blocked out, yeah.

Therapist: I'm not important?

David: That's right, I'm not important at all.

Therapist: What do you need from this side?

Up to this point, David had been following his therapist's suggestions (SASB 2-4) and had freely disclosed and shared his thoughts and feelings (SASB 2-2). He had been focusing inward, trying to differentiate his experience in an idiosyncratic way (EXP Stage 4; LCPP Level 5). After he expressed his feelings, his therapist focused him on what he needed.

David: Well, I guess I need some, maybe, some positive reinforcement. I guess that that would be the thing that I would need.

Therapist: So you would like some encouragement and support?

David: Encouragement, yeah, and support, yeah, right. That's the thing. So I need . . .

Therapist: So it's kind of, "stop criticizing me"?

David: Yeah.

Therapist: Is that part of it?

David: Oh, I would say so, yeah. You can give me some . . . [*crying*]

Therapist: This is really painful?

David: [*crying*] You can give me some support for Christ's sake.

Therapist: So "get off my back"?

David: Pardon me?

Therapist: "Get off my back. It's too much. Just give me some support."

David:	Yes [*crying*]. Just give me some support for Christ's sake.
Therapist:	What are the tears saying—that you have had enough?
David:	I guess it goes back. I never had support. I guess so . . .
Therapist:	You never had support, is that it?
David:	Yes, that's true.
Therapist:	That's what you really, really want; is that what you are saying?
David:	Yes.
Therapist:	So "I need you to support me"?
David:	Yeah.
Therapist:	"I need you to encourage me"?
David:	Yeah. I never really had that. I still don't have it at all. I've gone through life, you know, not getting any support, except well, I guess a few people helped me along the way, but most of it was, you know . . .
Therapist:	It was kind of sporadic?
David:	Yes, very sporadic, yeah.
Therapist:	It wasn't a continual kind of a support.
David:	Nothing, no nothing.
Therapist:	And that is what you need?
David:	Pardon?
Therapist:	And that's what you need?
David:	Yes, yeah.
Therapist:	What happened to the sadness?
David:	I feel a bit better. I mean, you know, just, I guess crying, I guess feeling sad for myself.

David was able to express his need and assert himself with respect to the critic. This represented new behavior as David tried to be more self-protecting and self-enhancing and set limits on the critic as well as ask for encouragement (SASB 3-3, 3-4). David tentatively proposed a new behavior and seemed on the verge of resolving a problem (LCPP Level 6). His behavior shifted, and he requested support instead of blame and criticism (EXP Stage 6). Along with this, David's mood shifted, and he did not feel so sad. However, at the same time he recognized the bigger problem, that he had never had support throughout his life.

Therapist:	Come over here. How does the critic respond to your request for support?

David: I don't know . . . um. I am not sure I know how to be supportive. It is hard for me to change and to stop being critical. It is hard for me to understand why you need support. I am scared that if I change everything will fall apart.

Therapist: So this side is scared of changing?

David: Yeah, that's it.

Therapist: So what does it need of this side?

David: I guess I need support too. I am sorry I let you down. I was trying to look after us, but now I realize what a terrible job I have done.

Therapist: Come over here. How do you respond to this side when he says "sorry" and "I did not mean to hurt you"?

David: I don't blame you; it's not your fault. If you were less critical, I could give you support.

Therapist: What is happening over here?

David: I am beginning to feel a little hopeful.

Therapist: OK, move over here [indicating the other chair]. What do you say to this side? He is asking you to stop being critical.

David: I will try to be supportive, though I am not sure how.

Therapist: Perhaps you can start by being gentler with yourself and setting limits on the criticism and be more reassuring.

David's mood shifted. He did not feel as sad and was a little more hopeful that things could be different. He was now more clearly aware of what he needed; however, he was still uncertain of how to act differently. David made a major shift in this session (EXP Stage 6; LCPP Level 7); he acquired a new perspective on his experience. He treated himself in a more nourishing and caring way. He was being more self-protective and enhancing, although he realized that he needed to learn how to act in other ways that are self-enhancing and supportive. At this point the critic admitted that he was not sure whether he could be supportive. The therapist acknowledged this lack of support and for the next few sessions the two continued to work on David's sadness about his childhood and early adulthood. During this period the therapist concentrated on empathically responding to David's pain as well as introducing specific tasks when specific task markers arose.

At the next session, David reported that he had had a good week. He was able to be assertive with a colleague and expressed his needs to his wife and son without becoming angry. He also took care of himself by setting up his music collection, something he had wanted to do for months. He noted that he really had a sense of how critical he was of himself and that he needed to take better care of himself. He said that the fog seemed to have lifted and that his brain did not feel so cloudy. He engaged in a two-chair exercise with his critic, who once again softened and undertook to be more caring and less critical. This time the experiencing chair became angry, blaming the critic for keeping him depressed for so long. Once again David realized how unloved and unsupported he had felt as a child.

In Sessions 5 through 9, David explored his childhood. He spoke about his sense of loss after his mother died and the responsibilities that he had had to assume. He and his therapist did some empty-chair work to help him mourn his mother's death and the absence of a loving, nurturing presence during his childhood. David recalled that he had felt mistreated, ignored, and unloved as a child. His father did not talk to him. David described him as absent while physically present. His mother was angry and abrupt in her interactions with him. His therapist suggested doing some empty-chair work to try to resolve these lingering negative feelings from childhood. In his first empty-chair task, David expressed his sadness to his father about their lack of communication.

> *David:* Why did you not talk to me?
>
> *Therapist:* "I wish you had talked to me and parented me." What else do you want to say to him?
>
> *David:* You wouldn't look at my marks. I couldn't share what I was doing at school with you. I wanted you to be proud of me, but you were always late for school functions, and then you would come in drunk. I felt so angry with you, Dad.
>
> *Therapist:* "I was so disappointed. I needed you to be interested in me."
>
> *David:* Yeah. I felt so alone—like an animal by myself. I was so scared and vulnerable.
>
> *Therapist:* So you just felt so scared and vulnerable. Come over here. How does your dad respond?
>
> *David:* "I didn't know how. I didn't get it. I didn't begrudge you because you were angry with me. I tried to be fair. At the end, I didn't understand school. I just didn't get it. But I was proud of you. I should have told you. I was very shy and fearful. I really did not know how to help you. I didn't know what to do after Mum died. I am so sorry."

After expressing his sorrow and unhappiness to his father (SASB 2-2), David was able to respond as his father and take his father's perspective. His introjected view of his father was able to acknowledge David's pain and to apologize. As his father, David was also able to say that he was proud of his son and acknowledge his own deficits. Thus his father was portrayed as more supportive, loving, and nurturing (SASB 1-2, 1-3, 1-4). This was a major shift for David because he saw that his father did love him and wish him well but that he was severely handicapped and unable to participate in his son's world (EXP Stage 6; LCPP Level 7). David formed a new perspective that allowed him to see his problem, himself, and his father differently. After this David was able to recall some good times with his father and resolved to remember these.

At the next session, David was concerned about work. He was worried about losing a contract and expressed a fear that the person in charge might not like him. As a result, he descended into a deep depression during the week. It felt like a dark hole. He recalled that he often felt like that as a child when his mother was angry and criticized him. At those times it felt dark inside, and he was scared, as if he had no foundation, as though he was nothing. His therapist suggested a two-chair task to explore how David scared himself and put himself in the dark hole.

Therapist: How do you make David anxious? What do you say? "You screwed up."

David: Yes, you screwed up.

Therapist: How do you make yourself anxious?

David: You could lose your job; then what will we do? If you make her angry, she will retaliate.

Therapist: Come over here [*indicating the other chair*]. How do you feel when this side threatens you?

David: I feel very scared. It makes me go into the black hole. I feel under attack, vulnerable, and uncertain of myself.

Therapist: So this side feels very scared. What do you need?

David: I need protection. Stop scaring me; stand up for me. Why are you doing this?

Therapist: So this is very hurtful. It is undermining you.

David: Yes, we live together but you don't help me, don't protect me.

Therapist: How does this side respond?

David: I can see it is hard. I just don't know what to do.

Therapist: Come over here. Can you tell this side what he needs to do? Can he stop scaring you?

David: Yes! Stop scaring me. We need to work together. You need to be more lenient, less hypercritical.

Therapist: Come over here and see how this side responds.

David: I don't know if I can change. I get so scared. I need reassurance. Perhaps you can tell me we will get other work.

Therapist:	OK, so "give me reassurance." Could he also tell you about good things you have done?
David:	Yes! You could remind me that I am good with people, that I am caring and interested in people, curious about the world.
Therapist:	What about being a good problem solver?
David:	Yes, I am a good problem solver, and I am good at my job.
Therapist:	Come over here [*indicating the other chair*]. How does that feel?
David:	Better [*begins to cry*].
Therapist:	What is happening?
David:	I have been in so many holes. I missed so much, but I do feel better. I appreciate what you are doing. I felt like I was in a tunnel; now I can see the light.

At the next session, David reported that he had been feeling more energetic. He went shopping for some clothes for himself and was able to be more expressive and assertive with others. He said he felt more relaxed and bubbly with ideas and plans that he wanted to implement. At work he felt stronger and more capable. He received positive feedback during the week that felt very good. He noted that he was not as self-critical and was trying to be much more supportive. During this session he wanted to work on his relationship with his wife. He realized how much she reminded him of his mother and how distant she appeared to be. After doing an empty-chair exercise, David realized that his depression prevented him from doing the little things around the house that his wife appreciated. He also realized that he could set limits on her critical behavior. He said that he had asked her to stop criticizing him and not to call him names. After this session he reported that he was trying to do little things for his wife to show that he cared.

At Session 8 David spoke about feeling sad about an elderly neighbor who had been kind to him when he was young. He wished he could have expressed his appreciation. The therapist suggested that they do an empty-chair exercise with the neighbor.

Therapist:	Would it be easier to sit on these chairs?
David:	[*laughs*] No, not at all. That's just fine. Thank you for being caring [*laughs*].
Therapist:	So what do you want to say to her?
David:	I guess the other thing, maybe is that, you know, I, for what you gave me, I guess I wanted to pay you back.
Therapist:	"I wish I'd been able to pay you back."
David:	. . . for what you did.

Therapist:	. . . to reciprocate?
David:	Yes, exactly. I wish I could have reciprocated it. I never offered anything to you to help you or to care for you, and I guess I would have liked to have cared for you once I realized that . . .
Therapist:	So you wish you could have cared for her?
David:	I guess that's maybe the problem here, is for what she did for me, I would want to pay her back, and really I can't pay her back because she has passed on and because I haven't . . .
Therapist:	But how does she respond to you? I mean, imagine her sitting there and you saying, "I wish I'd been able to reciprocate." What does she say?
David:	Liz would say, "Well that's OK David. I understand. Life was hard for you. I know you cared."
Therapist:	She would say there was no need?
David:	There was no need.
Therapist:	"Because it was a delight for me to have you kids, I didn't have my own."
David:	Exactly, yeah.
Therapist:	Tell David about that, how special it was to be able to help.
David:	"You know, it was, I had a bad life myself. My husband was drunk a lot of the time; I lived on the farm with him. I had no children; he didn't want any children; I wanted children. Then you and your family would come and see me, and I guess I adopted you. I adopted you as my second family, as my family" [*crying*].
Therapist:	"You were like my family?"
David:	Pardon me?
Therapist:	"That was all the thanks I needed; that was very special for me. You didn't have to do anything."
David:	That's right.
Therapist:	"It was my pleasure."
David:	That is true. I guess the other thing is, as I think about that, also is the, I guess maybe there is some resentment against my parents. In the sense . . .

Here David expressed his remorse (SASB 2-1) and was forgiven by his neighbor. David realized that she valued being able to care for him and his brothers, that it provided some joy in her bleak life. David was becoming more self-accepting, more forgiving, and less critical of himself (SASB 3-2,

3-3, 3-4). These represented important changes in how David viewed himself and the world. At this juncture David shifted his attention from his feelings about his neighbor to his feelings toward his parents. The therapist followed his lead, and they began an empty-chair exercise with his parents.

Therapist: What is the resentment about? Can you imagine your folks?

David: Well, the resentment that I have is that I couldn't get any love. I mean, they didn't show any love to me. You're supposed to be my father and my mother [*crying*], and I had to go to Liz for love.

Therapist: Right.

David: But I got all my love from Liz, and I don't think that's right.

Therapist: So "I wish you guys could have been there for me."

David: I wish you could have. I mean, why . . . ?

Therapist: "I needed you to help me."

David: And love me, and you never did. It was fortunate, very fortunate that Liz was living next to us.

Therapist: "I feel resentful that I had to look for it elsewhere."

David: I wish you could have been there for me.

Here David was able to express his feelings (EXP Stage 4; LCPP Level 5) indicating that he was engaged in internal differentiation. In terms of the working alliance, David was following his therapist's suggestion and engaging in the task (SASB 2-2, 2-4) and freely disclosing his feelings while trying to protect his interests with respect to his parents (SASB 3-4). The therapist then asked David to imagine how his parents might respond.

Therapist: OK, come over here. How do they respond to you when they hear you say, "I wish you guys could have been there; I wish you had expressed your love for me and I didn't have to go to Liz or someone outside." How would they respond?

David: My father wouldn't respond, but I guess my mother would be . . . she might get very angry.

Therapist: What would she say to you?

David: She would say, "Well, we've done, I've worked hard for you. I worked day and night to help you go to school."

Therapist: "So I wanted you guys to go to school and I worked very, very hard to make that happen." What else would she say? Did she say I love you?

David: No, she wouldn't say that. That's about all.

Here David was unable to see that his mother might have cared for him. The therapist continued to explore his memories of his mother and what she did for him to see whether new information would emerge.

Therapist: Why did she work so hard?

David: Well, she was ambitious.

Therapist: So it was ambition that drove her?

David: I think so, yes, ambition. The fact that she wanted us to have a better life and a life that she talked about, going to university, when I was . . .

Therapist: She wanted you to have more?

David: Well, at that time I didn't think it was. I mean, I thought that like when you live on a poor farm, and they talk about university, like my mother, I never believed her.

David expressed his mother's point of view (EXP Stage 4). He moved from an analytical view of the situation and of his parents' behavior to a more internally differentiated view that saw more of the complexity (LCPP Levels 4, 5). He realized that his mother's actions suggested that she wanted to improve her children's living conditions (SASB 1-4, 1-5) and that she was trying to look out for their futures. Although David recognized that it was her way of showing love, he stated he needed more warmth and kindness (SASB 2-1, 2-2).

Therapist: But now, looking back, does it seem as if she wanted more for you?

David: Well now I do, yeah.

Therapist: So do you think she did love you?

David: I would say yes.

Therapist: Can you say this to David?

David: "I did love you. I worked hard. I worked to let you go to university so that you could have a better life than what we are living now. This is a hell life. I mean, you cannot live like this. I'm just trying to help you."

Therapist: "I didn't want you to have my life."

David: "I don't want you to have this life; I want you to get off the farm; I want you to have a good profession; and the only way you can do that is go to university."

Therapist: "So I have to work night and day."

David: "And I have to work night and day for that."

Therapist:	"But it's because I love you."
David:	"And it's because I love you."
Therapist:	Come over here [*switching chairs*]. How do you feel when you hear her say that?
David:	Well, I feel a lot better. It's the reinforcement, at least. I always felt that you loved me, but you never really expressed anything to me.
Therapist:	"You didn't tell me a lot."
David:	You didn't tell me.
Therapist:	"But I realize that you did."
David:	But I realize that you did. I think you did work hard, and I still remember when I took the departmental exams; I mean, you took over all the chores that I had to do so I could study.

Here David came to a new perspective of his mother (EXP Stage 6; LCPP Level 6) as he reevaluated his mother's behavior. He was able to take in his therapist's suggestion that his mother loved him (SASB 2-4, 2-3) and continued to freely express his thoughts and feelings (SASB 2-2).

Therapist:	What's happening inside right now? What do the tears say [*speaking softly*]?
David:	[*crying*] Well, I think it is the same old problem. I mean, I never had . . . I never had any chance to sort of . . . express this to my mother. I mean . . .
Therapist:	What would you want to express to her David?
David:	Well to say that, to thank you, to thank her for what she did.
Therapist:	Can you say it to her now?
David:	Well, I'd like to thank you . . . thank you for all the . . . all the . . . all the sacrifices that you made for us . . . or for me. And, uh, you know, and I guess . . . I guess, you know, like I say, I think I—I know that you love me, but I guess you used to get angry . . . you used to get angry at us and me.
Therapist:	Tell her what it was like when she got angry with you David.
David:	It was very, very scary.
Therapist:	"I was so scared of you."
David:	I was so scared of you. And you knew that I was scared . . . because even when I was young, I remember I used to run under the bed when company came, and we all did run under the bed and hide like a bunch of animals. I always remember you were

	embarrassed because of our fears [*crying*]. But you did nothing about it [*crying*].
Therapist:	"You didn't reassure us or comfort us."
David:	You never comforted us; you never showed really any caring, I know you worked hard, that's for sure, but I mean, you never gave anything to us, nothing [*crying*].
Therapist:	"We needed to hear it."
David:	We needed someone to protect us . . . from the fears.
Therapist:	"We needed someone to reassure us."
David:	To reassure us and to show . . . show . . . show some compassion. I mean, you would get embarrassed when company came because it must have bothered you that we would run and hide like a bunch of animals, but you didn't . . . never reacted. You never did anything about that, you know. You must have known we were fearful—you were embarrassed about it.
Therapist:	Uh-huh.
David:	But you never did anything. You did nothing.
Therapist:	So is it possible that she didn't actually understand that you were fearful?
David:	Maybe so, maybe she was fearful too. Maybe she was just transmitting her fears . . .
Therapist:	Uh-huh.
David:	. . . to us.
Therapist:	Do you think it was hard for her as well?
David:	Yes, my father wouldn't . . . didn't do much supporting, that's for sure [*laughs*]. Maybe I shouldn't say that but . . .
Therapist:	So she had to sort of carry the load?
David:	Yeah, she did.
Therapist:	Was she a shy person?
David:	Pardon me?
Therapist:	Was she a shy person?
David:	She was quite shy. She didn't really talk much and only when she got angry though, she would talk a lot. And uh . . . like I say, she was always very severe.
Therapist:	Tell her what it was like for her to always to be severe. What did it feel like?

David:	For her?
Therapist:	No, for you.
David:	Well, like I say, I was full of fear and then you would get angry with me or say something.
Therapist:	"I was always just so scared of you, Mom."
David:	And I was so scared. I was very afraid of you, Mom, extremely afraid that when you got angry I was like nothing. It was like . . .
Therapist:	"Oh—it was like I had disappeared. I felt annihilated."
David:	Yeah, annihilated . . . I felt nothing.
Therapist:	Uh-huh.
David:	So scared . . . uncertain, I didn't . . . couldn't think properly.
Therapist:	Right.
David:	And as I look back, I mean, you didn't, I mean I know you didn't mean or know or know any better, but, uh, I guess I have to accept that because I . . . you know . . .
Therapist:	"But what did you want David? I wish you just could have been softer and kinder."
David:	And shown love.
Therapist:	"And shown me that you loved me"?
David:	And shown me. I mean, for me it wasn't enough just to say that you were working hard so that we could get off the farm. I mean first of all, I didn't even know what you were talking about when you first started talking about university, I didn't even know what university was when you were talking about it. And secondly, after I get older, I said to myself "how could we get . . . how could you get the money like to send me to university" [*crying*].
Therapist:	What are the tears about?
David:	Because we had no money.
Therapist:	So you . . . thought it was a pipe dream?
David:	Yes, I never believed her even though I did it [*laughs*].
Therapist:	"I did do it."
David:	Isn't that funny?
Therapist:	Uh-huh. Can you tell her that?
David:	I did it for you mom—you know?

Therapist: "I made it to university."

David: I did it. And then when I went back to school and took an oral exam. I was so afraid that I couldn't even hear the end of the questions, and I flunked, Mom. And I guess then I realized that I was doing all of this for you and not for myself. Even so I—but I did—I got a bachelor's and a master's degree, and I did it. After I flunked the exam, I guess then I realized that a lot of this, I wasn't even doing it for myself. I was doing it for you.

Here David shared with his mother his feelings of love as well as how scared he was as a child (SASB 2-2, 2-4). He was able to say what he needed and to assert himself as well as take care of his own interests (SASB 2-1, 3-4). He was engaged in internally differentiating his experience (LCPP Level 5) and was able to reevaluate his mother's behavior. He realized that she too was scared and shy and that she did not really understand what he needed emotionally (EXP Stage 6; LCPP Level 6).

TRANSFORMATION:
GENERATING NEW EMOTIONAL RESPONSES

In the next three sessions, David continued to grieve his childhood. His therapist responded with empathic affirmation and validation. He expressed his sadness at losing his mother, the lack of affection at home, and his sorrow at not attending his mother's funeral. When he represented his introjected view of his mother, he had her respond with forgiveness and acceptance. His mother also acknowledged how proud she was of his achievements, that he was her favorite child, and how much she had appreciated his help when he was young. As he retold his mother's story, David recalled that his mother had lost her mother when she was 2 years old and had been left in the care of a neighbor. Only after his mother married did she feel she had a home of her own. Subsequently, David was able to recognize that life had been difficult for his father too and recognized how devastating it was for him to lose his wife. As he shared his story and the events of his childhood, he saw events differently and expressed surprise that so many people had loved him.

In the sessions that followed, David began to look at his current life situation more closely. He expressed his dissatisfaction with his marriage. He was irritated with his wife's negative responses to events and was tired of her criticisms. He contemplated separating but realized that it was he who had difficulty setting boundaries and that perhaps if he were more assertive and set limits with his wife, things might improve between them. He decided that he wanted to try setting boundaries before taking the more drastic step of leaving. At the same time, he explored his reaction to his daughter-in-law, whom he experienced as very cold and aloof. He realized that his daughter-in-law reminded him of his mother and that he felt sad, angry, and empty when he was with her and his family.

Given that David's description of his daughter-in-law was similar to the one he had offered about his mother, his therapist saw this as a possible marker of unfinished business with his mother and suggested an empty-chair task. During the task David again told his mother how scared he was of her. He told her that being around her when she was severe and angry was like being in an earthquake. He told her that as a child he had needed more love and reassurance. His representation of his introjected view of his mother expressed concern and remorse that he had experienced her as cold and un-loving. She noted that she did not know how to be different but that she had tried her best to love him and his brothers. After this session David felt more comfortable with his daughter-in-law. He accepted that she was a cold person and that she treated everyone the same way. He did not personalize her behavior toward him and felt freer to be himself around her and not worry so much about her responses.

At this point in the treatment, David visited his extended family. During his visit he reconnected with family and friends and acquired a new perspective on how his siblings viewed him. He was able to visit and thank people whom he recognized had helped him in some way after his mother died. As he reviewed his family's life history, he was able to distinguish his needs as a young adolescent from those of his brothers. He accepted that he wanted to leave home and that he was a good student, and at the same time he recognized that his brothers had missed him and felt that he had deserted them. At this point in therapy his mood had lightened considerably. He said it was as if a bright light had come on in his brain.

David resolved to stay in touch with his family and nurture the relationships that he had rediscovered. He was much happier with his life. He noted that he was enjoying his work, both his teaching and consulting, and began to make plans for the future.

SUMMARY AND ANALYSIS

On the outcome measures, David dropped from a 20 on the Beck Depression Inventory at the beginning of therapy to 0 at the end. His self-esteem increased by 16 points on the Rosenberg Self-Esteem Inventory, and his dysfunctional attitudes decreased by 25 points. He reported that he had fewer interpersonal difficulties and that he suppressed his feelings less and was more reflective about them to solve personal problems. David reported an extremely good alliance with his therapist. His score on the Working Alliance Inventory (WAI) ranged from 5.08 to 6.91 on a 7-point scale, and after Session 4 his score did not fall below 6.41 on the WAI. David also reported changes after every session on the Client Task Specific Change

Measure (CTSC). His ratings ranged from 3.75 to 7 on a 7-point scale. Session 8 marked a significant turning point. After Session 8 his score on the CTSC was 6.94 indicating that he felt more able to stand up to his criticisms, had let go of unresolved feelings toward a significant other, understood his reactions better, and had a sense of how his thoughts influenced his behavior. His score on the CTSC continued to reflect the changes he was making right up till the termination of therapy.

David made significant changes during his therapy. He was able to access and build a more accepting, self-nurturing, and self-protective introject. Consequently, he was less self-critical and able to set boundaries with others so that they would treat him with respect. He mourned the loss of his mother as well as the emotional deprivation he had experienced as a child. The support of his therapist not only made it easier for him to feel safe and freely self-disclose but it also provided a model for him of how to treat himself more kindly. Finally, he was able to see himself and his family in a new light. His relationships were no longer frozen in time but had thawed and were in flux, allowing new possibilities to emerge. Along with these changes he began to feel better about himself and learned to value his strengths.

3

GENERATING NEW
EMOTIONAL RESPONSES

Gayle was a 37-year-old married woman and mother of two children, a son and a daughter, who completed 20 sessions of psychotherapy. She was concerned about being viewed as a "bad mother," was dissatisfied with her parenting, and felt like giving up. She was afraid of perpetuating her family history with her children. She was also concerned with having been unfairly considered "the screwed up one" by her parents and her parents-in-law. She felt unsupported and judged by everybody. She also perceived her life as a "mess" and was afraid of being disdained for being depressed. The stressors that were identified when she entered therapy were her inability to parent her children, conflict with her family of origin, and lack of support.

Gayle depicted her mother as a woman who was hypoglycemic, bordering on diabetic, and who wanted Gayle to be her companion but was unsupportive and disapproving of her. Gayle was tired of trying to meet her mother's needs. She wanted to stop taking care of her mother and wanted to overcome her depression but was fearful that it would be followed by an emotional crash. She was feeling "screwed up," "not good enough," "stupid," and ashamed of her binge eating. She longed to resolve her conflict with her parents and gain her mother's approval. Her parents made her feel like she was a bother. She characterized her father as unsupportive and her mother's "puppet," and her grandmother as rejecting and playing favorites. As a child Gayle's brother had been physically abusive toward her, however her parents blamed her for his behavior. Although Gayle saw her husband as wanting to support her, he did not know how. She was afraid that he would eventually have enough of her depression and leave her. Although her parents-in-law were critical and rejecting of her initially, they had become more approving and supportive over the years.

Gayle was diagnosed pretherapy with major depressive disorder on Axis I; borderline, dependent (dramatic, emotional, and erratic), and some fearful and anxious personality features on Axis II; back and weight problems on Axis III; problems with primary support, discord with parents and brother, and discord between son and daughters on Axis IV; and an occupational problem, unemployment, on Axis V. She had a Global Assessment of Functioning score of 49. Her Beck Depression Inventory score at 33 was in the severely depressed range.

CASE FORMULATION

Gayle said she needed a steady flow of support and encouragement and that self-control was difficult. She was able to reach out to others but had difficulty supporting herself. She saw herself as needy, helpless, incompetent, and vulnerable to rejection, betrayal, and domination. She also felt deprived of emotional support and experienced herself as powerless, out of control, defective, and overweight. She judged herself to be a bad mother and a bad daughter. Her positive views of others, which unfolded over therapy, involved seeing her therapist, some nurses, and her mother-in-law as powerful, loving, and perfect. Her negative views of others involved seeing her mother, mother-in-law, brother, former boyfriend, former boyfriend's parents, and nurses as rejecting, controlling, betraying, and abandoning. Gayle cultivated supportive relationships, protested dramatically when not supported or validated, and became punitive toward those who signaled possible rejection.

At the beginning of therapy, Gayle struggled with feelings of anger toward her parents. She felt that her parents judged her feelings of anger as inappropriate; consequently, she felt guilty about them. Gayle wanted to overcome her guilt and need for approval as well as her maladaptive eating as a way of dealing with her emotions. By the end of treatment, Gayle had resolved her unfinished business with her mother by letting go of her need for her approval and asserting boundaries. Ultimately, she came to validate her own feelings and approve of herself.

In terms of her emotional processing, Gayle was highly expressive and had a total of 510 emotion episodes during treatment, a high frequency of occurrence of emotions in therapy and almost double the number for the average client. From Session 1 Gayle spoke in an emotional voice with tears. However, she had a complaining quality in her voice and blamed others for her difficulties. She spoke quickly with an external vocal quality (high energy with very regular stress patterns). The therapist used empathic responses to promote a focus on her bodily experience. Gayle appeared hurt and angry at her mother and the world and was immediately appreciative of the therapist's support. She expressed a lot of anger and sadness in the early sessions, and these feelings were somewhat underregulated. She felt guilty for crying so much, both in the world at-large and in the therapy sessions.

Gayle's core maladaptive emotion scheme was of sadness and a sense of abandonment. These feelings became the central focus of therapy early in the treatment within the context of working on her unresolved feelings toward her mother. The goals of therapy were to resolve her unfinished business with her mother and to have Gayle become less self-critical and more self-validating. Her therapist thought that she needed to separate her feelings of anger and sadness, which were fused into complaint and helplessness, to acknowledge the hurt and grieve the loss of not having a supportive family and to stop condemning herself for being sexually abused by a neighbor. Gayle appeared to be aware of her feelings; however, she silenced them to avoid conflict with others. One of the primary tasks was to help her change her behavior so that she could become more expressive of her feelings and needs and differentiate herself from significant others.

BONDING AND AWARENESS

During this phase the therapist concentrated on getting more information about Gayle and provided an empathic supportive environment to build a good working alliance. At Session 1 Gayle announced that she had quit her job because she was depressed and that she wanted to be happy. She said that her children needed more from her and that her husband did not want her to work. Also in that session she reported that she had been sexually abused as a child but never told her mother because she was afraid her mother would hate her. Gayle said that all her life she has been trying to meet her mother's needs, and she did not want to do that anymore.

Gayle was sad that she did not feel cared for by her mother; she wanted a good relationship with her but was not getting results. She felt angry that her mother was not supportive. Though she wanted her mother's love and approval, she recognized that it might never be there. She wished her parents would take some responsibility for her life being a mess instead of saying that they had done their best for her. She no longer felt her family of origin was normal. She wished she could separate from them and stop seeking their approval, a goal her husband supported. Gayle felt that she was not good enough and stupid. She often felt like giving up so that no one would depend on her. She expressed sadness that her parents made her feel like a bother, and she was worried that she treated her children in the same way. Gayle was ashamed and concerned that she was a bad mother because she degraded her son when he was acting up. In Session 1 she said she wished she could forgive and forget, be pain free, and be emotionally available for her children.

Gayle brought her wedding pictures to Session 2. She complained that she hated having to look perfect and that appearance was so important to people. The therapist listened and responded in an empathic manner to her narrative. Gayle recalled that she had had a hard time after she got married and coped with her frustration by eating. She expressed sadness and longing for the happy and peppy self she had been when 18 years old. She recalled that she had become depressed when a love affair ended and she lost the love of her life. She felt that people were critical of her and was angry that everyone saw her husband as the good guy and her as the bad guy. Gayle was angry with him because he pretended that everything was OK.

Gayle noted that she was better off when she did not see her parents. She felt some shame and pain when her parents told her to calm down and was angry at her parents for trying to control her. She was angry that her mom hid in bed or put up a front. She blamed her mother for a rotten childhood and at the same time felt guilty for being angry at her parents. Gayle also felt guilty for not protecting her daughter from her mother. Gayle struggled with feelings that she was not good enough, which led her to feel hopeless. Toward the end of the session, Gayle felt overwhelmed. Her therapist suggested a breathing exercise to help regulate her breathing in the session.

By Session 3 Gayle and her therapist had established a safe bond and a clear collaborative focus to work on her unfinished business with her mother and her need for support. From the start there was agreement on the utility of approaching and focusing on her emotions, and she engaged readily in the empty-chair dialogue. Gayle saw her mother as taking her brother's side when Gayle and her brother were in conflict, failing to protect her and invalidating her experience that her brother was the culprit in their conflicts. According to Gayle, her father was unsupportive of her and supportive of her mother. Although she initially experienced her husband as unsupportive, early in the process of therapy she came to recognize that he was supportive of her.

EVOKING AND EXPLORING FEELINGS

Having established a bond and developed a focus on the underlying determinants of the depression, Gayle's unfinished business with her mother and her associated need for support and validation, her therapist moved readily in Session 3 into the evocation phase by accessing Gayle's core painful experiences. This involved accessing her core feelings of anger and sadness related to her mother and her feelings of abandonment and shame at being criticized and unsupported. Once core maladaptive emotion schemes are accessed they can be exposed to new important experience and transformed.

In Session 3 Gayle arrived angry at her husband for not supporting her with home schooling. After discussing her concerns about her son, she expressed how angry she was at her parents for blaming her for the long-standing conflict with her brother. She felt her parents were unfair and that her mother made her feel like she was crazy and screwed up. Identifying her feelings of complaint and neglect as a marker of unfinished business, her therapist suggested an empty-chair dialogue to help evoke and express Gayle's anger.

Gayle: When I had the big argument with my mom it was like "You always fight with your brother, you know you need to grow up," and it's like all me, me, me, me, I'm the one.

Therapist: Ah, so she was saying it was your fault.

Gayle: Yeah. I'm the one that used to try and make his bed and show him my love and buy all these stupid things, where I was used like a dog and I said, "Don't tell me that I didn't try."

Therapist: You're really just brimming.

Gayle: Yeah. I'm, like I said to Barry the whole week, I said, "I'm like a volcano; I'm gonna explode, and I don't want to." But, you know, my mom keeps phoning me; I haven't phoned her.

Therapist: I'd like us to try something. I think it might be helpful.

Gayle: [*blowing nose*] OK.

Therapist: What I'd like to try is for you to imagine your mom here.

Gayle: OK.

Therapist: In this chair. Can you imagine her here and have a dialogue with her? How does that sound?

Gayle: [*laughs*] I don't know. I do it in my head all the time [*laughs*].

Therapist: Yeah. OK. Why don't we see where it goes, and I'll be right there next to you. We'll just see what happens, OK? Can you imagine your mom there?

Gayle: Sort of.

Therapist: What do you see?

Gayle: Well, she wants to be accepted, and she doesn't think she's doing anything wrong.

The therapist asked Gayle to visualize her mother. This brought up an episodic memory and sensory sensations associated with her mother to facilitate access to Gayle's emotional experience. Gayle then went on to express her anger and resentment that she was required to grow up and be mature even though her brother was difficult. She felt dismissed and blamed (SASB [Structural Analysis of Social Behavior] 1-6) by her mother. She responded by protesting and walling off (SASB 2-6, 2-8) from her mother, but she was freely self-disclosing to her therapist (SASB 2-2) and willing to go along with her therapist's suggestions (SASB 2-4). In terms of her emotional processing, Gayle was describing her situation with clear reference to her emotions (EXP [The Experiencing Scale] Stage 3). As she began to imagine her mother, the therapist encouraged Gayle to express her feelings.

Gayle: Yeah. You hurt me so bad as a kid, Mom.

Therapist: That's so deep, yeah. What do you want from her?

Gayle: I want some space right now.

Therapist: Can you tell her that? "Mom, I just . . ."

Gayle: [*sighs, blows nose*] I'm sorry.

Therapist: That's OK.

Gayle: I'm a cry baby. It's happened [*laughs*] . . .

Therapist: Good. That's why you're here. [*laughs*] This is the place to cry.

Gayle: Well, Mom, I'd really like some space. I know you don't understand, and it's not that I don't care, but I feel like you control me, and I can't be myself when you're around.

Gayle continued to engage in the dialogue and to follow her therapist's suggestions (SASB 2-4). However, she was somewhat dismissive of her own experience and critical of herself for crying (SASB 3-8, 3-6). She judged her behavior in terms of external standards and rules (LCPP [Levels of Client Perceptual Processing] Level 3). Although she was able to assert her need for more space (SASB 2-1, 3-4), she was concerned about hurting her mother. As Gayle's feelings of guilt emerged, her therapist asked her to play her mother to heighten the impact of her mother's behavior on her and facilitate Gayle's awareness of her needs.

Therapist: What's happening for you as you see her there?

Gayle: I just feel guilty.

Therapist: Oh, yeah?

Gayle: I'm the bad daughter [*pulling tissue from box and sniffling*].

Therapist: OK. Change. Make her feel like the bad daughter. What do you do as your mom? What does she do to make you feel that way?

Gayle: "I don't know why she's gone bad. She turned into a lion all of a sudden."

Therapist:	Can you tell her, "You're a lion"?
Gayle:	Yeah. She told me that "You're a lion."
Therapist:	Uh-huh.
Gayle:	[*sniffs*] "You're not the kid I raised. You're just somebody else, and I don't know who you are, and I don't know why you're acting the way you're acting. You just need to pull yourself up by your bootstraps and get on with life."
Therapist:	OK. Change. She says, "Just pull yourself up by your bootstraps." What happens for you when you hear that?
Gayle:	I told her I was going to kill myself [*pulling tissue from box*].
Therapist:	Uh-huh.
Gayle:	She said, "Why don't you get a job?" I said that if I get a job right now I will kill myself. I can only handle so much. I've been trying to handle so much pain.
Therapist:	Uh-huh. Tell her, "Mom, I'm in a lot of pain."
Gayle:	Mom, I'm in a lot of pain right now, and I don't need you to come down on me.
Therapist:	Yeah. "I don't want your criticism."
Gayle:	Yeah. And I don't even care if you understand.
Therapist:	Uh-huh. "I don't care. I don't care about you right now."
Gayle:	That's right.
Therapist:	Can you tell her that?
Gayle:	Yes. I don't care about you right now, Mom. It's my kids that matter the most.

Here Gayle moved away from judging her behavior by external standards and rules (EXP Stage 2; LCPP Level 3) and began to express her feelings of intense pain (EXP Stage 4; LCPP Level 5). She expressed her needs and asserted her limits with her mother (EXP Stage 6; LCPP Level 6) as she shifted from taking care of the other to protecting and taking care of herself (SASB 3-4, 3-2). During this exercise Gayle has been able to trust and rely on her therapist (SASB 2-4) and clearly express how she is feeling (SASB 2-2). Later in the session, Gayle engaged in another empty-chair dialogue with her father. At first she expressed anger and blame that her father condemned her and her husband (SASB 3-6, 3-7). Later she was able to express her feelings of hurt that he was not able to say he loved her (EXP Stage 4; SASB 2-2).

Gayle:	He needs to come to terms with all the screw ups he's made and not to turn around and condemn me or my husband for going bankrupt or . . .

Therapist:	Yeah.
Gayle:	I don't even see it as my fault, Dad. I see it as your and Mom's fault.
Therapist:	So what happens for you when he condemns you? Can you tell him how that—how does that leave you feeling?
Gayle:	It makes me really angry.
Therapist:	So tell him you are really angry.
Client:	I'm really angry because I see it, Dad, as not my fault. I've worked hard.

Later in the dialogue Gayle was able to express her pain and her needs vis-à-vis the other.

Therapist:	So is it sort of like, "Dad, I want you to accept me for who I am"?
Gayle:	[*sighs*] He isn't, he doesn't even say I love you to me.
Therapist:	Can you tell him that?
Gayle:	Dad, that hurts. My husband says he loves his kids, and I've heard his dad say I love you.
Therapist:	Yeah.
Gayle:	And his, Barry's mom and dad, say I love you to me and you don't.
Therapist:	Yeah.
Gayle:	[*crying*] It's like, oh well, I've disappointed you so . . .
Therapist:	Uh-huh.
Gayle:	Or "I'm too manly and have never been able to tell you that."
Therapist:	Yeah. "So when you don't tell me you love me it hurts."

Gayle began to share her feelings and express her pain (EXP Stage 4; LCPP Level 4). At the next session, she reported that she had had a good week and felt good about setting boundaries with her mother by turning the answering service off and unplugging the phone at night. She said that she enjoyed the peace from her parents and was relieved that her mother could not leave messages to make her feel guilty about being a bad daughter. She expressed anger that her parents had hurt her so much. She described her mother as abusive and felt that her mother abandoned her when Gayle stopped meeting her mother's needs. Consequently, Gayle felt the need to protect herself from her mother. Her mother was shaming, disapproving, and embarrassed about Gayle's looks. Gayle experienced her mother as controlling and was worried that things might never improve between them. She would have liked to see her parents without allowing them to have control over her. Her therapist suggested an empty-chair dialogue with Gayle's mother to try to resolve some of the negative feelings that Gayle had. During the dialogue, Gayle expressed some of the hurt and loneliness underlying her anger and said how abandoned she felt. She acknowledged hating her parents for what they had done to her.

Gayle: [*pulling tissue from box and sniffling*] And, Mom, I don't feel like I have to meet your needs anymore. I don't feel like I have to make sure you guys are given gifts and like showing each of you the attention you need and I'm not gonna be there for you to do that. You're an adult. You need to do that yourself.

Therapist: Yeah. "I don't want to do that anymore."

Gayle: I won't meet your needs anymore, Mom. You weren't there for me when I needed you, and that hurt.

Therapist: Yeah. Tell her about the hurt. What was the hurt like?

Gayle: Makes me feel abandoned.

Therapist: Yeah.

Gayle: Like I'm alone and I'm helpless, and I'll never get out of the situation I'm in.

Therapist: Uh-huh. "You abandoned me, and it's left me feeling alone and helpless and . . ."

Gayle: Yeah. It's like it's left a scar.

Therapist: Uh-huh.

Gayle: And even when I get up now, and I'm facing the battle I'm facing, you still hurt me.

Therapist: Uh-huh.

Gayle: And I'll never forget the scar, and I won't allow another wound to happen again.

Therapist: Ah.

Gayle: Because I know it's just going to happen again because I've gotten up so many times before and just thought, oh well, it's just me, and I know it's not me anymore [*pulling tissues out of box*].

Therapist: Uh-huh. So, "I'm protecting myself now."

Gayle: Yeah.

Therapist: Is that what you're saying to her?

Gayle: Yeah.

Therapist: "Yeah, protecting myself from you."

Gayle: It's time for me to look out for me, and I know I've always been taught everybody else should be first, but there's a time in my life right now.

Here Gayle clearly and freely expressed the hurt and pain she felt in her interactions with her mother (EXP Stage 4; LCPP Level 5; SASB 2-2). She accepted her therapist's suggestions (SASB 2-4) and was able to clearly state her needs and establish a definite boundary with her mother (EXP Stage 6; LCPP Level 7; SASB 3-4, 3-3). Subsequently, she expressed her core emotion scheme of loneliness and her sense of not belonging.

Therapist: Can you tell her what it was like for you to not get what you needed from her all those years?

Gayle: I don't even know.

Therapist: It's hard to say.

Gayle: It is as a kid you feel really bad . . . lonely.

Therapist: Yeah. Can you tell her, "Mom, I felt lonely as a kid. I was alone."

Gayle: Yeah. Mom, I felt lonely as a kid.

Therapist: Yeah.

Gayle: I felt like I fit in with you, but I didn't fit in with my brother or my father.

Therapist: Uh-huh.

Gayle: And now I feel like I don't fit in with you either, and the only reason why I did is because I did whatever you said.

Therapist: Uh-huh.

Gayle: And I was shamed into doing it. I wasn't allowed to be my own person.

Therapist: Uh-huh.

Gayle: And I want to be who I am.

Therapist: "I felt like I didn't fit."

Gayle: Yeah.

Therapist: "And now I feel I don't fit with you."

Gayle: Yeah [sniffs]. I feel like you're living a lie. I feel like you're pretending everything's okay.

Therapist: Uh-huh. "You came from an abused, physically abusive . . ."

Gayle: . . . family and you're not gonna perpetuate that. You made up your mind when you had us as kids you'd never perpetuate that.

Therapist: Uh-huh.

Gayle: And I don't think you have the realm, the scope to admit that you did perpetuate it, just in a different form, and even though you didn't mean to, you still did it.

In this segment Gayle held the other accountable and set limits with respect to how she wanted to be treated (EXP Stage 6; LCPP Level 7; SASB 3-3, 3-4, 2-1). A primary focus in this therapy was to help Gayle differentiate from her mother. The therapist worked with her to help her find her voice and express the feelings that she had silenced for so long. As she expressed her feelings, Gayle began to redefine herself vis-à-vis her mother and to assert her independence. Gayle moved from shameful inadequacy to anger to asserting her needs.

Gayle: And if you felt my hair would be better in a different way, you'd tell me to change it.

Therapist: Uh-huh.

Gayle: And you always said, "Oh I wasn't trying to mean anything by it." But I mean, what mother in the world does that to their kid? That's so stupid.

Therapist: "When you did that to me I felt like I wasn't good enough or adequate or . . ."

Gayle: Yeah. Mom, in a sense, you know, hate's wrong, and it only hurts my own self, but I really find it hard not to hate you and dad.

Therapist: Uh-huh. So, "I hate you."

Gayle: I find it really hard because I know I shouldn't, but I do.

Therapist: Uh-huh.

Gayle: I'm really angry.

Therapist: Yeah. So "I don't want you to hurt us anymore."

Gayle: Yeah.

Therapist: What do you want from her?

Gayle: I just want her to leave me alone

Therapist: Can you tell her that?

Gayle: Yeah, Mom, I just want you to accept the fact you need to leave me alone.

Therapist: Yeah.

Gayle: That you're not doing your grandkids any good.

Therapist:	Uh-huh.
Gayle:	They don't want your gifts; they want your love.
Therapist:	Uh-huh.
Gayle:	[*sniffs*] And they don't want your judgment and your opinions.
Therapist:	"So don't judge us; leave us alone." What's happening when you say that?
Gayle:	[*sighs*] It's almost a wall. Like I feel, like I know there's a wall there. It's like . . .
Therapist:	Uh-huh.
Gayle:	It's like I'm building a wall to protect myself and she can't get through. It sounds kind of funny, but
Therapist:	No, it's yeah.
Gayle:	I just want it to be there forever. You really hurt me.
Therapist:	Yeah.
Gayle:	[*sighs*] And I'm so sick of pain. I just want to shut you out.
Therapist:	Ah.
Gayle:	And I don't want any more pain.
Therapist:	Uh-huh. "I'm shutting you out so you can't hurt me anymore."

In Session 5 Gayle began to focus on her sexual abuse. She expressed concern that she was not able to face her issues in therapy. She reported that she felt she was a mess and that she was sexually abused when really little. She was embarrassed for allowing the abuse, feeling it was her fault instead of seeing herself as a victim. Gayle observed that her husband, who was physically abused, was angry with himself as well. Gayle then went on to explore how the abuse had affected her personal relationships. She felt that her ex-boyfriend had taken advantage of her when she was an adolescent. Her therapist suggested an empty-chair exercise to help process these lingering bad feelings. Gayle agreed. During the exercise, Gayle expressed her anger toward her ex-boyfriend for the way that he had treated her. She recalled that the way he had treated her made her feel worthless and that the fact he had pushed her sexually made her feel used and disrespected. She expressed anger at him for touching her and hurting her feelings when he broke off the relationship. She recalled that she had felt suicidal at the time because she had expected that they would marry. His callous treatment of her had had an impact on how she expressed herself sexually in her marriage, making her afraid of sexual contact with her husband for fear of being taken advantage of again. She expressed a wish for an apology from him and a desire to move forward, to put what happened behind her, and to stop feeling ashamed. Gayle did not fully resolve this dialogue, although she felt OK about expressing her anger at being exploited and relieved that she had expressed some of her feelings. She still felt pain and wished she could make the pain go away and forgive herself.

In Sessions 6 and 7, Gayle began to explore a number of other issues. She explored her concerns about her children, especially her son who had been diagnosed with attention-deficit/hyperactivity disorder, her husband, her in-laws, and her brother. Gayle agreed to focus on her brother's impact on her in an empty-chair dialogue because this felt like the most salient concern. After imagining her brother in the chair, she recalled how rejected she felt by him. She recalled that her brother threatened her life three times and that her parents didn't seem to care. She expressed anger that he scared her so much. She also recalled feeling hurt and embarrassed when her brother punched her in school. She remembered a girl laughing at her and saying she deserved it. However, a guy defended her and told her brother that he should not hit girls. Gayle wished that she had had a brother who loved her. During the empty-chair exercise, Gayle set a boundary with her brother saying that she wanted him out of her life (EXP Stage 4, 6; LCPP Level 5, 6; SASB 2-1, 3-3, 3-4). She expressed her disappointment that her parents did not do a good job of parenting so that she and her brother could have been friends. She recalled how her family twisted things around and blamed her for the difficulties with her brother. Gayle expressed a desire to be free from frustration and to have her brother out of her life because she was tired of his judging her. As in the earlier sessions, Gayle was able to assert her needs and hold others accountable for their behavior. She engaged in new behavior with respect to them as she expressed her needs and protected herself from negative behavior.

At the next session, Gayle reported that she had had a difficult week and that she had been crying. She reported that she felt like a volcano was erupting inside of her and wondered when it would stop. She was appreciative of her husband's support but was upset at how she treated him and the children. She noted that she had felt some relief after doing some chair work with her brother and felt she was beginning to understand what was going on and how she could be in control by setting boundaries and standing up for herself without being overwhelmed by anger. She was longing for a sense of calm that she loses with her mother's attempts to control her and make her feel guilty. She reported that she had burst into tears after a telephone conversation with her mother who refused to acknowledge Gayle's problems. Her husband responded with compassion and support. Gayle noted that she feels some compassion for her parents because of their history of being abused as children. She wished that she could share everything with her mother and felt sad that she had to hold herself back for fear of being hurt again. In addition, Gayle reported that she had applied for breast reduction and abdominal surgery and expressed anger at her surgeon for suggesting that she diet instead. Toward the end of the session, she observed that she was angry at her husband for insisting on sex the previous night. Gayle noted that she does not enjoy sex. For the most part, she does not have desire unless they have sex in the middle of the night because it feels safer.

In Session 8 Gayle reported that her husband had apologized for his behavior when he insisted on sex. She observed that her mother was inconsistent in her treatment of her, sometimes acting loving and at others being very disapproving. Gayle reflected on her need for approval, and during an empty-chair exercise said that she wished her mother would take responsibility for being a bad mother. She expressed feelings of guilt that she did not have as much contact with her mother as her mother would have liked. However, Gayle questioned whether she should feel guilty. She felt angry at her mother for making her feel guilty for not returning her phone calls. She was uncomfortable for not meeting her mother's needs even though she felt she did not have to do so and recognized that her mother did not care about her needs. Gayle recalled that she had been a mess when she did what her mother wanted her to do. She observed that her mother tried to control her with domineering looks and disapproval in her voice. Gayle expressed disgust with how her mother controlled her father and how her father was like a puppet. As a result, Gayle indicated that she felt robbed of a relationship with her father because she did not know who he was independently of her mother. She wished her mother realized how selfish she had been. The therapist suggested an empty-chair dialogue to help Gayle process how she felt when her mother was disapproving.

Therapist:	Right, somehow you always end up in these interactions feeling just yucky and . . .
Gayle:	Uh-huh.
Therapist:	So how does your mom do that to you? That's what I'm interested in getting to here.
Gayle:	The meaning.
Therapist:	Ah, the meaning. It's not what she says; it's what she means to Gayle. What would the meaning be?
Gayle:	The judgmental look. If we're watching, if the kids were watching a funny video that they really enjoyed . . .
Therapist:	Uh-huh.
Gayle:	And if there was a part in it that she didn't, she would say, this is stupid, and she sort of is rolling her eyes.
Therapist:	So rolling the eyes, the sigh, the finger.
Gayle:	Well, it's the whole body.
Therapist:	Yeah.

Gayle:	Just like . . .
Therapist:	Yeah, the gestures.
Gayle:	Exactly. It's total body language. It's like everything, and then when the kids come, it's like, oh, hello children. It's so fake, and they climb on her lap, and one thing that made me so mad was when Di was saying like, she was laughing at everything, and ha, ha, that was so cute.

Here the therapist had asked Gayle to enact her mother's behavior to heighten Gayle's awareness of its impact on her and to bring her feelings alive. After enacting the disapproving mother, the therapist asked Gayle to change chairs.

Therapist:	Tell your mother what it's like to sit there and see that gesture. What does it do to you, that look and the lie?
Gayle:	You make me feel inferior.
Therapist:	Uh-huh.
Gayle:	Incompetent.
Therapist:	Uh-huh.
Gayle:	You make me feel like I don't have good judgment.
Therapist:	Uh-huh.
Gayle:	Especially pertaining to things that are good for my children.
Therapist:	Uh-huh.
Gayle:	And like you have it all together, and I don't.
Therapist:	So "you make me feel kind of messed up."
Gayle:	Very messed up.
Therapist:	"I feel very messed up, yeah."
Gayle:	And I feel very intimidated.
Therapist:	Yeah.
Gayle:	Especially when I know something is displeasing you.
Therapist:	Uh-huh.
Gayle:	But it's something that I want to do, and I don't care if it displeases you, and it really is a battle inside of myself that usually makes me sick to my stomach.
Therapist:	Yeah, "so I get sick from my struggle with you."
Gayle:	And sometimes when you phone, I think, this is crazy, you are so wonderful, and you do love me, and there is a chance that I might get your approval.

Therapist:	Uh-huh.
Gayle:	And the next phone call I realize the approval is only with the game.
Therapist:	Uh-huh.
Gayle:	It's only your way of getting me to do what you want me to do.
Therapist:	Uh-huh. "So this game leaves me feeling disappointed."
Gayle:	I'm disappointed; I feel empty; I feel like I'm robbed.
Therapist:	What is she robbing you of?
Gayle:	You're robbing me of the sense of being a good daughter.
Therapist:	Uh-huh.
Gayle:	And you're robbing me of the approval that I'm doing okay with my kids.
Therapist:	Yeah.
Gayle:	That to be my own person is just like reaching out into the fog. I mean, I'm who I am.
Therapist:	Yeah.
Gayle:	I'm still trying to figure it out, and . . .

In this part of the dialogue, Gayle had accepted her therapist's suggestions (SASB 2-4) and had clearly expressed her feelings (EXP Stage 4; LCPP Level 5; SASB 2-1). Once she had accessed and expressed her feelings about her core sense of being invalidated, her therapist asked her what she needs.

Therapist:	What do you need from her in a sense?
Gayle:	Stop trying to control me.
Therapist:	Yeah, say that again.
Gayle:	Stop trying to control me; I'm sick of it.
Therapist:	Yeah.
Gayle:	And I want you to see it.
Therapist:	"I want you to own this controlling behavior."
Gayle:	Yeah, I want you to realize that you are doing it.
Therapist:	Yeah.
Gayle:	Your mother did it, and you're doing it, and I'm not going to do it to my kids. I'm going to do everything I can to stop myself.
Therapist:	Yes, yes, "trying really hard not to control my kids the way you controlled me, and I want you to take responsibility for what you did and stop it."

Gayle:	Yeah, because I need to be free, and my kids need to be free of this. It's not fair.
Therapist:	Yeah.
Gayle:	Yeah, I am very angry.
Therapist:	Yeah, can you tell her again, "I'm really angry at you."
Gayle:	I'm really angry at you, Mom [*cries*]. You've got no right to do what you do, and it hurts me.
Therapist:	Yeah.
Gayle:	[*sniffs*] And you have always favored my brother.
Therapist:	"It hurts that you favored him over me."
Gayle:	Yeah, it does. It makes me so mad. They deny his incompetence, and they tell me I'm incompetent, and that makes me really angry. You want me to be what I used to be, and it's not going to happen.
Therapist:	So it sounds like being their puppet didn't feel right to you?
Gayle:	No, it didn't feel right.
Therapist:	Yeah.
Gayle:	It felt like she was saying, "someday you will get straightened out, and you'll be what you used to be."
Therapist:	Uh-huh.
Gayle:	I used to be very happy all the time. But then I was in my room and depressed out of my brains and doing whatever she wanted, and I'm not going to do it again.
Therapist:	So can you tell her, "let me be who I am now"?
Gayle:	Yeah, Mom, who you see now, is who I really am.
Therapist:	Yes, "I want you to love me for who I am."
Gayle:	I want you to love me for who I am, I might not always do what you want me to do, but that's okay because I'm not you.

During this exercise Gayle enacted different behaviors with respect to her mother. This change indicated some resolution of Gayle's unfinished business in the session because Gayle requested that she be loved and accepted for who she is (EXP Stage 6; LCPP Level 6; SASB 3-4, 3-3, 2-1). This represents a major shift because Gayle did not try to block the other out and withdraw in protest but clearly stated that she expects to be loved and respected for the person she is. In the next few sessions, Gayle reported more changes as she began to consolidate the new sense of self that she was developing.

TRANSFORMATION:
GENERATING NEW EMOTIONAL RESPONSES

In Session 9 Gayle noted that she felt on the verge of seeing something new but couldn't see it quite yet. She reported feeling relieved and freer with respect to her childhood abuse issues. She was happy that she was able to assert herself with her sister-in-law when she felt angry with her and did not "pop" or "freak out." Previously, she would have felt responsible for others and guilty when she was angry and then she would have eaten until it hurt. In Session 10 she reported that she felt overwhelmed with problems with respect to her children, her house, and her family's difficult financial situation. She was resentful with her husband but relieved that she had recently become employed and would be able to get some time away from home. She needed some space from family demands.

Session 11 was important because Gayle dealt with her internal critical voice for the first time. She reported that she was frustrated with herself for being too slow at work and felt stupid and afraid of screwing up and losing her job. Up to now the therapy had focused on Gayle's relationship with her mother. She had been working toward greater differentiation and a more solid sense of self. The focus shifted as more markers of self-critical behavior emerged. The therapist suggested a two-chair dialogue at the following self-critical split.

> *Gayle:* I'm screwing up again; I can't do anything right. I'm not going to keep this job; I can't stick to anything; this job won't last long, I'm going to do something wrong.
>
> *Therapist:* "Something bad is going to happen, and it will be my fault."
>
> *Gayle:* Exactly.
>
> *Therapist:* What happens to you inside when you're thinking that?
>
> *Gayle:* I was all upset. I couldn't handle the kids; I couldn't handle any noise at all. Barry had to keep them really quiet.

In the dialogue, she realized that her critical voice was like her mother's, making her feel she was a failure and making her feel dread, fear, and guilt. It was telling her that something would go wrong and that she should stop trying. She wanted to set a boundary with that critical voice. The therapist asked her to give voice to the critical dialogue (EXP Stage 2; LCPP Level 3; SASB 3-6).

> *Gayle:* OK. I'm miserable. You're screwing it up. I knew you couldn't do it.
>
> *Therapist:* Yeah, it's a miserable, mean voice.
>
> *Gayle:* Yeah.

Therapist:	And I guess it makes you feel kind of inadequate and . . .
Gayle:	Right.
Therapist:	So how does . . .
Gayle:	[*saying to the other chair*] I don't know why you even bother trying at anything because you're not going to succeed.
Therapist:	Uh-huh.
Gayle:	Something's going to go wrong—haven't figured it out yet, but something's going to go wrong.
Therapist:	You're going to fail.
Gayle:	Yeah, yes. You're heading down the street; you've fooled everybody that you've got a job with the bank; and everybody's like wow, you're going to screw it up.

Now that Gayle had clearly accessed and represented the critical voice, her therapist asked her to switch chairs to access how Gayle reacts to the criticism.

Therapist:	She's just told you, "Go to your room, be depressed." [*Gayle laughs.*] "Don't even bother." How does that feel when you hear that?
Gayle:	To hell with you! [*laughs*] That's what I feel like.
Therapist:	So why don't you tell her?
Gayle:	I want to overcome that. I'm really angry.
Therapist:	Yeah.
Gayle:	I don't need the constant failure thrown up in my face.
Therapist:	Yeah.
Gayle:	Not everything that's gone wrong in my life is my fault.
Therapist:	Uh-huh.
Gayle:	Things happen, and I have to do what my mother-in-law told me, and go forward.
Therapist:	Uh-huh.
Gayle:	And if I listen to you, then I'm going to go backward.
Therapist:	Yeah.
Gayle:	I need to fight it.
Therapist:	So "I'm really angry at you, undermining my attempts to fight it."

Gayle:	Yeah. I'm really angry at you for trying to make me down again.
Therapist:	Uh-huh.
Gayle:	For uh, making me feel dread and fear and guilt.
Therapist:	Uh-huh. What happens for you when you hear that? It's almost like . . . ? Can you tell her what happens? It almost really destroys you.
Gayle:	When I hear that, that just makes me want to cry [cries].
Therapist:	Yeah.
Gayle:	It makes me feel that it's going to be another bad experience to put on the chalkboard, and why didn't I kill myself when I was a teenager.
Therapist:	Yeah.
Gayle:	Because then I wouldn't have to feel all this pain.
Therapist:	So "it wipes me out." Can you tell her that "it wipes me out when you're like that"?
Gayle:	You wipe me out when you're like that.
Therapist:	Yeah, crushing.
Gayle:	It makes me feel—like a nobody.
Therapist:	Yeah.
Gayle:	It makes me feel worthless and . . .
Therapist:	Yeah.
Gayle:	It's suffocating, and it's not healthy, I don't want it.
Therapist:	"Crushing me, taking the life out of me."
Gayle:	Yeah [sniffs]. It's a very abusive thing.
Therapist:	Yeah.
Gayle:	It's not needed [sniffs].
Therapist:	Yeah. Tell her, "I don't want that abuse anymore."
Gayle:	I don't want you to abuse me anymore. I don't want it.
Therapist:	"Yeah, and I'm really angry."
Gayle:	I'm angry at you for making me feel so pressured [cries], and I act out of guilt, and I do stupid things, and then I feel worse and it's just a vicious cycle.

Here Gayle once again asserted her needs and set limits on how she treats herself. She recognized that the behavior was abusive and that it needed to be stopped (EXP Stages 4, 6; LCPP Level 6; SASB 3-4, 3-3, 2-1). Subsequently Gayle began to work on her feelings of guilt for having been sexually abused. She said that it was not her fault and that nobody was there to protect her. However, she realized that she was afraid of being hurt again if she did not have the critical voice to protect her. She became angry that her critical voice was hurting her and doing damage and was afraid that her depression would wreck her life. She was both angry and sad that the abuse happened and that she was not protected by her mother. She expressed resentment that her mother did not see she was hurt, self-blaming, and in pain. She was afraid that if her mother had known about the sexual abuse, she would have thrown her out and hated her for it.

Gayle wants to give her children what she never received. She expressed sadness that her mother would not get help or repair their relationship. She was afraid of being like her parents and unable to grow but reassured herself that she was changing already. When thinking about feeling guilty about not meeting her mother's standards, Gayle said "I have to make my own standards and not feel guilty." Reflecting on the session, she felt surprised by how powerful it was to express her feelings. She said that part of her has been frozen and scared to death. She teared up recognizing how self-critical she was and how she had wanted to kill herself because of this. She then addressed the critic saying she needed to be allowed to be human and to make mistakes.

Gayle: It's been like a rope around my neck just waiting to be tight enough to choke my life out, and I have a life worth living, and I don't need to die. I can be productive, and I can stay productive if I can just get you to work with me instead of against me.

Therapist: How could she work with you? What do you need from her?

Gayle: To forgive me, to realize that it wasn't my fault.

Therapist: Yeah.

Gayle: To love me.

Therapist: So you want her to realize that the truth is that little children can't stop . . .

Gayle: Abuse.

Therapist: And it's not their fault.

Gayle: It's not their fault. Any little kid that gets hurt, they need help.

Therapist: Yeah.

Gayle: They don't need to be beaten down.

Therapist: Yeah.

Gayle: They themselves [blows nose] . . .

Therapist:	Yeah. So you need forgiveness, and you need comfort.
Gayle:	I need love. I need to be loved for who I am whether I'm loud or quiet or . . .
Therapist:	Yeah.
Gayle:	I can't think straight, or I can think straight, no matter what I do, I need acceptance.
Therapist:	Yeah, OK, change. [*Gayle changes chairs.*] What do you want to say to her?
Gayle:	I don't understand why you let it happen.
Therapist:	Uh-huh.
Gayle:	I still feel that you could have stopped it even though everybody says you couldn't, and I don't know how I'm going to change because it's been so many years that I've hated you and blamed you and felt guilt, made you feel guilty.
Therapist:	Uh-huh.
Gayle:	But I'd like to change; I'd like to help you be productive.
Therapist:	Yeah.
Gayle:	If we work together . . .
Therapist:	Yeah.
Gayle:	You could be normal.
Therapist:	What does it mean for you to accept that she, that it wasn't her fault? What happens to you, the critical voice?
Gayle:	It takes away my power.
Therapist:	Yeah. I guess you feel like you've got to disappear then.
Gayle:	But if I do that, she might make the same mistake again.
Therapist:	Uh-huh.
Gayle:	She might not use her head.
Therapist:	So tell her that. "I'm worried that you'll get hurt again."
Gayle:	I'm worried that if I don't constantly drive you by guilt and anger and I'm afraid you're going to get hurt again, and I don't want it to happen [*cries*]. If I disappear and it happens again, it will be all my fault. How are you supposed to stay safe unless I'm there?
Therapist:	Yeah. Change back. [*Gayle changes chairs.*] What do you want to say to her as the adult? She's saying that she is worried you will be hurt again.

Gayle: I can tell you that it won't happen again. Other people have tried to abuse me, and I have stopped it not out of guilt but out of perception. It doesn't have to be all negative. I don't have to live with the fact that I'm bad because something bad happened to me. I'm not bad, and something bad did happen [*cries*], and I'm not a bad person.

Therapist: Yeah.

Gayle: I was a kid; let it go. Stop torturing me with it.

Therapist: Yeah. "I want you to let it go."

Gayle: It's stopping me from getting my dreams and my goals and everything. I'm lucky that someone even married me and cares enough to stay with me because you're still torturing me.

Therapist: Yeah.

Gayle: You're not doing good. You're doing damage [*cries*].

Therapist: Yeah.

Gayle: You need to let it go; it hurts.

Therapist: So you want her to dwell less on the negative and more on the positive.

Gayle: Yeah [*cries*].

Therapist: What else can she do to help the depression to ensure that it doesn't come back?

Gayle: When things go back, I really need the help.

Therapist: Yeah.

Gayle: To not be depressed, because when I have bad days [*cries*], it's like I'm just drowning, and I'm, and I just want her to help me through that. I want her to put her arms around me and love me anyway, when things go bad, and to point out that everybody goes through those days and that life is not perfect. You'll never be perfect, and it's OK. Give me permission.

     As in previous sessions, while engaged in an empty-chair dialogue with her mother, Gayle requested that she treat herself with compassion and care (EXP Stage 6; LCPP Level 7). This was a major shift and represented another resolution session. Not only was Gayle setting limits on abusive behavior but she was requesting positive, nurturing behaviors instead. She asked the critic to be more understanding and accepting of her (SASB 3-4, 3-3, 3-2). The dialogue then shifted to one with her mother, and Gayle asserted her need for protection. Here the critic was finally releasing the self from blame and holding the mother accountable for not providing adequate protection when she was a child. This represented an important turning point for Gayle.

Gayle:	I was really angry [*crying*] that nobody was there to help me. Why wasn't my mother there when I needed her?
Therapist:	Yeah. Do you want to put your mother in the chair, Gayle, and tell her now?
Gayle:	[*crying*] Why weren't you there when I needed you, Mom?
Therapist:	Yeah.
Gayle:	Why did you let me go to a stranger's house, and you didn't really know them?
Therapist:	Yeah. Tell her what it was like for you.
Gayle:	I felt very mad and wrong, and I felt very ashamed and scared, and I wanted to be protected. It's like I couldn't trust you again because you didn't protect me.
Therapist:	Yeah. "So I didn't trust you after that."
Gayle:	And I always felt that I had to meet your needs because you never met mine, I needed to be protected.
Therapist:	"I was a little girl; I was only 5."
Gayle:	I was so little.
Therapist:	Yeah.
Gayle:	I was so little, and you were just so concerned with [*blows nose*] I was out of your way and not bothering you.
Therapist:	Yeah. Tell her why you were sad.
Gayle:	[*blows nose*] I really resent the hurt I felt for years and blaming myself and for you not recognizing the signs of the depression.
Therapist:	"So I resent you for not seeing my pain."
Gayle:	Yeah.
Therapist:	All those years?
Gayle:	And I bottled it so much to the point where it was just exploding, and you didn't see any of it; you didn't recognize it.
Therapist:	Yeah. "So you didn't protect me from the abuse, and then you didn't see pain."
Gayle:	And you didn't help me.
Therapist:	"As a result you didn't help me."
Gayle:	It was very painful.
Therapist:	What did you need from her then?

Gayle:	I needed it not to happen.
Therapist:	Yeah. "I needed you to be an adult."
Gayle:	And then when it did happen [*cries*], I needed you to hug me and tell me it was OK and that she would get disciplined and that you would still love me, that it wasn't my fault.
Therapist:	Yeah.
Gayle:	I needed you to help me feel better about myself because I hated myself for it happening, and I was just so afraid of you [*blows nose*]. I was afraid that if you ever found out you would hate me and throw me out of the house.
Therapist:	Uh-huh. "So you needed to feel that I could tell you to feel safe."
Gayle:	I feel like I've lost your love and approval, and you don't understand [*cries*] what I've been through.
Therapist:	Yeah. "You don't know me; you don't understand my pain."
Gayle:	Because you're not processing your own, so how can you process mine?
Therapist:	Yeah. So kind of like "because you're so out of touch with your own pain, you can't share mine."
Gayle:	No, even if I did, it was just bouts.
Therapist:	What do you want from your mother now?
Gayle:	I just want what I'm allowing myself. I want her to let me go as a kid. I'm not a kid anymore. Let me go; let me grow up. . . . I have to make my own standards. It doesn't mean that they have to be different. I can still want to be a good person and want to do good things.
Therapist:	Uh-huh.
Gayle:	But I don't have to run under the pressure of the guilt.
Therapist:	That's all we have as children when terrible things happen to us and nobody protects us. Our own minds take over and try to protect, and by trying to convince you that you're responsible, in a way what the critic is saying is that because you're responsible, if you do everything right it will never happen again.
Gayle:	That's why I'm so driven to perfection.
Therapist:	Exactly!

In this last excerpt, we see Gayle express her feelings clearly (EXP Stage 4) and state what she needs (EXP Stage 6; LCPP Level 6). In Session 12 Gayle reported that she had not felt guilty since the last session. She was sleeping better and felt rested, and her husband had noticed the change. She also felt calmer and more at peace. She was disappointed in herself for not finishing an assignment the day before but got some support from her husband and also from a girl with whom she worked who told her she was a good employee. She expressed anger toward her inner critic for making her feel like crying and casting doubt on whether people liked her or not. She wanted to stop doing that but felt defeated by her inner critic at times.

Part of Gayle was scared to trust the change. So rather than risk disappointment, perhaps it was better to remain depressed. She said her inner critical voice told her that she was not going to make it, and she was fearful. She was angry at her critic for blowing things out of proportion, making her feel inadequate and hopeless, and also for making people turn away from her. She was both sad and angry for the loss of people; she felt it was not fair. She regretted she did not love herself and held her critic responsible. In an imaginary dialogue with her critic, she found that the critic was concerned that if it did not protect her, things were going to get worse because she was a failure. She said that in the past, she was ashamed of herself "like everything was wrong," but during the previous week, when she did not hear her inner critic, she felt great. She told her critic to leave her alone, that she did OK without her, and that she had been punished enough. The abuse was not her fault; she was vulnerable, and her parents did not protect her.

Gayle observed that she got married because she needed someone to protect her. She felt some compassion for her husband because her critical side was ruining their marriage and wrecking everything she touched. She noted that her husband always wondered whether he had done something wrong. Gayle said that she was afraid of feeling violated like when she was 5 and blamed the critic for her fear. She said that her critic punished her. She felt guilty for feeling pleasure during the abuse; as a result she felt bad and did not want to let it happen again.

Gayle felt she deserved pleasure as an adult and that her critic made her feel it was not OK. In her chair work with her inner critic, Gayle asserted herself by saying, "Stop reminding me. Go away. The job is over. I can take care of myself now." She also expressed some recognition and appreciation for her critic having protected her in the hard years but now felt the critic was interfering. The critic forgave her and said that she loved her and was just trying to protect her. Gayle mourned the loss of the previous 10 years and regretted that no one was there to help her. She remarked how lucky and thankful she felt to be in therapy. She recognized that she has a good husband and felt compassion for him for trying so hard.

There was a 3-week break in therapy as Gayle underwent liposuction. In Session 13 she reported feeling calm and happy and said that one of her friends commented on her progress by reminding her that before therapy she would not have been so calm and happy. She said she did not tell her mother about the operation initially because her mother would have freaked out and that she liked that her mom was in the dark. She wanted this to be her own private decision. She found the postoperation situation really hard and was concerned at the hospital because she felt so dependent and felt that the nurses were not providing good care. Her husband stayed with her to give her support. She was frustrated that nobody could do anything to help with the bad pain in her stomach. However, she spoke to a doctor from her church who had called her to see how she was doing and who recommended a good medication. She was able to stand up for herself and allowed herself to cry, seeing it as normal.

During Session 13 Gayle expressed her joy at asserting herself with the nurses and getting support from the doctor. She felt a sense of efficacy and was angry with her mother for telling her she looked horrible. In Session 14 Gayle was upset at a nurse for asking her whether she could talk about what had happened without getting upset so that it could be videotaped and used to educate the staff. Gayle was embarrassed and felt exploited at the idea of being videotaped. She felt judged by the nurses and felt that she had been treated poorly because she had had cosmetic surgery; whereas the woman in the next bed was treated decently for her medical procedure. Gayle was pleased at how much she had changed. She felt that she was handling difficult situations well and felt more confident that she could make it. Her husband confirmed how well she was doing. Gayle reflected that she was no longer so hard on herself. When she talked to her mother she did not get upset and was able to set limits. Previously, she used to get angry because she expected her mother to recognize and pick up on her cues. Now Gayle allowed her mother to be who she was, and if her mother wanted to make her feel guilty, she responded differently. She was also aware that she responded better to her kids when they woke her up in the morning by taking a deep breath to calm down instead of losing control as her father did. Gayle said that she wanted to have marital therapy after the sessions were over. She noted that she was holding the good feelings longer and was moving beyond her fear that something bad was going to happen.

In Session 15 Gayle gave an update about her health after the operation and talked about issues in her relationships with her husband, her mother, her in-laws, and her brother and sister-in-law. She expressed anger, sadness, and some joy in relation to these relationships. In Session 16 she reviewed some issues related to her operation. She noted that her eating had improved. She was pleased with her progress at work and said that she no longer "freaks out" or feels overwhelmed when she makes an error and that she gets support and confirmation that there is a lot of pressure in her work.

In the next few sessions, Gayle continued to consolidate her changes; however, she was still angry at her mother for being unsupportive and critical. She wished her parents would admit what they did to her and hold themselves accountable to her. She did some empty-chair work to try to let go of her feelings of anger and disappointment with her parents. She acknowledged that she still battled her inner voice that said she should give up. During this period Gayle recognized that she felt good about herself as a mother. She noted that her kids didn't have to worry about her disapproval. She had started setting boundaries with her mother saying, "You are not allowed to treat me that way anymore, and you will not do it to my children." She also reported that she no longer overruled her own judgment. She recalled that as a child she was depressed and used to hide it with anger, but now she was setting boundaries. Gayle stated that she wanted to stop seeing her mother and that her mother kept a connection with her own mom out of guilt. Rather than experiencing fear of disapproval, insecurity, shame of unworthiness and failure, Gayle said she was experiencing a sense of pride, was assertive, was able to set boundaries, and felt entitled to be valued and respected for the person she was.

Gayle continued to work with her critical inner voice over the final few sessions. She identified how crippling the critical voice was and how tired it made her feel. She asked the critic to go away. She was angry that her inner critic was inducing fear and worry instead of providing encouragement and support and that it isolated her. Gayle saw her fear as her biggest enemy. She did not want to function out of fear but wanted to feel relaxed and receive encouragement. She mourned and acknowledged her sadness at never getting encouragement from her mother and began to let go her hope that she would ever receive it from her mother. She recognized that it cost too much. Gayle asserted that she was more important than her relationship with her mother and that she was separating from her to survive and avert another depressive episode. Gayle recognized that she was getting support from all kinds of people and realized that her needs didn't have to be met by her mother; she could, in fact, get them met elsewhere. Gayle observed that her manager liked her and saw her potential, although her mother didn't. She described the manager as supportive and patient.

This represented an important shift as she began to feel nourished even though she was not depending on her mother. At last she felt that she could survive independently of her parents, which thrilled her. She asserted that she was OK and realized that even if her mother did not approve of her, she was OK as she was. By Session 18 she was feeling better, was successfully battling her inner critic, was getting and seeking support from others instead of her mother, and was letting go of her need for her mother's approval. Change occurred with the emergence of resilience and the ability to cope with distress much more effectively, even though Gayle still felt self-critical and sad at times. She no longer became stuck in maladaptive states of fear and shame and was able to generate healthy anger that empowered her and healthy sadness that led her to reach out for contact and comfort. She grieved what she did not get growing up, which helped her to let go of her wish that her parents would provide it some time in the future.

In the final session, Gayle reported that she was sad that therapy was ending but that positive things were happening in her life. She was promoted at work, felt more at peace, and had come to terms with her mom. She said she felt joy and relief and was not afraid anymore. She told her mother, "If you don't like me, I'll get my support from elsewhere." She reported that "it felt good not being afraid anymore, really liberating." The therapist commented that this was wonderful and that it was the first time Gayle really said she could get support elsewhere and that enough was enough.

SUMMARY AND ANALYSIS

By the end of treatment, Gayle felt that she was going to be OK, that she had come to terms with her mother, and that she could get support elsewhere. She was no longer afraid of depression, was getting her needs met, felt proud of herself, had a sense of competence, could validate her own feelings, and was able to express herself and set limits without guilt. She had increased self-esteem, was no longer angry at her mother, and no longer needed her mother's approval because she approved of herself. She had learned to separate love from approval and that it was OK to be angry. She was handling her anger well and was not afraid of not getting support from her mom.

In her posttherapy report, Gayle said she got everything she thought she might get out of therapy, although people had said not to expect too much in 20 weeks. She reported that she was able to function normally, whereas before she wasn't. She was no longer afraid of becoming depressed. Her scores on the Beck Depression Inventory dropped dramatically from 33 to 0 at the end of treatment as did her scores on the Inventory of Interpersonal Problems and the Symptom Checklist—90—Revised, which were, respectively, 2.07 and 1.34 at the beginning of therapy and .02 on both at the end. These changes held at the 18-month follow-up.

4

VALIDATING AN
EMERGING SENSE OF SELF

Anna was a single mother in her 30s when she sought treatment for her depression. At the time, she was having difficulty getting out of bed and was struggling to maintain order and basic routines at home for herself and her children. She had separated from her husband and lost her job 5 years prior to her first visit to the clinic. Since that time she had been struggling financially. She had a number of part-time jobs to try to make enough money to keep her family fed and clothed. However, she was often short of funds and felt very worried and stressed by their straitened financial situation. She noted she often felt worse after the summer as she became overwhelmed by the demands of a new school year and the thought of Christmas. As a result of encountering difficulty finding a permanent full-time position, her confidence waned, and she feared that she had lost her job skills. She had recently returned to school to take some business courses to update and extend her qualifications.

Anna was a very resilient young woman who maintained a sense of humor in the face of all her hardships. However, she suppressed and invalidated her feelings and needs to fit in with other people. She was very self-critical and demanding of herself, often assuming responsibility for events that were beyond her control. She recognized that she had difficulty setting limits and saying no. Anna was diagnosed pretherapy with major depressive disorder on Axis I; no diagnoses on Axes II and III; problems with primary support group characterized by divorce, discord with mother and siblings, and economic problems on Axis IV; and occupational problems characterized by unemployment on Axis V. She had a Global Assessment of Functioning score of 60, indicating moderate difficulty with social and occupational functioning.

CASE FORMULATION

Anna recalled that when she was a child her mother had been volatile and unpredictable. She described a cycle of emotional abuse that had damaged her sense of self. She described a cycle of being subject to one of her mother's outbursts and withdrawing in fear and uncertainty. After some time the memory of the attack would fade, and Anna would begin to feel safe and loving toward her mother, only to have her once again lash out in anger. As a consequence, Anna became very mistrustful of her mother and gave up hoping for her to be warm and loving. Although her mother was more supportive of Anna as an adult, her parents were very critical of her when she filed for divorce and refused to speak to her for 2 years. Anna expressed regrets about her divorce. She had not realized at the time what a massive and difficult journey it would prove to be. She regretted uprooting her children and found her worries about money very stressful and disconcerting because she had never had to worry about finances before. Anna was a committed and dedicated mother who, even as she struggled to feed her children, put on a happy face to hide her stress because she did not want to worry them.

Anna's core emotion scheme was hopelessness and a sense of unworthiness. She felt that she was not important and did not deserve to be heard. She was self-critical and invalidated her feelings as she tried to take care of others at the expense of herself. As a result, Anna was deferential with her therapist, looking to her therapist to provide feedback and advice on her problems. Although Anna dismissed her feelings, she was very reflective and an astute observer of her own and other people's psychological processes. She spoke with an externalizing voice as she told her story, often adding a humorous or funny twist to what was happening in her life. However, when the therapist asked her to attend to her inner experience, Anna was able to label and express her feelings and present them freshly using a more focused voice. She was self-effacing at first, trying to appear less distressed than she felt as she tried to determine what was required of her in therapy. Overall, her emotional processing was quite modulated in the session.

Three main themes emerged over the course of treatment. The first concerned her desire to improve her financial situation and the pressures she faced earning a living, going to school, and parenting her children. The second had to do with her concerns about her relationship with a housemate, and the third concerned her struggle with the bureaucracy to ensure funding for herself and her children. The primary tasks that were identified as ways to intervene to begin to help Anna overcome her depression were two-chair work to address her self-criticisms, empty-chair work to process her feelings of rejection and the emotional abuse she had experienced as a child with her mother, and empathic affirmation to support greater awareness of and expression of her feelings to encourage a stronger sense of self.

BONDING AND AWARENESS

During Sessions 1 through 4, Anna's therapist worked to establish an alliance. In Sessions 1 and 2, Anna described her current life situation and the problems she was facing. She said she realized that she took on too much and was becoming, as a result, overwhelmed and burned out. Her goal was to try to be more attentive to herself because she usually did not notice things about herself, but rather she blocked out her experience or invalidated it. In Session 2 Anna spoke about her marriage and the difficulties that ensued when she decided to leave. One of her goals was to resolve her relationship with a man she met soon after she separated from her ex-husband. When she entered therapy she and Peter were sharing a house to survive financially. He wanted a more permanent, intimate relationship, but Anna was uncertain about her feelings for him, which made her feel guilty because she did not want to hurt his feelings. She thought that he was more attached to her than she was to him. By Session 3 Anna began to explore the ways in which she silenced herself, and she and her therapist came to some agreement about the goals of therapy. She began to realize that part of her depression resulted from feeling overwhelmed by her current life situation and from her attempts to avoid conflict. She agreed to look at how she silenced and sabotaged herself so that she felt unable to get ahead. Anna also wanted to look at her relationship with Peter to try to figure out what was wrong and what she needed.

EVOKING AND EXPLORING

In Session 4 Anna's therapist began to explore her feelings of being overwhelmed. It became apparent that Anna was not aware of her emotions and inner experience. Although she said she was learning to be more aware, she realized that she still found it hard to slow down and take her emotional pulse. Hence, she overcommitted to too many projects. She was very worried about her future and felt stuck. Since losing her job, she felt overly dependent on others and isolated by the loss of her car. In the 5 years prior to therapy she felt her confidence had been eroded and that she no longer trusted herself and her judgment. Her therapist suggested a two-chair task to begin to help her explore her feelings of being overwhelmed. Anna recognized that part of her was very tired and longed to rest, and another part invalidated her feelings. This part pushed her to do more. As her therapist explored the "pushy" side with Anna, it became clear that this part was sad. The pushy side wanted Anna to get her degree. She had a sense that time was passing and that they were not achieving anything. The depressed side feared that the pushy side would never be satisfied. The depressed side needed the pushy side to recognize how much she had accomplished and needed to be heard and accepted. Anna asked the pushy side to stop invalidating her needs. The pushy side was able to hear this request and say that she was sorry about how she treated Anna.

As she recognized how invalidating she was of her experience, Anna recalled how her mother had often invalidated her as a child and how awful it felt. She agreed to be more respectful of herself and to stop invalidating her experience. This was an important session because it framed one of the major goals of the treatment, which was to have Anna stop invalidating her experience and start accepting it and expressing it in ways that would enable her to have her needs met. At the end of the session Anna reported on a postsession questionnaire that she felt more compassionate to a side of herself that she previously could not accept, that she could stand up to her own self-criticisms, and that she was more aware of how her thoughts influenced her feelings and behavior.

During the next few sessions her therapist began to explore how Anna stifled her feelings and how this contributed to her sense of being overwhelmed and depressed. In Session 5 the therapist used a focusing technique to help Anna attend to her inner experience. Anna became aware that she was feeling anxious because she was wasting time.

Anna: I am not sure where to focus today.

Therapist: Why don't you attend to your body? How do you feel?

Anna: I feel heavy; my eyes feel heavy; and my head is heavy.

Therapist: Like you are under a shroud?

Anna: Yes, like a little cloud is hanging over me. I don't feel I am seeing things clearly, and I have knots in my stomach.

At this point in the session the therapist prompted Anna to attend to her inner experience given the marker that she was feeling confused (SASB [Structural Analysis of Social Behavior] 3-8). Accepting her therapist's suggestion (SASB 2-4), Anna turned inward to attend to and express her subjective experience and to differentiate it to become aware of the nuances and implicit meanings in her emotional experience (EXP [The Experiencing Scale] Stage 4; LCPP [Levels of Client Perceptual Processing] Level 5). Her vocal quality indicated that she was mildly to moderately aroused as she explored and freely disclosed her experience (SASB 2-4, 2-2) in a self-enhancing and self-protective manner (SASB 3-4). Her therapist continued to be affirming and accepting of that experience (SASB 1-2). This type of interaction continued until the therapist introduced a new task.

Therapist: So you feel anxious. What is that about? Can you give it words?

Anna: Ouch! [*giggling*]

Therapist: What is the anxious side saying? You are letting things slide?

Anna: Yeah, that's it. You are letting the minutes slide. You are not doing the things you committed to. I am part of a small group, and I agreed to type up the minutes of the meeting. This group could be very worthwhile; yet I haven't typed up the minutes. I have tried to get started two or three or four times, and I just can't do it, and I didn't do my yoga this week either.

Her therapist suggested a two-chair exercise to help Anna become more aware of the internal conflict between engaging in certain activities and procrastinating.

Therapist: Would you like to try an exercise? It seems part of you wants to do all these things, but another part is rebelling. Would you like to look at that more and see if we can find a solution?

Anna: OK.

Therapist: Put the part that wants to do all these things in that chair and the other part that does not want to do them in this chair.

Anna: [*in critic chair*] How come you didn't go to yoga? People are counting on you.

Therapist: So this side is saying, "What is the matter? You are letting people down."

Anna: Yes. They won't trust you if you are unreliable, and you are letting these good opportunities slip by.

Therapist: So she is saying that you are letting opportunities slip. Tell Anna what will happen.

Anna: If you let things slide, you will need to find another route to meet your goals.

Therapist: So "you are screwing up my plans."

Anna: Yes and this group could be beneficial. It will help you develop contacts. If you don't deliver, it will be a waste.

Therapist:	What will she waste?
Anna:	Time and energy.
Therapist:	What else will she lose?
Anna:	She will lose self-respect. Other people will see you as unreliable and not feel they can count on you.

The therapist asked Anna to elaborate on her inner experience and to become aware of the negative things she said to herself that made her feel anxious and scared (SASB 2-4). Although Anna was exploring her inner experience, she was applying prescriptive rules and standards to her behavior (EXP Stages 4, 2; LCPP Level 3). She was self-critical and accused and blamed herself so that she felt guilty and ashamed (SASB 3-6). She continued to trust and rely on her therapist (SASB 2-4) as she continued to self-disclose (SASB 2-2). Her therapist continued to be affirming and understanding (SASB 1-2, 1-4) as well as helping and protecting as she tried to guide Anna through the two-chair exercise. Once Anna expressed the negative self-statements, her therapist asked her to switch chairs to help make her more aware of the impact of these on herself. They continued in this mode, differentiating Anna's critical self-statements and her reaction to these.

Therapist:	So they will see you as flighty, unreliable. OK, switch chairs. How do you feel when this side says you will be seen as unreliable?
Anna:	I never lied; I won't be seen as unreliable. I haven't gone back on my word.
Therapist:	So what this side is saying is "I don't care; nothing bad will happen." [*Anna nods.*] OK, come over here [*indicating other chair*]. How does that make you feel?
Anna:	I feel humiliated and embarrassed.
Therapist:	What do you say to make her feel that way? "I can't count on Anna"?
Anna:	You are only as good as your word. You are what you do. You are bad.
Therapist:	How is she bad?
Anna:	You can't be counted on.
Therapist:	So she is unreliable. Say this to her.
Anna:	You are unreliable; you can't be counted on.
Therapist:	[*indicating the critic chair and trying to label Anna's nonverbal behavior and the attitude she is expressing to the experiencing chair*]

Therapist:	So what are you saying, "too bad"?
Anna:	Don't be sad.
Therapist:	"I don't want to make you sad and scared"?
Anna:	I guess so.
Therapist:	What are you scared about over here? That she wants too much?
Anna:	I'm scared of you . . .
Therapist:	Is it that she rides roughshod over you?
Anna:	Yes, I am worried about you.
Therapist:	So you are worried; you don't trust that side somehow. This is an important struggle. We need to end here today, but it is important to be aware of how these sides battle it out. Your homework this week is to try to be more aware of the two sides and to listen to yourself more.

This was a partial resolution. The two sides expressed their needs, and the critic expressed her feelings, so there was a softening but there was still no agreement on a unified course of action. After this session Anna reported on a postsession questionnaire that she felt more compassionate toward a side of herself that she previously could not accept. Although her level of awareness had been raised, she still invalidated herself and neglected her needs. The therapist continued to work with her on this in the next few sessions.

In Session 6 Anna recalled how self-centered her mother had been and what a bad temper she had had. Anna realized that she too was often impatient and irritable with others. Since her divorce, she had found her children more challenging. However, Anna had difficulty expressing her feelings of irritation toward them and others. Instead, she felt tense and irritable as she tried to swallow her opinions and feelings. This highlighted for her once again that she was intolerant of her feelings. It became clear that she dismissed her own hurt to protect others. She became aware that she did not express her opinions because she cared about how others saw her. This realization was quite jarring because she had thought of herself as very independent. By admitting to herself that she cared so much about others' opinions, she felt like a wimp. Exploring the issue further, she appreciated that caring for others and their feelings represented the sensitive part of herself that she valued. She was able to acknowledge that she needed to accept her sensitive side more and to learn how to express her feelings and not stifle herself because this interfered with having a good time. On the postsession questionnaire, Anna rated this session as very productive. She reported that she was able to reconcile two opposing sides, that she understood a puzzling reaction better, and that she felt more compassionate toward a side of herself she previously could not accept.

TRANSFORMATION:
SUPPORTING AN EMERGING SENSE OF SELF

At Session 7 Anna came in feeling quite depressed. Her therapist suggested a two-chair exercise between the side that pushed her to do more and the side that was tired and rebellious. The pushy, invalidating side felt defeated by the depressed side. As the exercise unfolded, the depressed side expressed that she was tired and felt overwhelmed by the demands of the pushy side. The pushy side said she did not want to hear about the tiredness. They had to accomplish their goals. The depressed side expressed her fear that the pushy side would walk all over her. She told the pushy side that she needed her to listen and acknowledge the things that they had managed to accomplish over the last few weeks. The pushy side agreed that Anna needed to take care of herself and that it was important to rest and have some fun as well as to work at realizing her goals. At this point Anna realized that she could take care of herself and did not need to see herself as defenseless. This was a resolution session (EXP Stage 6; LCPP Level 7; SASB 3-3, 3-4). After this session Anna felt able to engage in behavior that was difficult for her. She said that she felt able to stand up to her critic and was more aware of her thoughts and behavior and how these interacted.

Anna brought a poem to Session 8; it expressed her wish to relinquish her fears and trust that she would be taken care of. She had had a good week, although she had been really busy. She observed that over the week she had noticed points when her confidence was low. Her therapist suggested a two-chair dialogue to see how she sapped her confidence and if they could reverse it. Anna saw that she was very critical of herself. She shamed herself by accusing herself of being a slob. She wished she was more presentable, and felt she needed a haircut. The experiencing side said how humiliated she felt and how much the critical comments just made her want to hide so that it was hard to do the things she needed to do for her course. Her therapist asked the experiencing side what she needed. Anna said, "Stop shaming me, I need support and encouragement, and I deserve to be here; I have worked hard."

Anna observed that people treated her differently when she had less money. She realized that she was often shy with authority figures and that she became paralyzed and spoke with a childish voice. She recalled experiencing similar feelings with her mother. At this point the therapist asked her what her mother would do to shame her or make her want to hide. Anna's mother would accuse her of lying and dismissed her opinions. She remonstrated with Anna, saying she was wrong, and pushed her away, refusing to listen to her. Anna recalled that her mother's dismissive and rejecting behavior was hurtful. She felt really sad that her mother did not believe or trust her and that her opinion did not matter. Her therapist suggested an empty-chair exercise. Anna agreed, and when talking to her imagined mother, she expressed a wish to feel supported and to have a mother who believed in her.

She told her mother how she could not trust her and that she would give her mother her heart only to have it ripped up. She recalled that she found her mother very unpredictable.

After expressing her hurt and sadness, Anna assumed the role of her mother. Playing the role of her mother, Anna acknowledged her pain and apologized. She said that she had not realized the effect her behavior had had on Anna and wished that she could make it better (EXP Stage 6; LCPP Level 6; SASB 1-3, 1-2, 3-4). After this Anna felt a huge sense of relief and an easing of her sadness. This session marked a second resolution session in which a task was resolved and Anna was able to express new or different behavior toward herself.

Anna cancelled the next session because of a bad winter storm. At Session 9 she was feeling down because Peter's son had come to visit. She felt crowded by him and found it difficult to interact with him. She experienced him as blaming, nasty, and manipulative. Anna felt that Peter's son saw her as a threat to his relationship with his father. The therapist suggested a two-chair task to see how Anna made herself feel bad around Peter's son. However, it did not seem to move forward, so the therapist returned to trying to listen empathically for what was more salient for Anna during the session. As they explored Anna's feelings of hopelessness about the situation at home, the therapist became aware that Anna was invalidating her feelings once again and communicated this to her. Anna cried, saying that she did not feel that she was making progress. Her therapist noted that it sounded as if she was being critical and expecting a lot from herself. Anna admitted that she had begun to doubt herself again, but that she was trying to break old patterns. It is possible that the therapist's attempt to become more attuned to Anna during this session and to try to understand better what was happening, as opposed to pushing forward with the task, may have provided an antidote to the invalidating messages Anna had received as a child. Some confirmation for this was gleaned from Anna's responses on the postsession measure on which she reported that she understood a puzzling reaction of her own better, felt more compassionate toward herself, felt less burdened by negative feelings, and was able to let go of unresolved feelings toward a significant other.

TRANSFORMATION: CONSTRUCTING NEW ALTERNATIVES

At the next session, Anna arrived saying she felt much better. She had started developing a business plan, which was required for one of her courses, but was also something she hoped to implement in the long-term. She was able to clarify her relationship with Peter and felt better about it and less angry toward his son. She began to look at her own contribution to the relationship and decided she did not want to invest in it. Anna did not know what she wanted to focus on during the session, so the therapist suggested a focusing exercise, and Anna agreed. As she attended to all the issues that came up for her, including worries about money, her business plan, finding a job, her insurance company, and her children, she decided the most salient one was her insurance company. A representative of the company had written saying that they needed to investigate her finances because she was living in the same house as Peter, and therefore, she was no longer entitled to insurance to help support her and her children. Anna was quite despondent. She felt overpowered by the insurance company and felt that she was not able to defend herself. She explored the impact the letter had had on her. She felt very sad and had cried nearly every day since receiving it. She was fearful that her life would be ruined and that her dream of getting back on her feet financially would be smashed. She wished she had been more indignant about having to account for her finances. She felt humiliated by the process and quite vulnerable and unprotected. Her therapist used evocative and empathic exploration to help Anna process her feelings about the investigation. She described herself as "inching out of the pit only to be pushed back in." However, she resolved that she was determined to find a way out. She began to look at her alternatives for making extra money, including providing child care and doing some office administration for Peter. Because she was not enthusiastic about working with Peter, she resolved to continue looking for other jobs at the same time.

During this session Anna was very critical and down on herself as a result of the investigation. Her therapist suggested a two-chair exercise to see if Anna could be more supportive of herself. The critic accused Anna of being stupid. The experiencing chair responded that when she dismissed her and criticized her, it made her frightened; she felt as if there were something wrong with her. She told the critic that she needed her to stop criticizing her and be more supportive. The critic acknowledged that frightening Anna was not useful. She was able to access a soothing, reassuring voice that acknowledged that Anna had a different way of handling things that worked well for her (EXP Stages 4, 6; LCPP Levels 5, 6; SASB 3-2, 3-3, 3-4). She realized that she was feeling crowded by Peter and needed to take more time for herself and to soothe her fears. This was a third resolution session, after which Anna reported that she felt able to engage in behavior that had previously been difficult for her.

For the next few sessions, Anna did not report any changes. She seemed to be questioning herself as she questioned her relationship with Peter and tried to cope with the insurance company. At Session 12 Anna reported that she was feeling more stressed about her relationship with Peter and that the insurance company had cut off her income. She feared getting into a rut and staying with Peter just to make ends meet. Anna was feeling very overwhelmed and really anxious. She felt despondent that she had not been able to adequately defend herself against the insurance company. The therapist suggested that they do a two-chair exercise to explore how she made herself feel afraid. The client realized that she pushed herself by saying, "You have to do something. No one else is going to take care of you." Saying these things scared and paralyzed her so that she was unable to act. She began to cry and felt that she had put up a big wall to protect herself because she did not feel strong enough. She did not want to look over the wall because it felt too difficult. Her therapist, noting Anna's distress, began to explore ways that she could soothe herself. Anna said that she was trying yoga and meditation and would continue to try to use these techniques to soothe herself when she felt overwhelmed.

At the next session, Anna reported that her mother had taken her shopping. She looked brighter. Her mother had bought her clothes and had given her money. However, Anna felt a little overwhelmed and part of her was scared that her mother would turn on her and become angry as she had when Anna was a child. Anna felt uneasy and mistrustful during the visit with her mother and was upset that her mother would not listen to her. Consequently, Anna felt swamped by her mother's generosity. To cope during the shopping excursion, Anna became withdrawn as she experienced her mother as invalidating. Nonetheless, Anna was concerned about her mother seeing her as tired and as spending too much money.

In addition to her concerns about her mother, Anna was worried about Peter because he wanted to know whether she was moving out or not. Her financial situation felt so precarious that she was undecided and scared of moving. She realized that over the previous few weeks she had begun to question herself again. She felt that she was wasting time and was not making any progress. However, in spite of feeling helpless, she recognized that she had gained a lot. She noted that she was trying to listen to herself and find ways to soothe and reassure herself. On the postsession questionnaire at the end of Session 13, Anna reported that she felt that she understood herself better, was able to challenge her dysfunctional thoughts, was more aware of how her thoughts affected her behavior and feelings, was able to act differently, and felt less burdened.

At Session 14 Anna said that her depression had lightened, but she still felt overwhelmed. She wanted to focus on her relationship with her sisters during the session. She said that she felt left out by her sisters and that they were critical of her. The therapist suggested a two-chair exercise to see whether Anna could come to view her sisters differently or to develop a new way of being with them. Anna saw her sisters as viewing her home as untidy and not clean enough. She experienced them as disdainful of her and thought that they saw her furniture as old and tatty. In response to these criticisms, Anna expressed how hurt she felt. She told her sisters how much she missed them and that she wished they could appreciate the home that she had made with her children and see it as an expression of herself and her children. She told them that she wished they understood that she had chosen to spend time with her kids rather than keep a spotlessly clean house. She requested that they stop judging her and accept her instead. She asked them how they could claim to be her friend and yet criticize her behind her back.

During the exercise Anna realized how much she dismissed herself as she tried to brush away her viewpoint by saying that she was too needy and overly sensitive. As she heard herself saying these words she recalled her mother, whom she mistrusted. She realized that her sisters hit a nerve because they echoed her own criticisms of herself. Anna recognized that it was hard for her to trust herself and that she was worried that she might be crazy. Anna was able to tell the critical self how much it hurt when she was dismissed as crazy. She asked the critical side to have faith in her and to stop doubting her. The critic acknowledged the experiencing side's pain and said that she was trying to listen to that side more, but she was scared that she would fail; she asked the experiencing side for reassurance. The experiencing side was able to reassure her; however, Anna still felt a little sad because she was tired of having to be so brave and strong. This was another resolution session because Anna reported afterward that she had let go unresolved feelings toward significant people in her life and saw them in a new light; she felt less burdened by a recurring bad feeling. She also said she would be able to act differently in future.

In the final session, Anna reported that it had been a difficult week. She was still concerned about her insurance company and was a little uncertain about Peter. However, she recognized that she had achieved a lot over the 16 sessions. She was more independent and had accomplished a number of her objectives, such as driving into town on her own. She felt more confident in her abilities and, most important, had acquired a new perspective. She felt that she had some new ideas, was able to manage things better, and was able to look at things more positively. She reported that there was the possibility of a number of new developments at home. She had applied to rent another apartment, which would allow her to live independently of Peter and alleviate some of the financial pressure she was feeling. Anna expressed appreciation for her therapist's support and said that she would miss her.

SUMMARY AND ANALYSIS

Overall, by the end of therapy, Anna was more self-assertive and accepting of her own needs and feelings. She was able to clarify her relationship with Peter. She accepted that she was not attracted to him and did not want a sexual relationship, preferring to remain friends. She recognized that she was tired of pretending to protect his feelings and that it would be better to move out before the relationship was damaged. She stopped trying to be so independent and felt more able to ask others for help. To this end she asked someone to coach her on how to apply for jobs and present herself for job interviews. She resolved that she wanted to be heard, noting how much better she felt when she was. Although she recognized that being more expressive had helped her, she was still somewhat cautious.

An analysis of Anna's therapy shows that she had three or more task resolution sessions, indicating that she was able to engage in new behavior so that she was able to be more compassionate to herself and set limits with other people whom she experienced as demanding and critical. Anna was able to stand outside her experience and reflect on her own and other people's behavior, not in an intellectual, distant way but in an experience-near fashion. She was clearly in touch with her own feelings and perceptions as well as able to see events through other people's eyes. Anna was also able to focus on her own inner experience and able to freely self-disclose to her therapist, trusting and relying on her suggestions to process Anna's experience in new ways. There was a sense of collaboration as they worked together to find solutions to the problems that contributed to Anna's depression. From the outset Anna was aware of the life events and issues that were contributing to her depression, including her lack of a sense of self-worth, her current living arrangements, and the burdens she experienced as a single parent; thus she was able to frame the context and goals of the therapy. During the therapy she came to see how she invalidated her own needs and tended to take care of others at her own expense. Her capacity for empathy and ability to care for others made it easier for her to adopt a more caring, nurturing, and validating posture toward her own experience.

These changes were confirmed and highlighted by the data from the process measures. The ratings on the SASB indicated that Anna was able to move from self-criticism, neglect, and abandonment of herself to greater self-acceptance, care, guidance, and nurturance of herself. Her emotional processing indicated that she was able to differentiate her internal experience and pose questions about that experience to resolve issues in personally meaningful ways. She entered therapy at a midlevel on the EXP because she was able to narrate the events in her life in a coherent and self-relevant way and reference these events with her own inner perceptions and reactions. In terms of her cognitive processing on the LCPP, she was able to analyze her inner experience and dispense with external rules and ways of viewing her experience to synthesize new ways of viewing and monitoring her experience and to create new personally meaningful rules. These are best exemplified by the changes she made in her interpersonal relationships with her mother and housemate.

On the self-report measures that Anna filled out at the end of therapy, she dropped from 17 to 0 on the Beck Depression Inventory, meeting criteria for reliable clinical change in depression. In addition, she reported fewer symptoms on the Symptom Checklist—90—Revised and that she suppressed her feelings less and expressed her reactions more. There was little change on the Rosenberg Self-Esteem Inventory, the Dysfunctional Attitudes Scale, or the Inventory of Interpersonal Problems. Given the changes on the process measures, it is difficult to interpret the lack of movement on these outcome measures. One interpretation is that because Anna did not score in the clinical range at the beginning of treatment, she did not have that much room to move on these scales over the course of therapy. Another possibility is that in terms of her life situation she was still in a state of transition as therapy ended and may not have felt sufficiently settled to experience and note the changes in these other domains of functioning. Anna remained a self-reflective and somewhat self-critical person at the end of therapy and may not have felt willing, with many goals still to be accomplished, to endorse certain changes as permanent.

The therapeutic alliance as measured by the Working Alliance Inventory was very good. Anna's ratings on the alliance were consistently 4 and above on a 7-point scale. However, there was one question that she answered negatively after every session, noting that she did not feel that she and her therapist had discussed the goals of therapy explicitly. This comment highlights how important it is for therapists to clarify with their clients how they are conceptualizing their problems and to provide clients with some guidelines about how therapy might proceed. Some clients do not require explicit direction; they are happy to come in and talk and allow the process to unfold. However, other clients may need and prefer a more explicit statement of goals with more explicit guidance and structure.

III

CASES WITH POOR OUTCOME

5

BONDING INHIBITED

Richard was 47 when he presented for treatment for his depression. He was a soft-spoken man who tried to accommodate the needs of others. He was the middle child and had assumed most of the care for his aging mother after his father's death 20 years ago. He wished that his siblings would assist more but recognized that he had always considered himself to be different from and more sensitive than his two brothers. He noted that his depression had worsened after his father died.

As a child he had been shy and anxious and did not enjoy school because he found it too regimented and stifling. Although he did well, he was not interested in what he was learning. He disliked being evaluated and complained that the system evaluated the whole person and suppressed people instead of helping them to flourish. Richard was a creative person who left home at 15. He trained dogs but later changed careers to renovate and build houses; subsequently, he turned to writing as a profession. When he came for treatment, his career was at a low ebb, and he felt that he was not contributing sufficiently to the household income, though he was building a new house for himself and his wife.

Richard was reserved and did not form close friendships with others but got along well with everyone. He described himself as a private person, so much so that he did not even discuss his feelings of depression with his wife of 30 years because he was concerned about burdening her. He described his wife as supportive; however, she suffered from ill health and required care. Richard had difficulty reaching out even though he felt burdened trying to take care of others. He dreamed of escaping to a remote place and cutting himself off from people entirely; however, he felt bad about such dreams and tried to silence them.

Richard was unable to link his depression to a single event. He reported that his mother and father were good parents and his childhood was uneventful. He recalled that he had been depressed since he was a child and consequently was not optimistic about treatment. He had been depressed for so long that he had given up hope of overcoming his depression and was resigned to living with it. Richard experienced a lot of anxiety because he set very high standards for himself. He stated that he poured all of himself into projects, and once involved, he fretted and worried about the project incessantly. He was often overwhelmed by projects and tended to ruminate about his goals and objectives, lying awake at night trying to figure out the best way to accomplish them. Richard was diagnosed pretherapy with major depressive disorder on Axis I; paranoid, avoidant, and obsessive–compulsive features on Axis II; no diagnosis on Axis III; no diagnosis on Axis IV; and occupational problems characterized by job dissatisfaction on Axis V. Richard had a Global Assessment of Functioning score of 49, indicating serious difficulties with social and occupational functioning.

CASE FORMULATION

It became apparent early on that Richard had difficulty setting limits. He overburdened himself and set very high standards that were difficult to meet. He noted that even though he was forgiving of others, he expected perfection from himself. He was distant from his emotional experience, speaking with an external vocal quality with no reference to his inner subjective worldview and reactions except to state that he was depressed. Richard presented his situation quite objectively. He did not discuss his feelings or the details of his life, even when asked. He seemed reluctant to provide any information about his daily activities or describe the events in his life and used external rules and standards to judge his behavior. Thus his therapist had no sense of his context or how specific events were affecting him and how they might be contributing to his depression. Focusing on his deep sense of fatigue, his therapist observed that he seemed to overburden himself and had difficulty setting limits and asking for what he needed. His therapist suggested that this might be contributing to his depression and exhaustion. She suggested that they work on some two-chair exercises to become more aware of how exacting Richard was with himself and how he overburdened himself. Richard agreed.

Richard's core emotion scheme was rooted in a deep sense of shame and a sense that he was unacceptable to others. As he and his therapist began to engage in two-chair tasks, it became clear that Richard had very little empathy for himself. On the contrary, he was quite punishing and rejecting of himself. He acknowledged that he was very anxious and tended to ruminate about events as he strove to ensure the outcomes that he desired. He was unable to nourish and accept himself so much so that he saw his desire to move to a more peaceful environment as pathological and even shameful. Richard's deep sense of shame and reluctance to appear weak and acknowledge his vulnerability as well as his fear of burdening others impeded the successful resolution of his depression in 16 weeks.

BONDING AND AWARENESS

In the early sessions the therapist tried to foster the alliance and find a framework for working that would fit with the client's objectives. In Session 2 Richard admitted that he was a very private person and that he never confided in friends and never reached out when he was in distress. As he described his sense of hopelessness that things would ever be different, he remained calm and composed. There were no outward signs of emotion. He had a strong sense of right and wrong and carefully monitored his behavior so that he did not transgress. He complained that there was very little relief from his feelings and that he felt hopeless 24 hours a day. He was unable to pinpoint exactly when his depression started, but he recalled that he was aware of it as a child. He recognized that he had difficulty moderating his behavior and that when he became involved in a project he went at it "full tilt" and was either in or out with very little in between.

In Session 3 Richard spoke about feeling overwhelmed by the project he was working on. He said that he had difficulty sleeping and lay awake at night worrying about how he might do things differently because he needed it to be perfect. His therapist observed that one side seemed totally exhausted and the other side kept driving him to be perfect. She suggested a two-chair exercise to help Richard become more aware of the demands and expectations he had of himself and the impact the demands had on his well-being. Richard agreed.

Therapist: So what do you say to yourself?

Richard: You have got to get this right, no half measures. It has to work.

Therapist: So he drives you . . . can you come over to this chair? [*indicating the other chair*] How does this side respond? How do you feel in this chair?

Richard: I feel exhausted listening to him.

Therapist:	So he is wearing you out? What do you need over here?
Richard:	I need him to go away.
Therapist:	So you would like him to go away? Do you need him to stop?
Richard:	Yes!
Therapist:	Can you tell him to stop?
Richard:	Stop pushing me; I am tired.
Therapist:	OK. Can you come over here [*indicating the other chair*]? How does this side respond when you say, "stop, I am just too tired"?
Richard:	I can't let up or we won't do a good job. I am not going to listen to you. I won't lose. I won't stop. I am in charge in this relationship.
Therapist:	So he refuses to listen. Come over here [*indicating the other chair*]. How does this side respond when that side refuses to listen?
Richard:	When I hear that side I feel tired. This side is just too weak [*breaking out of the dialogue with himself to address his therapist*]. I feel more identified with the strong side. The weak side is more like other people. The strong side is scared that if I listen to the tiredness, I won't follow through and do things as well. The strong, controlling side never relaxes. If I am not useful, I am wasting my time.
Therapist:	So he is pushing, pushing.
Richard:	Yeah, you have to keep going. You are not good enough. You should be making more of a contribution. You are not doing enough.

In this excerpt Richard was extremely controlling with himself (SASB [Structural Analysis of Social Behavior] 3-5, 3-6, 3-7). He was overburdening himself; even though he was exhausted, he did not want to listen and forced himself to push on regardless (EXP [The Experiencing Scale] Stages 2, 4). Although Richard differentiated his inner experience (LCPP [Levels of Client Perceptual Processing] Level 5), he used external standards to judge his behavior (LCPP Level 3). His therapist continued to try to activate his experiencing side to see if he could treat himself with more compassion.

Therapist:	Come over to this chair. How does it feel when he says you are not good enough?
Richard:	I feel frustrated and tired. These two sides are always in conflict. He makes me feel stirred up and anxious.
Therapist:	Tell him how you feel.
Richard:	I feel tormented. I have hit a wall. I can't push myself any longer. Part of me wants to shut out the conflict. I feel ashamed showing it. It is hard to admit what I am doing. I should be strong

enough to deal with it. I feel I am giving in when I admit how badly I am feeling.

Therapist: So it is hard to talk about it?

Richard: Yes, I find it hard to talk about myself. It is very unsettling. I am always concerned about other people and find it hard to shift my attention to myself. I feel weak.

Therapist: So what do you say to him? "You are weak"?

Richard: Yes, you are weak and not interesting. It is selfish to talk about yourself.

Therapist: So it is hard to make room for you. You blot him out?

Richard: No one ever asked me how I felt. It is so hard.

The task ended with Richard acknowledging how difficult it was for him to change and to engage in the work of psychotherapy. He was able to articulate his tiredness and so seemed to be engaged in the task with his therapist (SASB 2-1). However, he admitted how hard it was for him to freely self-disclose (EXP Stage 5; SASB 2-8, 3-5, 3-7). He acknowledged that he felt weak when he talked about himself. Richard was making a proposition about himself and how he functioned that was a marker for further exploration that might have led him to an alternative way of viewing himself and his experience. However, the session ended, and he did not explore these feelings further or resolve them, so they continued to get in the way and block his progress.

Richard's deep sense of shame made it difficult for him to disclose and reveal his feelings and how he was treating himself (SASB 3-7). His therapist tried to explore his feelings of shame and to support his need to talk about his feelings (SASB 1-2; 1-3). However, Richard felt bad about admitting how depressed he was. He felt weak and vulnerable. He was more identified with the aggressive, punishing, and controlling side of his personality than the side that required rest, compassion, and nourishment. More of an introvert, he compared himself unfavorably with his more extroverted colleagues and friends and felt that there was something wrong with him (SASB 3-6). The therapist continued to communicate empathy and acceptance in the hope that Richard would overcome his sense of shame (SASB 1-2). Given Richard's ambivalence about sharing his vulnerability and weakness, his therapist might have suggested a two-chair task to try to help him resolve his ambivalence about the work of therapy.

EVOKING AND EXPLORING

In Session 4 Richard said he felt a little better and that the two-chair task had been useful in making him analyze how he was thinking. He realized that his thinking was very agitated. When his therapist asked how he made himself agitated, Richard responded that he needed to make perfect decisions and felt he could not make a mistake. He acknowledged that it was very difficult to soothe and calm himself. So much so that he often lay awake at night worrying about the outcome of events. When his therapist inquired about his concern that things be perfect, Richard replied that he was scared of losing his freedom. He said he had struggled to attain the standard of living that he currently enjoyed and was worried that if he made a mistake he would lose everything and be back where he started because he did not have a safety net. The therapist suggested a two-chair exercise to explore Richard's anxiety to see if it could be moderated. The therapist was still trying to facilitate his awareness of what he was doing to establish an agreement on the goals and tasks of therapy. Richard agreed.

Therapist: So how do you scare this side?

Richard: If we screw up, we will be in trouble.

Therapist: Come over here. How does this side feel?

Richard: This side feels responsible, like I am to blame. I feel like I am not valued, not important.

Therapist: So what do you need?

Richard: I need that side to back off.

Therapist: Come over here. How does this side respond when this side says "back off"?

Richard: OK, but I am worried.

Therapist: Tell him why you are so worried. What is so bad about making a mistake?

Richard: It just feels so bad.

Therapist: What do you say to yourself when you make a mistake?

Richard: It has to be perfect. Anything less is not good enough.

Therapist: Come over here [*indicating the other chair*]. How do you feel when he says that?

Richard: It is so exhausting. I feel flattened, like I can't do it. It's too much pressure. I need him to accept that it's OK not to be perfect all the time. Lower your sights. I can't get it right all the time.

Therapist: OK! How does the other side respond?

Richard: I was feeling a little sorry for him as he said that. I just don't want to give up.

Therapist:	So are you saying you will try not to push him? What do you need?
Richard:	I am scared of the chaos. I don't feel he is capable of being in charge. Mistakes are just unacceptable. If he makes a mistake, we lose control.
Therapist:	So this side does not trust him. Come over here. What do you want to say in response?
Richard:	I need you to share the power. Stop trying to beat me into submission.
Therapist:	Can you say that again?
Richard:	I need you to share the power.
Therapist:	How does this side respond?
Richard:	He listens but is doubtful. I'm not sure you can handle the responsibility. I need to see you manage.
Therapist:	Come over here. How do you respond to him?
Richard:	Give me a chance; let me show you.
Therapist:	How do you feel?
Richard:	More powerful.
Therapist:	OK, change. What is happening over here?
Richard:	He feels a little open to the idea. It feels good that he can do it. I feel a little more confidence in him.
Therapist:	So you will give up control?
Richard:	Not sure about that. This side is so strong; it does not want to give up.

Here Richard approached a partial resolution as the controlling side softened and felt a little sorry for the exhausted side (SASB 3-3, 3-4). However, the controlling side was reluctant to relinquish control and trust the needs of the exhausted side and once again overrode his feelings in favor of perfection and control (SASB 3-6). As Richard softened slightly, his therapist was still hopeful that with time he would become more compassionate toward himself and less controlling. The critic monitored and restrained Richard (SASB 3-5) while the experiencing side alternated between protesting and walling off and asserting and separating (SASB 3-1, 3-7, 3-8). When prompted by his therapist, Richard was able to express his feelings (EXP Stage 4; LCPP Level 5) and disclose what he needed to the critic. The critic became momentarily a little more self-accepting and understanding (SASB 3-1, 3-2). However, he reverted to doubting himself and refused to give up control. The critic's reluctance to share power was evident in the sessions that followed as he continued to exert pressure on Richard.

In the next few sessions Richard and therapist continued to work with the split between the part of Richard that expected him to continue functioning and the side that was exhausted and needed the controlling side to be less demanding. It became clear that these two parts of his personality were locked in a power struggle to the death because they each felt the other side needed to be extinguished for things to change (SASB 3-7). It was very difficult for the controlling side to give ground and respect the needs of the other side. Richard was also very attached to the powerful side; he saw it as confident, in control, and the part of his personality that other people liked and respected.

As Richard explored his experience, he became aware that he was constantly agitated. He felt unable to let himself go or be in the moment. He was continuously monitoring his behavior (SASB 3-5). He felt that if he were to stop he would disintegrate. He did not trust the exhausted side because he felt that if he gave in to it, things would come to a halt and unravel. The exhausted side recognized how brutal the controlling side was being. In the face of the controlling side's relentless beating, the exhausted side said he felt "extinguished" and thought it better to play dead than continue fighting for acknowledgment of his state (SASB 3-7). He said he felt "hopeless, totally defeated." He was feeling particularly vulnerable when he came for therapy. He noted that any small thing seemed to hit a raw nerve and that he did not feel very resilient in the face of small setbacks.

Richard remained analytical and detached as he confided these feelings. His voice had an externalizing quality, and he betrayed very little emotion, even as he spoke of his struggle. He did express curiosity about the cause of his feelings and why he treated himself in this way. However, he was unable to come up with an explanation. His curiosity had a disengaged, distant quality, as if he were idly musing as opposed to actively searching for the reason. When he considered his childhood, he was confident that it was positive and there were no events that he could relate to his feelings of depression. His therapist continued to work with making him aware of his feelings and trying to negotiate specific goals that could be achieved in the 16-week treatment. A primary reason the therapist encouraged Richard to stay in touch with how painful it felt for him to treat himself in such a punishing fashion was to try to help him become aware of his needs in relation to the pain he was feeling. In this way his therapist hoped to access Richard's more compassionate and caring way of treating himself.

In Session 6 the therapist suggested a two-chair exercise to explore Richard's feelings of anxiety. Richard realized that part of him felt numb as he silenced his needs and feelings.

Richard: You have no right to complain.

Therapist:	So this is how he silences you? Say this again.
Richard:	You have no right to complain. You can't let others see you.
Therapist:	Oh, so others shouldn't see him? Tell him why.
Richard:	They will think less of you. They won't understand. This side has no input.
Therapist:	So it is like you silence him?
Richard:	Yeah. I just give up.
Therapist:	Come over here. How does it feel over here when he silences you?
Richard:	I feel I have no value. You don't listen to me. I am never heard [*speaking to other chair*].
Therapist:	What do you need?
Richard:	I need to have more say. I need you to listen to me.
Therapist:	Come over here. How does this side respond?
Richard:	I am scared. If he has more input, people will see me as depressed.
Therapist:	What are you scared of?
Richard:	People see me as in control. If they see I am depressed, they will see me as weak. I would feel ashamed.
Therapist:	So "I am scared. I would feel so humiliated if they knew how depressed I was." Come over here. How does the exhausted side respond?
Richard:	I don't want to be humiliated either.
Therapist:	What does this side want [*indicating the exhausted chair*]?
Richard:	I need you to stop being so emotional. You are browbeating me. I need you to quiet down and give me space. Trust me.
Therapist:	So you need this side to trust your judgment? How does this side respond [*indicating the other chair*]?
Richard:	I feel more reassured. I will try to give you space and see what you do with it.
Therapist:	So how do you feel over here? Is there some relief?
Richard:	Yes, yes, I do. This side is worn out with trying to silence the other side.
Therapist:	So "I need a breather"?
Richard:	So if I felt that side could handle it, it would relieve me. It feels more reassuring.

Here Richard came close to a partial resolution as he asked for more space. There was a sense that each side might be able to listen and respond to the other (SASB 3-1, 3-4). There was less of a sense of struggle and more one of compromise as the controlling side realized it might be good to relax. The client was processing his emotions as he differentiated them and expressed how he was feeling (EXP Stage 4; LCPP Level 5). Although there was a hint of reevaluation and Richard saw a glimmer of an alternative perspective (EXP Stage 6; LCPP Level 6), by the next session the controlling side was once again in the driver's seat. Richard became more aware that he treated others with more compassion than he treated himself but remained unable to treat himself in the same way, though he wished that he could. As the struggle continued, the exhausted side began to lose hope and to wish the other side would die or go away because it was so brutal and relentless (SASB 3-6, 3-7).

In Session 9 Richard explored his anxiety about visiting friends on the weekend. He dreaded seeing them but felt that he must for his wife's sake. He said that she needed social contact, which he felt that his depression restricted. He criticized himself for being selfish by putting his needs first. He worried that he lacked social skills and intelligence and did not feel confident around others. He did wonder whether other people criticized themselves as much as he did. He then questioned whether he was really depressed but had to acknowledge that he did not look forward to anything and that he did things for other people and did not live for himself. However, he had reached a point at which he felt that he had no strength left to keep going. He wished he could crawl into a corner and rest because he was tired of going through the motions. He expressed a desire to live and to have the controlling side be less demanding. However, he admitted that he did not think he was mentally stable so forced himself to keep busy, though he longed to go at his own pace. His therapist responded with empathic affirmation at this marker of vulnerability.

Therapist: It doesn't seem worthwhile to you to do this. There's nothing that you'd like to hang around for?

Richard: I guess I just feel a bit burned out or whatever. I don't know what. That's the way I feel.

Therapist: So you're exhausted . . .

Richard: Uh-huh, totally, like and I find like that's really what sort of keeps you going is more that these other people depend on you.

Therapist: So that's the only thing that keeps you going on right now is your obligations?

Richard: Uh-huh.

Therapist: That you can't let other people down?

Richard:	Right.
Therapist:	That part of you would just like to let it all go and sort of just let it all slide away?
Richard:	Yeah.
Therapist:	You're tired of holding this load?
Richard:	Yeah, like I don't feel that there's any equipment or whatever to go forward, like there's nothing there to draw upon.
Therapist:	Uh-huh.
Richard:	Like there's no strength or anything there.
Therapist:	Uh-huh.
Richard:	But sometimes you can feel down temporarily or what have you, but there's always that little thing you call on. Like it's just, to me its like, it's just like there's really nothing there.
Therapist:	So the spark's gone out?
Richard:	Right.
Therapist:	And you don't think it'll ever come back?
Richard:	Yeah, I mean, I guess I, as long as I can remember, that I've always had this kind of personality. But I guess there was more strength to me then, like down, trying to talk myself up.
Therapist:	So you've always been very critical of yourself?
Richard:	Yeah.
Therapist:	Where does that come from?
Richard:	I don't know where it comes from. It just, I don't know, I guess. I guess for a long time I just thought that that was how it was.
Therapist:	That people are born that way?
Richard:	Yeah, right. I thought everyone was like that and though, if I just try and observe other people through doing that, I came to the [*laughs*] conclusion that they're not.
Therapist:	No, well, people are critical but maybe not quite as harsh with themselves as you are right?
Richard:	Right.
Therapist:	I mean, a lot of people are, obviously, but it seems that you've been too harsh on yourself. So harsh that you know it reaches a stage where you are kind of beaten and lying by the roadside virtually unable to get up, look around, and enjoy your surroundings anymore?

Richard: Uh-huh. Sometimes I wonder if that's kind of the major thing or what. I don't know.

Therapist: You're not sure that that's the reason?

Richard: Well, I don't, maybe it is, I don't know. I don't know if that . . .

Here Richard expressed uncertainty about the therapist's formulation about his depression (SASB 2-1). He acknowledged that he had thought the critical, controlling way in which he treated himself was normal and that he had only recently come to recognize that most people do not treat themselves in this manner. In this session there was a sense of someone waking up to realize and acknowledge that he or she was in an abusive relationship and that not all relationships are damaging and hurtful in the way that this one was. However, even as Richard came to this view, he was still mistrustful that he could cure his depression or even that his treatment of himself contributed to his depression. His therapist encouraged him to ask his body for confirmation of whether the view fit as opposed to rationally inquiring whether it made sense as they began to explore Richard's doubts.

Therapist: What does it feel like in you, I mean, if you go to that place where you kind of sense and feel things in your body as opposed to think about them?

Richard: I guess I never thought about it in those terms of being [*clearing throat*] self-critical. When you mentioned that, and I recognize that that's, you know what I'm probably, what I'm doing.

Therapist: Uh-huh. Part of you doesn't buy it. Is that what you're telling me?

Richard: No. I buy it. I'm just trying to think [*sighs*] if that's all it is. Like if I could . . .

Therapist: You think there must be something more?

Richard: Well, I think, well, I wonder if I could defeat that, like if that's it, if that's what's causing it.

Therapist: So hang on, hang on. Are you saying that seems too simple?

Richard: [*laughs*] Sometimes . . .

Therapist: I'm not sure. You said you wonder if you could defeat that?

Richard: Well, I guess I wonder if that's what's causing it all.

Therapist: But you're not sure?

Richard: No, I'm not sure.

Therapist: What's the uncertainty about?

Richard: I guess because, to a degree, I do it all the time, but sometimes it's worse than others. So in between [*laughs*] those times I think, then life should look better in between those times when you're doing, you know, when you're in one of those bouts or whatever. Then, like I guess I think if that's what's doing it, then how come I never get like even 5 minutes of sort of a break from it?

Therapist: So there's something missing in the middle, but the self-criticism doesn't allow it to grow?

Richard: Uh-huh.

Therapist: So it feels like it's empty in there?

Richard: Uh-huh.

Therapist: Do you know what I mean? I can see there's a real critic and this other person that's real kind of strong, but it's like there's actually nothing in the middle that's you inside?

Richard: Uh-huh, right.

Therapist: So even when the critic isn't being that loud, it's still there, right?

Richard: Right.

Therapist: There's that part of you that, one of the things or one of the objectives is to try and give more voice to that part of you. I mean, this is why I ask you, that's when I say you don't respect yourself.

Richard: Uh-huh.

Therapist: You know my sense is the critic stomps very hard on the part of you that has some wants, some needs and desires. It's kind of squashed all the time. I mean, we see it and we hear it, right; this side doesn't have a voice, I mean, you said that, right; it doesn't know what to say; it doesn't know what to feel; and that's the life part, isn't it? You know the other is a sergeant major. It keeps the army going, but this is the part that you need to experience to not feel depressed anymore.

The therapist worked to have the formulation fit Richard's experience of himself. She was trying to negotiate the tasks and goals of therapy so that they could share a joint vision of what they could work on together and what approach they could take (SASB 1-4; 1-2). Richard agreed with how the therapist presented the tasks and goals as they continued to explore and forge a joint understanding of his problems (SASB 2-4).

Richard: Right.

Therapist: This is the part we need to kind of somehow find a way of giving a voice to. He has been stifled for so long.

Richard:	Would it be . . .
Therapist:	He hardly knows the language?
Richard:	Like the one thing that I have a hard time with, too, like if there's any kind of adversity or whatever, I don't know would that affect that because . . .
Therapist:	I think it's part of the same thing of not being resilient, right?
Richard:	Because I'll go for days [*sighs*], you know, without sleeping and things, if something comes up.
Therapist:	Uh-huh.
Richard:	I stay awake for 24 hours.
Therapist:	So there's also a real sense of being vulnerable?
Richard:	Well, yeah, it's like if some small little thing happens, it's like there's no cushion there to absorb anything . . .
Therapist:	Yes.
Richard:	It's just like it's just hitting, like, a total raw nerve—like just like something that would, that other people would just take in stride.
Therapist:	Bounce back from and not notice?
Richard:	Right.
Therapist:	And it just knocks you over in some way?
Richard:	Right.
Therapist:	Uh-huh.
Richard:	So through that I develop a sense, too, that I can't really accomplish anything because if I try anything there's bound to be adversity or whatever in my life, and I seem to be staying away from it because of that [*laughs*].
Therapist:	So it kind of, it's gotten to the point where the best protection is to kind of to withdraw because you can't keep being knocked over really any more?
Richard:	Right.
Therapist:	Is that it?
Richard:	Uh-huh.
Therapist:	"I've had enough of being buffeted"?
Richard:	Right. You can't take it anymore so you just don't want to do anything because you subject yourself to something that you can't take.

Therapist:	Uh-huh.
Richard:	So you just try and withdraw from things as much as possible.
Therapist:	Uh-huh.
Richard:	And then I guess that could [*laughs*], then you have a whole other thing growing. You should be doing this, and you should be doing that. You know all I do . . .
Therapist:	So it's hard to kind of accept that as the solution. It's another part that says, "No, that's not acceptable; you should be going out; you should be making plans to do such and such"?
Richard:	Right, well, I mean, to have a career and to move forward, I mean, you have to get out there; you have to do things; and it's [*laughs*] difficult to live in this world the way things are going.
Therapist:	Uh-huh.
Richard:	To be able to . . .
Therapist:	So hang on, hang on. Am I right in getting the sense that part of you would just like to kind of crawl away into a corner and just let it all kind of go on without you?
Richard:	Right.
Therapist:	Uh-huh.
Richard:	Part of that.
Therapist:	But that doesn't seem like a real option, even that you plan to go to work and make a living . . .
Richard:	It's kind of a waste of your own life, you know? I mean, if I just crawled away into a corner and stayed there for [*laughs*] the next whatever, I don't think that's a reasonable way out of this.
Therapist:	Uh-huh. So it doesn't seem reasonable or . . .
Richard:	No. Do you think it is [*laughs*]? What would I be doing, you know?
Therapist:	So that's a conflict in you then, the part that kind of just wants to withdraw and hide and the other part that says, "No, you keep going, keep going, keep going"?
Richard:	Well, I think I have certain talents and things that I do, and I like to be able to make use of them, work on some things that I get enjoyment from.

Here Richard expressed his concern that if he did stop and rest and give in to the side that was exhausted, then he would waste his life (SASB 2-2, 3-6). This was a clear expression of his fear that the tired side would take over and that he would lose any sense of purpose. His therapist suggested that they work with this to see if it could be resolved. To this point the therapist had assumed that the critic had all the power. However, having heard the fear, she began to suspect that the power resided with the depressed, exhausted side, and the critic was actually scared of being overwhelmed by the depression. At this point she changed her approach to try to see whether the controlling side's fear could activate the depressed side to encourage more dialogue between the two sides.

Therapist: Can we separate that out? Can we put that part of you that wants to hide away over here, and you're speaking out from the part that says, "Hey I got a contribution to make right"?

Richard: Uh-huh.

Therapist: Can you tell this side just what you've told me, "I've got talents and I want to make a contribution"? Is that what you were saying?

Richard: Right. Well, there are certain things in life that I want to move forward and be able to do and be able to do them constructively.

Therapist: Uh-huh. Tell this side what you want to be able to do.

Richard: The actual thing?

Therapist: Tell this side what your dreams are, what your goals are.

Richard: Well, like I've been writing books and so forth, and I'd like to be able to carry on doing that because I do get enjoyment out of it. It is something [*laughs*] that you can actually work on by yourself, and it sort of fulfills my personality and stuff like that. I like to try and do something that I feel has some kind of meaning, and I can work on different stories and so forth but . . .

Therapist: So "I want to write more books."

Richard: Right.

Therapist: Anything else?

Richard: I'd like to be able to, I guess, look forward to the next day would be a treat.

Therapist: Can you say that? "I'd like to look forward to tomorrow."

Richard: Right, OK. I'd like to look forward to tomorrow.

Therapist: Uh-huh. What's it like not looking forward to tomorrow? What does it feel like?

Richard: It feels like there's no sense to your existence, I guess.

Therapist: So life's lost real meaning?

Richard:	Yes, it feels like going through the motions.
Therapist:	So "I'm tired of going through the motions." Can you say that?
Richard:	Right, I'm tired of going through the motions.
Therapist:	What do you want? Am I right to say, "I want to live"?
Richard:	Right.
Therapist:	Could you say that?
Richard:	I want to live.
Therapist:	Say that again.
Richard:	I want to live. I think I'd be happy with that [*laughs*].
Therapist:	Come over here [*asking Richard to switch chairs*]. This is the side that just has given up and wants to hide away. How does it respond right here as that side is saying, "There are things that I want to do; I've got talents. I want to write more books. You know, they express me; they fit with me; and more than that I want to live. I'm tired of being depressed." How do you respond?
Richard:	I don't know, I guess I'm going to have to learn to not be able to deal with things in some kind of way where I'm not affected so much. Like I just feel that it sounds great, but I wonder how practical it is [*laughs*].
Therapist:	Is that your head talking?
Richard:	Right.
Therapist:	The side that wants to run away, what is that side saying? "What's the point of this— it's just pipe dreams"? Are you putting it down? Is that what you're saying? "What's the point"?
Richard:	It doesn't make sense. I guess that is what he's saying.
Therapist:	That's what he's saying. It's like those are pipe dreams, and it's . . . it's not worth it. Is that what he's saying?
Richard:	Right.
Therapist:	It's not worth it. Say this to him, "It's not worth it."
Richard:	Well, that it's not worth it, that it's easier to just be by yourself and [*laughs*] not try and do it.
Therapist:	So this is the way that you stifle him, right? This is the way you take away his life and his hope. "It's not worth it, there's no point."
Richard:	Well, I also tell him stuff like that that I can't deal with it.
Therapist:	How come, is it you're exhausted?
Richard:	I guess that's it, but . . .

Therapist:	Uh-huh.
Richard:	Because to do something, to move ahead along the way, like there's various things that you have to deal with, and I just don't feel like I can do it.
Therapist:	"I can't do it."
Richard:	Right.
Therapist:	Tell him why you can't do it; it feels too much?
Richard:	It feels too much. I guess it feels that I've done it so many times, and it has been so hard to do it that I feel that I'm just not up to it anymore—that if the least little thing happens—things just come crashing down again.
Therapist:	So, what—"I feel like there are no reserves anymore"?
Richard:	Right.
Therapist:	"I'm tired of pushing and pulling and getting things in place." Is that what you're saying?
Richard:	Yes. Oh, well, that I'm tired from always trying to push myself into doing this, and that I don't feel like there's really anything to work for or anything to . . .
Therapist:	[*Richard switches chairs.*] How does this side respond when it feels that side saying, "I'm just too tired. I'm tired of pulling and pushing, and I can't get my hopes up; there's no point." What do you feel over here?
Richard:	Well, I guess this side feels a bit deflated.
Therapist:	You feel deflated over there?
Richard:	Yeah, because he's trying to get up and says, Are we going to do this or we got to get going, and he listens to the . . .
Therapist:	Are you scared of the deflation?
Richard:	Right.
Therapist:	Tell this side about feeling deflated, like, "I feel the air goes out of my balloon."
Richard:	Right. Like I'm just trying to get up about things and get back and get involved, to be part of life, and basically he's telling me that there's no sense; you can't do it; forget about it.
Therapist:	Uh-huh. What is it like being over here? Do you feel crushed?
Richard:	Hopeless.
Therapist:	You feel hopeless. So when this side says, there's no point, this side feels hopeless?

Richard:	Right, and it sort of wants to do it, but it's like this great big ball and chain around it. So there's that dialogue all the time . . .

Here the therapist and Richard identified the cycle that occurs between the depressed side and the controlling side. Richard was beginning to recognize the impact that his behavior had and to see its effect on him.

Therapist:	So what's it like having a ball and chain on all the time? Tell him about the ball and chain; tell him what happens having the ball and chain on?
Richard:	Well, it takes away any happiness in you to try and get on with your life because there's always a downer part and then I don't want to get involved anymore.
Therapist:	The lights have gone out; there's no happiness; there's no joy in our world anymore?
Richard:	Right.
Therapist:	What else is happening? What else does it mean to have a ball and chain around you? There's no joy?
Richard:	Well, it feels like an impossible situation because regardless of what I come up with . . .
Therapist:	Uh huh. You said you feel deflated, with kind of this enormous weight around you. What's it like to be carrying that weight? [*speaking softly*] What does it need?
Richard:	Need?
Therapist:	Do you need this ball and chain to be taken off?
Richard:	Yeah. Well, that would be nice.
Therapist:	Can you say that?
Richard:	Well, I need the ball and chain to be taken off.
Therapist:	So "I need you to take at least the ball and chain off. Let me walk freely."
Richard:	Right.
Therapist:	Can you say that?
Richard:	That I need you to release the ball and chain and to let me walk freely, and to do what I want to do.
Therapist:	"I need to be able to roam."
Richard:	Uh-huh.
Therapist:	Is there anything else you want to say to this side?
Richard:	No.

Therapist:	OK, come here [*Richard switches chairs.*]. How does this side respond when it says, "I need you to release the ball and chain. I need you to let me walk away, to live with joy in my life."
Richard:	I find it hard to, I don't know. I can't seem to reach these places for whatever reason.
Therapist:	Well, what . . .
Richard:	I want to walk out of here and . . .
Therapist:	Yes, but maybe this side needs something too, so what are you saying, "I'd like to release you but . . ."
Richard:	I don't feel I can, I guess.
Therapist:	You don't want to release him; you want to keep him chained up?
Richard:	I guess if I really think about it, I don't need to trust him or I can't let this side, like there's no feeling that oh OK, you know, go ahead.
Therapist:	So hang on, this side's scared?
Richard:	I think so.
Therapist:	"I can't trust; but if I let you free, I can't trust you." What are you worried about? What are you concerns about this side?
Richard:	I guess I'm having trouble because there's just this the underlying thing that's just so overwhelming that it's something that I cannot do, that I can't get beyond that feeling.
Therapist:	Why can't you do it? What is the, "I can't do it," about? What is it screeching no for? "I can't afford to"?
Richard:	That I just don't have the requirement like mental stability or the mental strength to do it.

Here we see that Richard does not believe he can change. He does not feel strong enough. In Session 10 Richard revealed how depressed he was. His wife had become angry with him during the week, and he felt bad. He was tired of meeting other people's demands. He blamed himself for not taking care of his needs and not being able to say no. He tried to distract himself from his feelings by staying busy all the time. His therapist pointed out how much he beat up on himself. He agreed but noted that he was trying to be more accepting because she had reassured him that it was OK not to be as sociable as his wife. However, a part of him did not care whether he was dead or alive, and he was only staying alive for others. His life felt empty and without fun. He did not feel he was getting anything out of it. He agreed with his therapist that he was very critical and observed that the critical voice was very vicious with no empathy. They engaged in another two-chair exercise with the critic. The experiencing side was able to tell the critic to back off. The critic was surprised that the experiencing side said this, and although the critic listened, he was just waiting to find another way to undermine the experiencing side and beat him down. The critic admitted that if he stopped criticizing the other side, he feared he would die and the other side would take over.

After this session the therapist began to accept how hard it was for Richard to change his behavior. His fear of being exposed and seen as "sick" precluded him from engaging in behaviors that he viewed as weak. The power struggle between the controlling side and the side that wanted relief seemed to grow more intense and did not diminish over time. The two sides seemed entrenched and unable to negotiate their differences. Although the therapist had been hopeful initially as Richard partially resolved some splits, she began to feel discouraged as she realized that there was little movement in the therapy. Thinking about the process, the therapist became more aware of how abstract their exchanges were and what little information Richard provided about his daily life. He had also remained quite analytical and dispassionate about his experience. The therapist decided to pull back from focusing on the tasks and Richard's internal processes to try to see whether she could open up or explore his experiences in a slightly different way. She resorted to using more empathic responses with the aim of trying to build a more positive and nurturing introject and to see if there was an alternative way of formulating his depression. In retrospect it might have been more helpful to focus on Richard's fear and ambivalence about change. However, the therapist continued to try to heighten and make him aware of the toll that his behavior was taking of him and to accentuate how annihilating and brutal it was.

In Session 11 Richard said he had had a good week. He had played squash. The game took his mind off his depression as he was totally in the moment. His therapist explored how much physical exercise he did and encouraged him to do more because it would be beneficial for the depression. The therapist noted that he invalidated himself during the session. Richard agreed but said that if he were to do as he wished he was not sure what he would become. He did not feel he could stop fighting because if he did, he would give everything up and move to a cabin in the wilderness because he did not fit in. However, he felt insecure about this as society kept telling him how much money he needed to amass to retire. He berated himself for wasting his life and not looking for clients to increase his business.

During a two-chair task to work with the critic, the controlling side expressed astonishment at the experiencing side saying, "How dare you! Where do you come from? I am the driver. I call the shots." The controlling side acknowledged that he felt vulnerable and that he feared losing his authority and importance. He was scared that he would be diminished and useless. The experiencing side expressed concern for the critical side's fears and tried to reassure him that he did not want to extinguish him. The critic was attentive to the experiencing side's reassurance. He observed that the experiencing side seemed stronger, so he had to take him more seriously. However, the controlling side was still not prepared to relinquish power or come to a compromise. Instead, he said in an aside to his therapist, "This is a serious attack. I will have to wait to ambush him." His therapist emphasized that it was important for the two sides to find a way to live together.

At Session 12 Richard came in feeling depressed, but he was unable to pinpoint the trigger for his depression. When his therapist observed that he did not share the details of what happened to him during the session, he replied that he was worried about burdening her, and he wanted to say that things were good. He still had the feeling that he should not burden other people, even though he knew that was ridiculous. However, he noted that he did not usually spend an hour just talking about himself and was not consciously holding back. Because Richard said he felt useless, his therapist suggested that they go back and explore what happened during the week that might have contributed to his depression. Richard became aware that he was exhausted paying attention to other people's needs. He found it hard to say no to the requests of others and to put his own needs first. The therapist expressed concern that there did not seem to be any progress. Richard said that he had had a few new insights, but it was hard to change his thinking. His mind was so quick and just seemed to gallop off. He was unable to stop or interrupt his critical thoughts.

Over the next two sessions, Richard and his therapist continued to explore what was holding him back. He reported that he was more active during the week. As he explored his depression with his therapist, he noted that since he started working alone he had more time on his hands with no distraction and that allowed him to think about how hopeless he felt and how bleak the future looked. He said his whole life had been a battle, but it was worse for the last 3 to 5 years. He said that he felt totally exhausted and that small things set him off. His therapist observed how he did not speak of the details of his life. Richard said he did not know how to do this. His therapist suggested that it was important for them to unpack what was happening, so that perhaps they could identify the triggers for his depression. Richard said he was uncertain what his depression was about, but he felt as if he were wasting his life. He would rather be doing more creative things but felt trapped and unable to change direction. His therapist suggested a two-chair exercise to explore his conflict about feeling trapped.

Therapist: [addressing the critical side] So what do you say to him?

Richard: You are too sensitive and disorganized.

Therapist: What happens over here?

Richard: I feel attacked. Feels like I can't do anything. Just feel constantly attacked.

Therapist:	So it is like being under fire?
Richard:	Yes, I feel like giving up.
Therapist:	What do you need?
Richard:	I need you to stop.
Therapist:	Anything else?
Richard:	I need you to say something positive.
Therapist:	So be supportive?
Richard:	Yes, give me a sign he is changing.
Therapist:	Come over here. How does this side respond?
Richard:	I'm uncertain; I'm not sure whether to listen.

Once again Richard came to his feelings of fear that the other side would demolish him. He was concerned that the other side would produce shoddy work and lower his standards. He continued to be driven by his external rules and expectations (EXP Stage 2; LCPP Level 4; SASB 3-6, 3-7, 3-8), which he was reluctant to give up or modify.

At Session 14 Richard observed that when he was busy he did not feel so bad but recognized that he was only avoiding the feelings and that his depression had not moderated. He noted that he had been thinking about why it was difficult to disclose in the session and realized that he was out of touch with his feelings. He felt that he couldn't reach his feelings, that inside he felt "blank." He was concerned that time was running out and that his therapist was feeling frustrated. She reassured him that she understood how hard it was for him to express his feelings. Richard expressed how hopeless he felt. One side of him did not believe that he could change, and the other wanted to hope. He acknowledged that he was frightened of talking about how bad it was because he had trouble coping when he felt really bad, and saying it out loud might make it more real. His therapist observed that he seemed to interrupt himself. Richard agreed but said that he felt dead inside. He said looking for his feelings was like "looking into a black room." His therapist focused him on his body to try to help him get in touch with what was happening for him. He observed that he became critical and then felt anxious because he did not know what he was feeling. His therapist reassured him, saying that when you don't pay attention to your feelings they can become like an overgrown garden. It sounded as if Richard had lost the way in and so no longer knew what was inside. Richard agreed, saying it was very difficult to talk about himself. Yet he recognized that it was one of the reasons therapy had been helpful and that he had never had the opportunity to talk so freely with anybody else before in his life. He also felt that to talk about himself was very self-centered. He felt he could not confide in his wife and that he needed to be strong and stable for her.

His therapist focused him on his body to help him become more aware of his feelings. Once again Richard observed how tired he felt and how tense his shoulders and neck were. He felt bad about not being able to say clearly what he felt. He needed the controlling side to leave him alone. He noted how destructive he had been. The controlling side backed up but was unable to respond in a sympathetic way. So his therapist asked him how he would respond if it were his wife or a friend who was making the request. He said he would feel sorry and would make an effort to help by trying to understand and by giving them some peace and quiet. The therapist asked if he could give that to himself. "Can you reach out a hand and do that for yourself?" Richard said he did not feel like that toward the exhausted side. His therapist responded, "So you are going to continue kicking him?" Richard stopped to think and wondered how he could switch so quickly from feeling concerned and sympathetic toward someone else and treat himself so callously. He realized that his gut did not feel he deserved a break. To think about himself was selfish and wrong; he should be concerned only for others. His therapist emphasized that he was killing himself. Richard acknowledged that he could see that he was and that he cared for the other side and did not want him to die. This marked a turning point as Richard recognized that he needed to take care of himself and listen to his feelings and needs. However, there were only two more sessions, and there was no time to work with him on becoming more in touch with his feelings, needs, and wants. In a sense the therapy was just beginning as it was about to end.

In the next session, Richard and his therapist continued to work with the split between the side that wanted to give up and the side that wanted to survive. He realized that he was always chivying himself and thinking about how he could make things better. To try to counteract his fear of drowning in his depression, his therapist asked him what would happen if he allowed himself to withdraw and give into his depression. Richard acknowledged that he would withdraw for a day or two but then become tired of lying in bed and get up to see what was happening. His therapist tried to reassure him that his curiosity and desire to live would reassert itself without his having to push and kick himself so hard to do things. She also tried to help him focus on what he needed moment by moment as opposed to living according to other people's rules and standards. In this session Richard was able to ask the depressed side to be more positive.

Therapist: Do you want to look at those two voices? Does that make sense or is there something else that you want to do today?

Richard: No, I just, you know, whatever . . .

Therapist: So which side are you most in touch with, the side that says, "I want to just give up. It's enough," or the side that says, "Come on, you got to keep going, come on"?

Richard:	Probably the giving up side is the one feeling I have more often.
Therapist:	OK, so what does that feeling say? What does that side say?
Richard:	The side about giving up?
Therapist:	Uh-huh.
Richard:	Well, it's, that's where I find it hard to put sort of a voice on that or because it seems almost more like, it's like a feeling more than a voice.
Therapist:	What's the feeling?
Richard:	It's just feeling like really numb, like physically numb, mentally numb.
Therapist:	Can you stay with the numbness?
Richard:	Uh-huh.
Therapist:	Can you give a voice to the numbness? What's the numbness about? What does that numbness say? "I want to stop feeling that, I've had enough" or "it's too much, leave me alone." What does it say?
Richard:	All of that.
Therapist:	Say that to him?
Richard:	Well, that it's, I just feel that. I think that I want to turn off really all feeling, to just not feel anything . . .
Therapist:	Tell this side why you need to turn off those feelings.
Richard:	Why I need to is maybe I just have trouble dealing with them. I don't . . .
Therapist:	Uh-huh. What's difficult about dealing with the feelings?
Richard:	Like this is where it gets like to where like you know it's frustrating because like I don't know why I can't think of that. It seems pretty basic.
Therapist:	The feelings are hard?
Richard:	Well, to try and understand . . .
Therapist:	They hurt?
Richard:	I don't even know. I just, the answers won't or . . .
Therapist:	What comes to mind when you say that? What do you feel when I say that?
Richard:	I guess I'm trying to think about the answer, and it won't come, and then I think, where is, like do I . . .

Therapist:	But hang on. So there isn't anything in there; it's just a blank numbness?
Richard:	Uh-huh.
Therapist:	That says, "I'm tired of feeling. It's too hard to feel anymore"?
Richard:	Yeah, that's closer to it than . . .
Therapist:	"It's too hard to carry on. I've had it." Is that what it says?
Richard:	There's not much inner dialogue that goes on about that.
Therapist:	No, I realize that.
Richard:	Right.
Therapist:	But what we're also trying to do is just give words to the feelings?
Richard:	Oh, right.

Here Richard expressed his disagreement with the therapist about the task of labeling feelings. He did not feel he was engaged in an inner dialogue; rather the feelings just happened to him (EXP Stage 4; LCPP Level 5; SASB 2-1, 2-2). The therapist suggested that they try to label the feelings and Richard agreed. The therapist responded in an accepting way and tried to explain her understanding of the process (SASB 1-2, 1-4).

Therapist:	So it's like, "I've just had enough." It's just, "I want to switch off. Leave me alone." Anything else?
Richard:	Right, no, nothing I can think of.
Therapist:	It's just too hard, too difficult?
Richard:	Like, I mean, I don't tell myself that really, but it's like you say, like trying to put some words to it, like I don't tell myself it's too hard or tell myself it's painful or anything like that. I just feel that way.
Therapist:	Uh-huh. So that's what the feeling is. So that captures the feeling, even if it's not, you know, you don't have a sense of it. That's what you say to yourself?
Richard:	Right.
Therapist:	OK, come over here [*Richard switches chairs.*]. What happens over here when you hear this side saying, "You know, I just want to switch off. I've had enough. It's just too hard to feel." What happens over here?
Richard:	Well, I don't even know if it's over here, but just when I listen to that, I guess it's the sense of giving up or something.
Therapist:	Do you feel hopeless over here?

Richard:	Well, that was the first thought that came to my mind.
Therapist:	Yeah, what's the hopelessness about?
Richard:	When I try and think of it, my mind just kind of goes blank. It just . . .
Therapist:	Uh-huh. So, but what happens when you hear this side saying, "I don't want to carry on"? This side just sort of feels really hopeless, really defeated.
Richard:	Uh-huh.
Therapist:	What do you need from this side?
Richard:	I guess more positive energy or thoughts or something that's more uplifting than fear of that.

Here the therapist was encouraging Richard to label his feelings and to try to represent them in words (SASB 1-4). Richard went along with his therapist's suggestions but still had a little difficulty accepting that he said or thought negative thoughts. Nonetheless, he voiced his thoughts and expressed his feelings and needs to the other side (EXP Stage 4; LCPP Level 6; SASB 2-2, 2-4) and began to see how he might treat himself differently (SASB 3-3, 3-4).

Therapist:	Right, so it's just so hard to see you so defeated. I wish you'd be more positive. I need you to be more positive.
Richard:	It's like, well, it's like living with somebody who's constantly just going on about things that are depressing.
Therapist:	Uh-huh. Tell this side what it's like to live with someone who's constantly depressed.
Richard:	Well, it's hard to give much energy, I guess, to life or positive feelings when you're dealing with somebody who's feeling like that 24 hours a day. Like you can do it sometimes, but it's sort of, I guess, you feel that it seems to be a hopeless situation so why bother.
Therapist:	So you're feeling burdened. Can you say that to this side, "I feel burdened by your depression"?
Richard:	Yeah. I feel burdened by your depression.
Therapist:	Uh-huh, "I feel drained."
Richard:	Right. Well, I feel drained and I guess I don't see much sense to keep trying to get him going because he seems like a bit of a dud.
Therapist:	"I can't keep pushing by myself."
Richard:	Right.

Therapist:	Can you say that?
Richard:	I can't keep pushing by myself.
Therapist:	Uh-huh. What do you need from him?
Richard:	I think I need a better attitude.
Therapist:	Uh-huh. You need a better attitude. Do you need him to stop dragging you down?
Richard:	As far as thinking more positively?
Therapist:	Positively, yeah, thinking more positively. It feels like he's just dragging you down, for you to do the work. It's a burden.
Richard:	Well, it would make me feel a lot better to be with . . .
Therapist:	So it would help you more if a lot of things were more positive.
Richard:	Right.
Therapist:	Right. "I need you to be more positive."
Richard:	Right.
Therapist:	Uh-huh. What happens when you hear this side saying, "But I feel so kind of defeated and burdened when you're so hopeless. I just feel like I'm giving up. I need you to be more positive"?
Richard:	Well, I guess I feel that I'd like to be, but I don't know if I'm able to.

Here Richard expressed himself clearly to the depressed side as he freely shared his needs with the other side and tried to take care of himself (EXP Stage 4; LCPP Level 5; SASB 1-2, 3-4). His therapist used empathic reflection and conjectures to try to help Richard express his needs (SASB 1-2, 1-4).

Richard expressed a wish to be different but was uncertain of what to do (SASB 3-2). He and his therapist went on to explore how the side that wanted to survive could support and help the depressed side be different. Richard was beginning to see glimmers of how he could change. However, by the time therapy ended he and his therapist were still working to make him more aware of his feelings and to evoke and explore his experience. There were glimmers of transformation, but new ways of behaving had yet to be constructed, and new meaning that would help him view things differently had not been generated. It was clear at the end of treatment that Richard needed to continue in therapy. Session 16 was devoted to assessing what Richard had found useful in therapy, exploring his goals for the future, and discussing further treatment options.

Because Richard was part of a research protocol and because he had not responded to the treatment as quickly as hoped, his therapist decided to refer him to a cognitive–behavior therapy clinic in the city. However, in a follow-up interview 12 months later, Richard observed that he had had difficulty with the cognitive–behavioral approach as well.

SUMMARY AND ANALYSIS

A review of the outcome measures shows that Richard reported more distress at the end of treatment. He was more depressed, with his score on the Beck Depression Inventory rising 10 points, from 24 to 34, and his score on the Dysfunctional Attitudes Scale rising 31 points, from 154 to 185. He also reported that he was less reflective, suppressed his feelings more, and was slightly more reactive at the end of treatment on the Ways of Coping questionnaire. There was little fluctuation in his self-esteem and his report of his interpersonal problems.

In contrast, a review of the Working Alliance Inventory data showed that Richard reported a good alliance with scores from 4.67 to 5.33 on a 7-point scale and a mean of 5.04 over the 16 weeks. Further inspection of the data showed that he did not express confusion or disagreement about the tasks and goals of therapy but seemed more uncertain about whether his therapist appreciated and liked him. This was contrary to what was observed in the therapy transcripts in which Richard seemed hesitant to accept his therapist's view of the factors that were contributing to his depression. Although he reported that he very often felt that he and his therapist were working toward mutually agreed on goals, that he trusted his therapist to help him, and that they trusted each other, he only occasionally felt his therapist liked or appreciated him. This suggests that Richard had some difficulty with the bond of the alliance or trusting that others would care for him as opposed to disagreement about the goals and tasks in therapy.

In fact, he reported that therapy often provided him with new ways of looking at his problems. This view was further supported by another postsession measure that inquired about the changes that Richard experienced during the session. Three questions that focus on changes that may have occurred as a function of the therapeutic relationship were consistently rated 6 or 7 on a 7-point scale. The items were "Feeling understood by my therapist helped me get in touch with my inner sense of direction"; "My therapist's acceptance made me feel better about myself"; and "My therapist's genuineness enabled me to feel more trusting and open to exploring my experience." Thus it appears that he did feel understood and accepted by his therapist at times and that he saw her as sincere and genuine in her interactions with him; however, he was not sure that she liked him. His scores on the Barrett-Lennard Relationship Inventory showed that he was below the mean for the group in terms of his sense of whether his therapist accepted him. In contrast to Richard's view, his therapist reported that she felt empathic toward him, regarded him warmly, and was accepting and congruent. Her scores were close to the mean for the sample overall. However, it seems Richard did not perceive or have a consistent sense of this according to his responses on the postsession questionnaires.

It is of concern that Richard felt worse at the end of treatment. However, the worsening of his depression was not apparent in a review of the therapy tapes or in his reports of how he was feeling in the session. One notable change was that Richard did seem to be more open about revealing how depressed he felt as the treatment progressed. One explanation for his worsening symptoms may have been his growing appreciation of how bad he felt. An important focus of the treatment was to encourage Richard to treat himself with more kindness and compassion. Alternatively, he may also have felt more able to honestly say how bad he was feeling by the end of treatment. He observed during therapy that he had not previously shared his pain with anyone, doing his best to hide it and pretend that he was fine. He also said that he was afraid to admit how bad he felt for fear of making it more real.

Another factor that may have contributed to his reporting that he felt worse was that therapy was ending early, before he had made any substantial gains. He may have felt hopeless about ever getting better given that the treatment had not helped. This may have been exacerbated by his knowledge that his brother's depression had ameliorated after he received a brief cognitive–behavioral treatment. In comparison with his brother, Richard may have felt like a failure or that he had received the wrong type of therapy. His therapist's knowledge of his brother's improvement influenced her decision to refer him to a cognitive–behavioral clinic. In addition to these factors, there may have been some sadness that the relationship with his therapist was ending that contributed to his higher scores on depression. Richard had said on a number of occasions that he had not had the opportunity to focus on himself with anyone in his life before nor did he have a confidant with whom to share his pain. He was very appreciative of the opportunity to speak with his therapist. Thus losing the relationship with his therapist created a void that he may not have been able to fill readily.

Richard's score on the Beck Depression Inventory at his 18-month follow-up was 21. He reported that he felt that neither therapy approach, cognitive–behavioral therapy, nor emotion-focused therapy, had cured his depression, but each had been somewhat helpful. He was able to use different techniques from the two types of therapy and was more accepting of himself. In the interim he had bought a cottage and was looking forward to relocating to it, as he felt more relaxed and happy there.

A number of factors may have contributed to Richard's poor outcome. First was his stance toward the change process; second, he was embedded in his experience and unreflective of it; third, Richard did not yet have a narrative or story that provided a framework for his depression; and fourth, his emotional processing skills were limited because he had silenced his feelings for so long. We examine how these factors may have impeded Richard's progress and look at what type of interventions might have been more appropriate for him.

First, in terms of the stages of change model, Richard was still contemplating whether he could change. When he began therapy, Richard was not convinced that therapy would help his depression given that it had endured for so long. For therapy to be effective, clients need to take an active, engaged stance toward their problems and see the possibility for change by reflecting on their own and other peoples' behavior as well as their life situation to devise alternative ways of behaving. At the beginning of therapy Richard was quite passive. He admitted that for a long time he saw his condition as normal and that this was the way life was. It was only toward the end of therapy that he began to question his behavior and develop a view that perhaps he could be different. After he began to compare himself with others and observe their behavior, he realized that most people did not walk around depressed. When Richard entered therapy he was in transition from a precontemplation phase to a contemplation phase of change. Consequently much of the therapy was focused on moving him from a contemplation phase to an engaged one. This suggests that short-term therapy is not efficacious for clients who are at the contemplation stage. In the future it will be important to assess where clients are in terms of the stages of change model to determine whether a short-term treatment will be beneficial for them or not.

Second, Richard was embedded in his life experience. He was not able to identify and name difficulties in his life. He had difficulty standing outside his life experience to see what might be contributing to his depression in a personally meaningful way. Thus he continued to be the subject of his experience and not the agent. He described his childhood as unproblematic, yet he left home at a very young age. He did acknowledge that ever since he was an adolescent he had seen himself as different because he was more sensitive than other people in his family and that he was resentful that his siblings did not help with his ailing mother. However, he did not see these factors as important or related to his depression, nor did his therapist focus on these. This may, in part, be explained by the fact that she felt constrained by working within a research protocol that required that she focus on how the client was treating himself, his problematic reactions, and unfinished business. Although these tasks are useful, they are premature if a client has underdeveloped emotional processing skills and is unable to be compassionate and validating of the self.

Third, Richard did not have a narrative of his life experience. He needed time to explore his life to begin to construct a story that would encompass his experience. A story would have provided a framework and context that would have provided an explanation for his symptoms. It would have enabled him to become disembedded from his experience so that he could observe it from outside. Richard and his therapist needed to spend more time reconstructing the events in his life to see what was contributing to his depression. This probably would have taken time because Richard was not at the stage in which he viewed talk therapy as a way of solving his problems. Consequently, the initial task was to build a common view of how to work with Richard's problems in therapy. Without this fundamental agreement in place, it was very difficult for Richard and his therapist to move forward and implement changes.

Fourth, Richard's emotional processing skills were underdeveloped. There was a sense that he had neglected his emotional life and had learned to silence his needs. He had stifled his feelings so much that when asked what he was feeling he went blank and felt panic. An important task in the therapy prior to the initiation of more advanced tasks such as two-chair work or empty-chair work would have been to facilitate Richard's awareness and labeling of his inner experience. He had difficulty symbolizing his experience and needed to learn to do this in the context of a supportive, empathic relationship. Without these skills in place, it is very difficult to engage in chair tasks. The therapist could have used more focusing exercises and empathic reflections to help Richard symbolize his emotional experience.

Fifth, Richard struggled in therapy to be compassionate and nurturing of himself and his experience. Although he had no difficulty being understanding and considerate of others, he was unable to apply the same care and concern to his own well-being. An important focus in therapy would have been to help him develop a kinder, more caring attitude toward himself in the context of a safe, supportive, and empathic relationship with his therapist. It takes time to develop positive introjects, and is usually not possible in a 16-week treatment. If short-term therapy is to be effective, clients need to come in with well-developed, positive introjects and not require these to be developed in the context of the therapeutic relationship. Richard's ability to be compassionate toward himself was also hindered by his deep sense of shame at his condition and his difficulty reaching out to others for support, care, and guidance. This suggests that Richard may not have learned to trust and rely on caretakers early in life. These difficulties are indicators that a longer term therapy was necessary for Richard to build a positive introject, overcome his shame, and learn to accept caretaking so that he could depend and rely on others for support and comfort. These skills can be acquired in an empathic, responsive relationship in which one has the opportunity to explore one's experience safely and without threat of criticism, retaliation, or invalidation.

In retrospect, most of the sessions were spent trying to develop a working alliance with Richard. When he came to therapy he was not yet ready to believe that his depression could be alleviated. His therapist spent the sessions highlighting how he treated himself and building his awareness of his feelings so that he could begin to see how he might be different and get a sense of how he might change. It was only in the last few sessions that he began to become more engaged in therapy as he started to pose questions about his functioning and sought to understand why he did things in a more personal way than in his earlier more intellectual musings. However, no further progress was made on his issues because therapy terminated after 16 sessions as prescribed by the research protocol. Even though his depression was not relieved by the end of treatment, Richard expressed appreciation on numerous occasions for the opportunity to talk about himself in a way that he never had with anybody else.

It is likely that Richard would have benefited from a longer term treatment. If he was to change, he needed a warm, consistent, and empathic therapeutic relationship that would enable him to start symbolizing and examining his life experience and to understand how he had developed his ways of being. He would have benefited from learning to process his emotional experience so that he could use the information to develop more satisfying ways of treating himself. He had difficulty being aware of and attending to his feelings and reflecting on them to solve his life problems. He needed to develop a stronger sense of self that was not so dependent on the approval of others. These changes would have required him to reconsider the rules and standards that he used to evaluate his behavior and apply them less rigidly to his life. However, to effect some of these changes, Richard needed to move beyond a stage of contemplating them to a stage of preparation and action. He needed to come to believe in therapy; to be open to his feelings; and to be more accepting, compassionate, and nourishing of himself. To combat his feelings of depression he needed to learn to respect his feelings, to give them a place in his world, and to express them to others in a way that would enable him to meet his needs better.

Richard was beginning to make some changes toward the end of therapy. He began to question how easy it was to feel compassion for others but not himself and to recognize that he needed to be more compassionate toward himself. Before being able to engage fully in therapy, Richard needed to recover from his deep sense of shame and begin to believe that he could be different. During and after the therapy, his therapist expressed the wish that she had been able to do more or respond in a way that would have facilitated Richard's feeling less depressed and better about himself.

6

FEAR OF EMOTION

Sean was a 40-year-old man who completed 16 sessions of therapy. When he began therapy, Sean was employed and married with a son. His chief concern was that he was depressed. He had been depressed since he was a teenager and dealt with it mainly by sleeping. He was concerned that his depression was getting worse and interfering with both his work and his personal relationships. He attributed the onset of his current depressive episode to experiencing a financial crisis 3 years prior to entering therapy, when his business went bankrupt; his wife lost her job; and his father died. At that time he saw a psychiatrist. He complained that his wife did not understand his difficulties and was irritable with him. He had difficulty maintaining employment since he lost his business and was currently having difficulty getting along with people at work. Sean was diagnosed with major depression on Axis I; depression and avoidant features on Axis II; no diagnosis on Axis III; and problems with primary support characterized by discord with his mother and wife and occupational problems characterized by discord with colleagues at work on Axis IV. He had a Global Assessment of Functioning score of 59 on Axis V, indicating moderate difficulty in occupational functioning.

CASE FORMULATION

Sean described his mother as a predator who attacked weaker personalities. He said she was a frustrated, angry, drinking, loud, and embarrassing woman who, when he was a child, punished everyone regardless of who was guilty and judged him negatively when he cried. He described his father as withdrawn with a wife who "hated his guts." His father was disengaged because he did not want to be involved in conflicts between his wife and children. In contrast to Sean, who had been careful not to be punished by his parents, his sister was careless, unafraid of punishment, dyslexic, and wrongly labeled as retarded by teachers.

In terms of Sean's style of emotional processing, the therapist observed that it was difficult for him to focus on his internal experience, and although the therapist's empathic responses were well received, they did not promote a deeper focus on his bodily experience. Sean was emotionally constricted, processing most material conceptually rather than experientially, and he appeared cautious and on guard. Sean admitted that he was afraid of his feelings and avoided both his anger and his sadness. He was afraid of his emotions and wanted to push them away to keep them under control. He was embarrassed for feeling anxiety and judged himself harshly. He spoke quickly, often with a limited, wary, and fragile vocal quality (high pitch but low energy) or with an external vocal quality (higher energy with a very regular stress pattern) giving his story a rehearsed quality. Although there was a lot of anger and fear present as he spoke about the events in his life, he overregulated these as he tried to avoid and control his emotions. This resulted in Sean's experiencing a sense of hopelessness and resignation.

His core maladaptive emotion schemes were fear and anger. He had difficulty acknowledging his anger, fearing that it would drive people away, and was afraid that others would attack him. He felt worthless and ashamed as a result of his mother's denigration of him when he was a child. He viewed himself as weak, subject to vicious attacks, fearful of rejection, and misunderstood by his mother. As a consequence of growing up with a parent who ridiculed his feelings and was abusive and threatening, Sean had learned that his feelings were dangerous. His feelings of social vulnerability, avoidance, and inhibition were overdeveloped, and his self-assertion was underdeveloped. He viewed himself as vulnerable to depreciation, socially inept, and incompetent and saw others as critical, strong, demeaning, dangerous, and superior. The goals of therapy were to resolve Sean's unfinished business with his mother with respect to her abusive treatment of him; to help him allow and tolerate his feelings; and to try to change his harsh internal critic, which made him feel worthless and prevented him from asserting himself with others.

BONDING AND AWARENESS

Sean's therapist listened within an emotion-focused frame of reference as she began to develop a good working alliance, promote bonding, and raise Sean's awareness of his emotions. She tried to be attuned to Sean's affect, providing empathic understanding as she listened for markers of cognitive–affective processing problems. The first few sessions were spent developing an alliance and establishing a focus on the underlying determinants of Sean's depression. By Session 3 a safe bond and focus had been established. In the early sessions there was some disagreement about the utility of approaching and focusing on his emotions, especially anger. Sean said he wanted to have more distance from and control over his anger, so feeling it seemed counterintuitive to him. The therapist repeatedly offered the rationale that it was important to approach and process emotions to help manage them and that one way out of his anger was to acknowledge it and go through it. Sean expressed some doubt but was willing to go along with the therapist's sug-gested tasks. At times he said he found the empty-chair task of dialoguing with his mother difficult and found it easier to talk to the therapist than to an empty chair. By the middle of treatment, however, a good alliance had been established, and Sean accepted that he needed to process his emotions rather than avoid them.

In Session 1 Sean came in apprehensive but said he wanted to be rid of his depression and was afraid it was getting worse. He was having difficulty sleeping and feared that his employer was trying to get rid of him. He was not getting along with people at work and felt that the only people he could trust were his wife and son. However, he felt misunderstood by his wife because she often expressed impatience with him, wondering what was wrong. Fear-ful of rejection, he was reserved and protective of his inner self.

His therapist listened empathically to his feelings and gathered infor-mation about Sean's early and current relationships with his mother, wife, and son while simultaneously observing his style of processing emotions. He described how his mother always made him feel as if he were doing some-thing terribly wrong while he was growing up. He recalled a situation in which his mother had dropped a casserole on the kitchen floor as a reaction to his not listening to her. He noted that he was terrified of being terrorized and related this to his mother's saying, "What the hell is the matter with you," when he was upset. He observed that his wife used the same phrase when she was angry with him. As a child he was afraid that if he tried and failed, it would have been worse than not trying. As an adult he felt he set himself up for failure and feared that he would be fired and not be paid the money he was owed. He felt he deserved to be criticized.

Sean was angry at his mother for being manipulative and for making people feel that they were indebted to her. However, he had difficulty confronting his mother because he feared she would manipulate her way around it. At work he experienced his boss as intimidating and as much of a bully as his mother. He observed that he usually lost focus around bullies, telling himself "You're an idiot. What the hell is the matter with you?"

EVOKING AND EXPLORING

In Session 3 the therapist began to try to access the core painful aspects of Sean's experiences. These were his core feelings of fear and shame and his feelings of anger and sadness related to his mother. When Sean arrived he said he was dreading coming to therapy, fearing that he might discover that he was worthless. He felt embarrassed discussing his feelings of worthlessness with his therapist. As the therapist empathically explored his feelings about his relationship with his mother, he began to express how angry he was at her and how hopeless he felt that she would ever change. He also said he was angry with his wife for being like his mother and angry at himself for being angry at them. He said that it was easier for him to talk to his wife on the phone than to her directly and that it was easier to talk to his therapist about his problems with his wife than it was to talk to her because his therapist was not judgmental.

In an attempt to evoke some of his feelings toward his mother, his therapist introduced an empty-chair dialogue. As he began to express his anger he became afraid and ashamed that he could not do anything about how he had been treated. He said he was fearful of standing up for himself at work and angry that he had to do it. He wondered what the point of expressing anger was because it would not solve anything; instead it would leave him vulnerable.

Therapist: Let's try something. This is sometimes very helpful. You've been telling me what you would say to her. What I'd like you to do is to just imagine for a moment that your mom is sitting there. Can you see her there? Something is happening.

Sean: [sigh] . . . [sigh].

Therapist: Lots of big sighs.

Sean: I've just been calming down [chuckles].

Therapist: So what was it you're . . . what are you trying to calm? Just imagining her there brings up a lot of feelings, doesn't it? What are you trying to do?

Sean: Oh, I guess the usual, take control of the situation internally— trying to look at the other side of the situation of it . . .

Therapist: OK, so let's just—you don't have to go too fast. I'm just curious, what happens when I say, "Imagine her sitting there," 'cause I

	could see lots of stuff is happening. How would she be if she was sitting there? What does she look like?
Sean:	If she was sitting there now?
Therapist:	So could you come sit here for a minute? I want you to do what she does; be her; take on that defiant kind of look at Sean there. [*Sean moves to other chair and looks, sighs.*] So you're looking down your nose at him?
Sean:	"Why don't you grow up?"
Therapist:	OK, so you just, that's what she says, "Why don't you grow up?"
Sean:	That's, frankly, exactly I think what she would say.
Therapist:	OK, come back in this chair. "Just grow up S.! Whatever your problems are, just grow up." What happens when you hear that?
Sean:	I suppose for the most part, I figure she's right.
Therapist:	So what else would you say to her? What do you feel or need?
Sean:	I guess what I would really like is for her to realize that I do hurt still, a lot, and she has something to do with it. At least acknowledge it's me, just once.
Therapist:	OK. Do you want to say to her, "You know, I still really hurt"?
Sean:	Yeah, but she can't hear that because she can't admit that she has any responsibility.
Therapist:	Yeah, but can you just say it? Imagine her there and just say, "Mom, I really hurt."
Sean:	I really hurt.
Therapist:	Uh-huh. Can you tell her what hurts? What hurt you?
Sean:	I feel that I always disappointed you, never measured up. I didn't know what the rules of the game were and was expected to excel at them, and then you made me feel that I never could.
Therapist:	So "I, I feel hurt that you always made me feel less than or inadequate."
Sean:	Yeah, I guess part of what makes me feel angry is that sometimes I think you did it on purpose! [*sighs*] And the rest of the time it was just carelessness.
Therapist:	There is a big sigh there, right?
Sean:	Sometimes I wish you'd just behave as if you care. I don't believe you really do or you could.
Therapist:	Say that again. "I don't believe you, you really . . ."

Sean:	I don't believe you really cared about me.
Therapist:	[reaching for a tissue] That hurts.
Sean:	She told me one time when I was a kid [sniffs], "The only reason you're here is because I got your father drunk!"
Therapist:	Wow, oh that one really hurts, doesn't it?
Sean:	Yeah.
Therapist:	Yeah, just this real sense of not being wanted and not being cared about and . . .
Sean:	Just being a goddamn pawn! I guess that's part of—keeping it under control, 'cause if I ever, as I said, I've only been real mad in my life twice.
Therapist:	Yeah.
Sean:	Both times, the situation was between my wife and I, and she . . . It was a serious issue, but she triggered it with behavior patterns of my mother. She still does.
Therapist:	And then it all came out . . .
Sean:	Well, it came out, but I focused on the issue at hand at the moment. She kept pushing. I could have hit her; I didn't.
Therapist:	But you were that angry.
Sean:	And I'm still that angry that I got that angry.
Therapist:	That you lost control?
Sean:	Almost, and it was scary.
Therapist:	So a lot of energy goes into keeping in that anger?
Sean:	Yeah. I guess by bottling it all up so, it kills any zest or power in life. I probably could . . .
Therapist:	Uh-huh. What are you feeling right now?
Sean:	Well, all kinds of things—angry, cheated, ashamed, and the terror, and I guess too is that, as a kid I used to feel terror.
Therapist:	Yeah.
Sean:	Not just afraid, I mean, afraid is to get on the skates or the bicycle or to go down the big slide or to jump off the high board, that's afraid.
Therapist:	But what you felt was much much stronger than that, terrified of what?
Sean:	Things might get worse. Probably I tried to just become a piece of wallpaper—disappear and it would all go away, try to become invisible.

Therapist: That's what you've tried to do isn't it?

Sean: Yeah and still do.

In the preceding dialogue, Sean expressed his unresolved feelings of anger and sadness, and his therapist evoked the core maladaptive emotion schemes of fear and shame, which Sean began to process. Sean described how he felt rejected and put down by his mother (SASB [Structural Analysis of Social Behavior] 1-6, 1-7). At first he was reluctant to engage in the task (SASB 2-1); however, with coaxing he began to follow his therapist's suggestions (SASB 2-4). He was able to label and describe his feelings (EXP [The Experiencing Scale] Stage 4; LCPP [Levels of Client Perceptual Processing] Level 4) but was quite judgmental of his behavior at times when he became angry and lost control (LCPP Level 3; SASB 3-6). As he engaged in the task, he realized how angry he was at his mother (EXP Stage 5). The session ended with Sean acknowledging that his problem was rage.

Sean: But then when I do try and stand up, I mean, I get this huge rage, and I'm on the edge of snapping.

Therapist: That rage is what we need to tap into here because there's a lot of rage, not surprisingly.

Sean: What's the point? That I'm not . . . how do you mean tap into it?

Therapist: Well, deal with your anger.

Sean: That won't solve anything, will it?

Therapist: It won't change your mom; it won't change your boss; it can change you if you get its message and see what needs to be done about it. You're walking around with a powder keg inside of you, and things trigger it all the time, but underneath the anger I think is the terrible fear and shame.

Sean: I never thought of myself as angry.

Therapist: Well, just think about it and see. Maybe you don't express anger, but just give it some thought over the next week, and pay attention to how often you actually feel frustration.

Sean: I just never really thought I was angry at my mother. I thought it was the other, all the other shit that goes on, on a daily basis.

Therapist: So now it's occurring to you that you have a fair bit of anger at your mom as well.

Sean: And not just for current or future behavior.

Therapist: No, because of the hurt from the past as well.

Sean: I guess I'm angry that she does not acknowledge it.

In Session 4 Sean reflected on his anger and wished he could get beyond his anger without having to deal with it. He felt that he was always in emotional turmoil and was angry at having to go through life on a roller coaster. He told his therapist that he felt some anger at her for making him talk about things that were scary to the point that they made him feel like he was standing at the edge of a cliff or an abyss. The therapist offered him the choice of walking away or facing it. By the end of the session he was beginning to feel more comfortable with his feelings but still did not know what to do with them. He felt that anger and fear came together as a package for him, and he was afraid of his emotions getting out of control, especially his fear.

Sean entered Session 5 saying that as he expected he had been fired from his job and that he was afraid that he would not get paid. He had been offered a new position, but it came with a lot of unknowns that made him fearful. He was angry at his ex-employer for unfairly accusing him of mishandling a bid. Sean felt that he was always angry, if not at others, then at himself. He was angry at himself for having stayed with the company knowing he might be fired and for his difficulties with finding and keeping a job. Sean and his therapist began a self-critical and self-interruptive dialogue in this session, one that focused on how Sean kept himself boxed in and was unable to stand up for himself.

In Session 6 Sean noticed that he was able to feel angry without feeling guilty. He was angry at his ex-employer for making him fight to get his money and was depressed at his powerlessness. He blamed himself for not listening to the warning signs at work and angry at his mother for having ridiculed his anger. When thinking of doing chair work with his mother, he worried that he would get angry and feel hopeless because he would embarrass himself and accomplish nothing. Sean talked about having confronted his mother the previous week. Although she couldn't change her behavior, he felt some joy at getting things off his chest. He considered the possibility of saying to people "You can't do that to me" but was afraid of getting too angry and of being judged negatively. In this session during the dialogue with his mother he became blocked, as seen in the excerpt that follows.

Therapist: Can you imagine her sitting there?

Sean: That's the tough part.

Therapist: Yeah, just turn your chair around a little bit so that you actually can see her.

Sean: I mean, I spend all my time trying to block her off, so . . .

Therapist: So how do you block her off? Do that. How do you want to block her off?

Sean: So this is not a daily influence. Her, her behavior is not a daily influence on my life and the way I feel. It's stirring up all these emotions. I mean, you'd think it was the only thing I was focused on in my life.

Therapist: Uh-huh. So just actually imagining her there brings up this feeling of . . .

Sean: Actually, it's just trying to imagine her there. I mean, something else just cuts right in and says, oh well, and cuts off my anger.

Therapist: So something is stopping you?

Sean: Actually, yeah, it's a funny situation. When I started talking to the lady that came over to dinner last night, stuff started to come up when she was describing her father's behavior. I started to get really angry but not at her father. I've never met the man, but at my mother.

Therapist: So you didn't block then?

Sean: Yeah.

Sean was having difficulty engaging in the task initially because he usually blocked out his mother (SASB 2-8). He also expressed some discomfort with stirring up the feelings (SASB 2-1, 2-2). As he began the task, he reflected on his own behavior and realized that it did not make sense (EXP Stage 5; SASB 3-4). Later in the dialogue talking to his mother in the empty chair he said,

Sean: I mean, you could be proud of me when I performed well and very easily disappointed with me when I didn't perform to expectations, but that's it. Unless I was performing one way or the other, I didn't exist; action or reaction, that's all that counted. Yeah, I could hear her come back and say, "Well you never cared about anything that I had to think or say; you never asked anything." Well, that's true, 'cause when I was growing up, I thought that was the way it was supposed to be. That's the way you behaved toward me, so why would it occur to me that that's not the way it's supposed to be?

Therapist: "I learned it from you."

Sean: Yeah.

Therapist: . . . to not care.

Sean: I had no way to know there was anything any different. It's [chuckles], I was reading a poster on the way in here today, and something, that a fish doesn't know it's in water until it discovers air. You know, it wasn't until I grew up that I discovered air. You just don't seem to understand and never will, which I guess I feel sad about and angry.

Sean acknowledged that he felt uncared for (SASB 1-8). He expressed the hurt and sadness that caused (EXP Stage 4; LCPP Level 5) but accepted that was the way his mother was (SASB 1-2). The session ended with an expression of resignation.

Therapist: What is it like for you, Sean, to talk with her today?

Sean: I have no idea, well, what to say.

Therapist: I mean, you, you know you've really been saying a lot of the stuff that's really hurtful and . . .

Sean: And without the anger and emotion.

Therapist: What are you feeling as you say it?

Sean: Resigned.

Sean commented in the next session that he noticed an absence of fear and anxiety in thinking of inviting his mother for Christmas. While doing chair work with his mother in the session, he was able to stand up to her dismissiveness.

Sean: [as his mother] "I don't know what your problem is. If you can't be specific, maybe these things never happened. It's all in your mind."

Therapist: "You're making it up."

Sean: "You're making it up, so I can't be held responsible for something like that, and I won't be. So whatever your problem is, I suggest you get over it!"

Sean, however, began to assert himself (SASB 2-1). He resented his mother's calling him stupid. He was both angry at himself for not being able to say or do anything about it (SASB 3-5, 3-6) and angry at his mother for silencing him (SASB 2-6). He decided that he was not going to put up with his mother's behavior any longer (EXP Stage 6; LCPP Level 6; SASB 2-1).

Therapist: And what do you want to say to her, if she was sitting right there?

Sean: Want . . . I want to say to her, Get the hell out of my life.

Therapist: Yeah and what else?

Sean: And if I don't start seeing any change in your behavior, it's going to get worse. I can cut you off completely and absolutely, and I want you to get that through your head. You're not in control here anymore; you don't control anything anymore. Your actions push buttons; I react, but that's me. I have to deal with that, but you're not going to do it anymore; you're not going to be the cause of it anymore. I'm not, no only, yeah, you hurt me.

I'm not going to let you hurt me anymore, and I'm sure as hell aren't, I'm not going to allow R. [his son] to get hurt by you either.

Therapist: How did she hurt you? What did she do? Tell her what she did.

He had difficulty labeling his hurt because he had buried it for so long and concluded saying,

Sean: Yeah, and it's, I guess it's part of me that I tried to suppress it for so long. I allowed it to stay below the surface for years and years and years, decades. I, maybe, couldn't handle it, so I buried them so deep that it's only one particular incident I remember. As I say, you know, something happens or somebody says something or describes a story or whatever and a trigger goes off. Then it comes up, and I can't articulate it, but you know, it's like I've got a file folder, and I'm collecting all these little things, but then I can't remember what I have filed away.

TRANSFORMATION: CREATING NEW MEANING AND CONSTRUCTING ALTERNATIVES

In Session 8 Sean recalled he was never allowed to say no as a child but that he was learning to say no to his wife when she dismissed him or when she wanted him to answer the phone or the door. He felt some sadness for the two messages he got from his mother: "Do as I say" and "You are not capable" (EXP Stage 4; LCPP Level 5; SASB 1-5, 1-6). Doing an empty-chair exercise with his mother, he experienced her as looking at him with a challenging expression. She was disdainful and impatient as he struggled to articulate his wish that she understand him and that they have a relationship free of conflict. He felt sad at the thought that his mother might never meet his needs and afraid that he would be swallowed up in his sadness (EXP Stage 4; LCPP Level 5). He continued to deal with his anger as shown in the following dialogue.

Sean: Yeah, I was afraid most of the time, and yes, I wanted to hide. I mean, I wasn't being, even when I showed fear, I was being shamed, so that was part of the, one of the controlling techniques as well. She liked to shame me.

Therapist: So if you showed any kind of . . .

Sean: And I suppose she still does.

Therapist: So that's why sitting here and, and just imagining her there . . . you just feel a sense of "I'm not going to be, make myself vulnerable, 'cause if I am, she'll shame me."

Sean:	This is the way I feel. I feel angry that she's trying to blame me. I didn't do it.
Therapist:	Uh-huh. So tell her.
Sean:	It's not my fault, I didn't do this, OK. I mean, you've created the situation, and I'm angry that you created it, and worst, you perpetuate it.
Therapist:	"I'm sick of feeling like this."
Sean:	And I won't do it anymore. That's why you're at arm's length.
Therapist:	"No more!"
Sean:	Well, at this stage it's a little more than no. I would say it's more like, Go to hell.
Therapist:	Right. "Go to hell, Mom."
Sean:	Yeah. Have fun; enjoy it. I've been there; I know what it's like.
Therapist:	OK, so you can be angry with her; you can even set a limit with her, but when I ask you to tell her that you feel hurt or you feel sad, that's where you . . .
Sean:	In order to, I don't know, for, for some reason, in order to do that I start feeling hurt and that's when I become vulnerable and that's when I know I can still be hurt again.
Therapist:	Uh-huh.
Sean:	So, I don't want to do that.
Therapist:	OK, so when you are actually just sitting here and talking with an empty chair and imagining her, it's still quite powerful isn't it? That feeling of "I could still be hurt by her, and I was hurt by her, and the way that she hurt me, one of the worst ways is that she, she. . . ." At your most vulnerable time is when she shamed you.
Sean:	Yeah, she is an expert at sensing when you're vulnerable. As I said before, she's like a shark; once they smell blood . . . So what I'm saying is that I'm coming to the realization that the relationship is never going to be what I would have liked it to be or what I would like it to . . .
Therapist:	She is who she is.
Sean:	I've, I guess part of me blamed me. It was my response, my fault for that.
Therapist:	Now you've seen that it wasn't your fault.
Sean:	Some of it, I guess, I'm now coming to terms with, just letting it go. Up to this point in my life there was some hope . . . I have to give up the hope, and that's hard to do.

Here Sean accepted that the relationship with his mother will never be different (EXP Stage 6; LCPP Level 6), and he worked to be more self-assertive and self-protective (SASB 3-4). In Sessions 9 and 10 Sean continued to work productively on his anger and on being more assertive. In Session 10, which follows, he touched on his own sadness through talking about his son's success. He relayed an incident in which his son was involved in a judo demonstration and lost his balance and slipped.

Sean: I mean, I don't care if she gets it or not. What I do care is what he did; he kept trying [*moved to tears*].

Therapist: Yeah, that's what really touched you.

Sean: He did it again and lost his balance, and he walked away with his head down but his shoulders back. The next boy went up and actually didn't make it, and then R. went again and he got it.

Therapist: Wow.

Sean: First time, he, I found out . . . His coach said, "That's the first time R. has ever done it." So this isn't a case, he knew he could do it—just keep trying and knows he'll get it. At that moment he didn't know that he could do it.

Therapist: Yeah.

Sean: And that's in front of everybody.

Therapist: That really, it says a lot to you doesn't it?

Sean: I was so proud of him, and I guess what I attach to that is, if he can do that then I can do this.

Therapist: Yeah, and you are doing it.

Sean: I'm emotional now, eh [*sniffs*]?

Therapist: Well, it's, it's OK. Are you, are you comfortable with feeling your feelings?

Sean: A little bit.

Therapist: It's, it's really touching, what you're telling me. You know, it's very touching; I feel touched. I can feel it, you know, in me, and I can see how proud you are of him but also how his struggle has mirrored your own.

Sean: Yeah.

Therapist: And just, you know, how he keeps getting up, and he's not, he's not ashamed, and he's not hiding and . . .

Sean: Yeah.

Therapist:	He's just gonna be . . .
Sean:	He didn't quit. He has in the past; he gets pissed off, and he'd say, "The hell with it; I don't need to do this," which is really just an excuse to not have to deal with it. I know that.
Therapist:	Right, and I guess that's the thing for you, isn't it? For a lot, a lot of years it's like, "What's the use of trying"?
Sean:	Yeah, exactly. I basically lived my life that way up till now.
Therapist:	Yeah.
Sean:	Which I'm not proud of [*sniffs*].
Therapist:	Yeah, I guess that's partly what's struck you. It isn't that he just kept on trying even though it was really hard. So it was a real moment for both of you, wasn't it?
Sean:	Yeah, so if he can remember that for the rest of his life, as far as I'm concerned, I've achieved, really.
Therapist:	You feel like he got what you didn't get right? And that's why you're crying, for what you didn't get and . . .
Sean:	Yeah, I mean, it's—he doesn't have to go through what I went through, feeling the way I always felt about myself.
Therapist:	Yeah.
Sean:	He won't have to; he won't have to live with that.

Here Sean was able to appreciate and express pride at his son's perseverance in the face of hardship (SASB 1-2, 1-3). In terms of his emotional processing, he was clearly in touch with his feelings and able to represent his inner world and values as he described the situation (EXP Stages 3, 4; LCPP Level 5). Sean began Session 11 by dealing with his conflict with his wife about her coming down hard on their son. Sean was afraid of confronting his wife on her parenting. He said his wife was a little like his mother in that "she is who she is." In this session he again engaged in a chair dialogue with his mother in which he felt sad at giving up hope that she would ever be the mother he would have liked. He said he was disappointed for having to guard himself against her and disappointed that she was not there for him but observed that his disappointment had changed (EXP Stage 6; LCPP Level 6).

Sean:	Oh, yeah, I'm still disappointed always. Always will be, but, ah, no, it's not intense; it's not, it's not debilitating anymore.

In the dialogue he was angry at his mother for not having a relationship with him, for manipulating his emotions by making him feel guilty, for judging and dismissing him, and for not seeing him. He was able to express his need to be recognized.

Sean:	I want you to see me as a person not an extension of you, not as one of the children, a problem to be endured or dismissed.
Therapist:	"I wanted you to see me for who I was."
Sean:	I wanted you to see me!

Sean was able to assert himself and ask for what he needed from his mother (SASB 2-1). This represented an important shift for him as he began to look out for his own interests and nurture and protect himself (EXP Stage 6; LCPP Level 6; SASB 3-3, 3-4). By the end of the session, he affirmed himself (SASB 3-3).

Sean:	I'm disappointed again, and I guess I'm angry, and what did I ever do to deserve, to deserve that? But it's just the way it is, and I guess now I've come to the conclusion that, really, I didn't do anything to deserve it so I'm not going to feel guilty about it anymore.
Therapist:	"I didn't do anything; I'm not bad."
Sean:	Oh, I may have misbehaved, but I'm not a bad person.
Therapist:	Can you tell her that again?
Sean:	I'm not a bad person.
Therapist:	Again, "I'm not a bad person; I'm not."
Sean:	I'm not a bad person, and you can't convince me otherwise anymore.
Therapist:	How do you feel when you say that?
Sean:	[sniffs] I guess a little . . . several things, I mean, on one level it makes me feel better; on the other level it hurts too. The hurt part is that if I was to, in a sense lay myself bare, I couldn't trust her not to abuse that power because basically I'm handing the power over to her, and every time I've done that in the past, it's been abused. So, I just, I'm not one to take the risk anymore.

In Session 12 Sean said he felt more empowered realizing that he had a choice about how to handle a confrontation with his wife. He was angry at his wife for yelling at their son. Although he hated confrontation, he felt less bothered by his wife's loud arguments than in the past when he used to panic. Sean said he was no longer afraid to challenge his wife and wished he could be like that with others as well. He did an empty-chair exercise with his wife and expressed his anger at her for dragging him into conflicts between her and their son. During the chair work, he realized that telling his wife to back off felt like he was putting a red flag in front of a bull, which made him shut down. His therapist suggested they work on how he interrupted himself and shut himself down. Toward the end of the task, Sean realized that when he was younger he had received the message, "Don't challenge me or I won't love you anymore," and believing it, had lived by it.

In Session 13 Sean focused on his apprehension about doing a presentation in front of a group at work and of being afraid of not getting paid by his ex-employer (EXP Stage 5). As he talked, his therapist identified an anxiety-provoking, self-critical dialogue.

> Sean: Oh, nervous apprehension, I mean, just thinking about making the phone call gets me worked up. But I have to do it 'cause if I don't, they're just going to take me . . . They will just take the attitude, "Oh well, he's not very . . . so why should we?"

> Therapist: And what does the other voice say? I mean the loud voice, the one voice, the loud voice is saying, "Wait, don't do anything, don't."

> Sean: You may screw it up; you'd probably make it worse. I don't know, it's just, you know, for me it's a big deal. I don't know if it is for everybody else or not.

Sean felt an overwhelming need to be loved while feeling that he did not deserve it and that he wanted it too much (SASB 3-5, 3-6). He was afraid of "screwing up" in the presentation because as a child he got in trouble when he was noticed (EXP Stages 4, 5; LCPP Level 5). The idea of calling his ex-employer brought up fears similar to those he might have experienced being on the icy deck of a ship. He wanted to take control but was afraid that if he lost control, he would slip and become a "basket case" (EXP Stage 4, 5; SASB 3-5). He always felt exposed and wanted to cover up. He was afraid of being vulnerable, as though something might hit him (EXP Stage 5; LCPP Level 5). He said that this was how he felt with his mother. He was unable to tell his wife that he was in therapy because he was afraid he would lose her respect and she would see him as weak. He complained that nobody had any idea of what was going on inside of him.

In this session Sean's therapist focused on his bodily feeling of fear of failure.

> Sean: You have this sick feeling in your gut.

> Therapist: Yeah.

> Sean: Yeah, and what I'm saying is that, you know, most people, they would feel like this, you know, half a dozen times in their lives, you know. But I feel it all the time.

> Therapist: Uh-huh. Well, let's focus on that.

> Sean: So it's that intense for me!

> Therapist: OK, so it's like there's two parts. There's a part that's saying, "Don't, you'll screw it up; just leave things like . . ." and then . . .

Sean:	Well, just. I guess what I'm trying to say is first there's the gut feeling, and then I try to intellectualize what it is and why it's there.
Therapist:	Uh-huh.
Sean:	So I would put it in that order, like this: First the feeling of nausea hits me, and I go, What's going on? Why? What? you know. Oh, so I'm trying, I'm trying to explain why I get it, but [*inhaling*], and then if I fight my way through it, . . . I'm finding now that it, faster than if I try and ignore, because it goes away but it, and then there's something triggering, I'll remember, Oh, I got to make that call, and boom, I start feeling it again.
Therapist:	Are you feeling that sick feeling now when you talk about this?
Sean:	Uh-huh.
Therapist:	So can you describe it a bit?
Sean:	Well it's, literally, it's like a very light car sickness nausea.
Therapist:	So you just feel like you could throw up almost?
Sean:	Well the very vestiges of it, yes. I, I, I wouldn't get that bad.
Therapist:	But your stomach is sort of churning?
Sean:	Yeah.
Therapist:	Or turning over?
Sean:	Yeah, it has that, that, you know.
Therapist:	Kind of real unsettled. If it had a voice, what would it say? Churning and twisting and . . .
Sean:	It's not twisting, I've had that . . .
Therapist:	Just churning.
Sean:	. . . before too, but, you know, it's not, it's just like up against the diaphragm.
Therapist:	So it's pushing up?
Sean:	Yeah, so to speak.
Therapist:	And you're trying to push it down? Is that what you're . . . like you want to just push it down, or is it just going down on its own?
Sean:	I guess pushing it down. Take a deep breath and physically pushing it down.
Therapist:	So there's something in you that wants to get out, and you're kind of wish . . .

Sean: I suppose. No nothing wants to get out with anything. It's run and hide.

Therapist: Oh, OK. So it wants to get away.

Sean: Yeah. I guess as a, as a kid, when I was noticed I was in trouble [*chuckles*].

Therapist: Right.

Sean: So not to be noticed.

Here Sean was exploring his experience (EXP Stage 4; LCPP Level 5). With his therapist's guidance and empathic responses, he was able to differentiate his feelings (SASB 2-4, 1-2). In Session 14 Sean reported that his reactions to stressful situations had changed. He was not fearful and did not have nauseous feelings (EXP Stage 6; LCPP Level 7). He expressed some sadness for not being able to be as compassionate to himself as he was to his son. He still had problems with self-worth that he wanted to change but felt hopeless about succeeding because he heard himself saying, "Just hang on, if you let go you might lose everything." He was sad realizing that what happened in the past when he was his son's age still hurt him. He was also sad that it had gone on so long without his noticing it. He did not want his son to have low self-esteem as he did. He did not want to blame his mother and felt that he was scarred but that he was healing. Although he was sad, he decided to be more aware of his son and of himself as well.

Therapist: Just this sense that there is not this sort of, ah, it's not a festering kind of wound anymore. It's almost like, "OK, it happened. She is who she is, and that's the way that . . . and I have to . . ."

Sean: Yeah, the scars are still there, but they're healed kind of thing.

Therapist: Right.

Sean: Yeah, and I can see the scars still.

Therapist: Right.

Sean: I remember when you did that, and I remember when you did that, and . . .

Therapist: Is she still a shark?

This represented an important shift for Sean (EXP Stage 6; LCPP Level 7) as he recognized that the wound was not as painful and that he could heal himself (SASB 3-4). During this session he dialogued with his child self and decided that he did not have to face his pain alone and that he could support himself (SASB 3-3, 3-4).

Sean: Oh yeah, I mean, you know, that wasn't just me being me [*chuckles*]; that's the way she is.

Therapist:	If a little Sean, an 8-year-old Sean, were here, what would you be saying to him?
Sean:	I'd probably say, You weren't kidding.
Therapist:	Yeah.
Sean:	You don't know how. I don't expect you to know how.
Therapist:	"But I'm here for you."
Sean:	All you have to do is ask; don't be afraid to say it hurts. I really do understand.
Therapist:	Yeah, yeah.
Sean:	[*crying*] You don't have to face it alone.
Therapist:	Yeah.
Sean:	Sorry.
Therapist:	You don't have to apologize. It's good that you are crying. It's something that's very important. This is like just . . .
Sean:	That you could say those things . . .
Therapist:	And maybe that's what you need to, maybe that will help you is to, to ah, when you're struggling, when you're feeling afraid, and when you feel the nausea, think of it as 8-year-old Sean needs to be reassured. Big Sean, the adult Sean, is, understands, 'cause you do.
Sean:	Yeah, that's what I need.
Therapist:	So, where does that leave you? I mean, you feel comfortable enough that you cry about it.
Sean:	[*exhaling loudly*] Well, it's a little . . . I never really thought of myself as a, you know, 8-year-old Sean. I just, but I guess and truth, I mean, I watch tearjerky little movies and I get this . . . I can get very emotional like this over it, so I mean, it's not something that never happens to me. As a matter of fact, it can happen a lot.
Therapist:	It just never happened in relation to you.
Sean:	I never made that connection or maybe I never made the separation.
Therapist:	Uh-huh.
Sean:	So maybe I'll try and make the separation.
Therapist:	Yeah, little Sean is not alone, is not alone anymore, OK?

In the penultimate session, Sean reported feeling weird since he had worked on his child self. He was feeling some sadness around not having had his needs met and felt that he needed too much. He was afraid of his sadness and worried that he might not be able to get out of it. He described the history of his emotions as first experiencing sadness, then getting angry because he was sad for so long, and then being afraid it would never go away. Although he was able to get some control over the anger, he was not able to soothe the sadness underneath. He found it hard to justify compassion for himself, although he could feel it for others who, like he, had spent many years feeling really sad and alone. He felt there was something wrong with feeling sad about his own sadness and remembered that his mother used to tell him "to get over it." He recognized that his depression was triggered by feeling sad and was afraid that the cycle of depression would never end and perhaps even get worse. "I guess, for me, it's like a tight little circle that, you know, it doesn't end. It's, for whatever reason, I'm feeling sad, then I start feeling sad because I feel sad and then, it just, I'd be spinning at that point. Then usually the depression kicks in."

He felt sad for not having had someone there for him when he was a child and also for being told that he shouldn't need so much. He felt he was deficient and needy. He always felt that no one was looking after him, but at the end of therapy he felt that he had a new perspective on himself, thinking that possibly his parents saw him as the older brother and expected him to behave like one. He missed his uncle whom he liked because his uncle challenged him, coached him, and believed in him when his own parents failed to. Sean noted that he taught his son the same way his uncle taught him. He noted that he was tired and afraid of his sadness. He wanted to replace his depression with self-confidence but was afraid that this would not happen given his age.

His view of the difference between sad and depressed was that feeling sad was feeling very sensitive and vulnerable, whereas depression was lethargy, unwillingness to do anything, wanting to hide from it all, not feeling anything, and being drained and tired. A sequence from the session in which he acknowledged some sadness follows.

Therapist:	What are you feeling right now?
Sean:	Waves.
Therapist:	Of sadness?
Sean:	Yeah.
Therapist:	Can you tell me about the sadness? What's the sadness? When it comes in the waves, what are you feeling sad about?
Sean:	No, I can't. It comes and goes, I mean, it's all [*sighs*] . . . Right now it's all linked to my son. I can't explain why.

7

DISPARATE THERAPEUTIC GOALS

Hilary came to therapy feeling broken and depressed. After 63 years, she believed she had accomplished little and felt ashamed at her inability to provide for her family. Approximately 10 years prior to the beginning of therapy, she had lost a job as an executive and her marriage of 20 years had ended. The reason given for the termination of her employment was that the restructuring of the company rendered her position redundant. Hilary described herself as educated with a lot of redundant skills; however, she had been unable to secure a position with the same status and salary since her employment was terminated, at which time she became depressed. She had tried consulting work and was currently employed in a clerical position working for the government. For the past decade she had felt both dissatisfied with her employment and financially insecure.

Hilary was living with a partner and had three grown daughters. She was satisfied with her situation, although she often felt unsupported by her partner and did not feel they communicated well because they were somewhat disengaged. Hilary was busy 3 nights during the week and spent most of her free time alone. She and her partner had been in couples counseling 6 years ago, but Hilary had not found it helpful. Instead she felt worse as a result of the counseling and blamed the counseling for her partner's behavior. The main concerns that brought her to therapy this time were that she felt depressed, worthless, and hopeless about the future and wanted to improve her relationships with others. She often found herself irritable and intolerant of others. At the beginning of therapy, she reported that she had unresolved conflicts with her mother. She had recently had contact with her after 12 years and had felt melancholic ever since. In Session 1 Hilary mentioned that her father had died 13 years previously, bequeathing a large inheritance to his children and grandchildren, but that she had been excluded. In fact, she felt that she had been conspicuously left out of the will. Her father had left most of his estate to Hilary's three daughters and a stepbrother from her father's second marriage. Hilary experienced this as a painful rejection with financial ramifications that lingered to the present day. She recounted this to her therapist in Session 1.

> *Hilary:*   But my father died, you know, 13 years ago this summer, um, and to a very large extent I hold, I hold him particularly responsible for some of the disappointments which I mentioned about matters of the inheritance and the transfer of paternal affection away from me towards my stepbrother. He and my stepbrother got on so well. I thought that he would stand by his word that he gave to my mother at the time of his second marriage, that, um, it would have no effect on his relationship with me, but it, but it did. I mean all, all sorts of obscure cousins were, were beneficiaries in, in tangible terms from his estate. I just couldn't believe the will when, when I finally saw it.

Hilary had a difficult childhood. Her parents' marriage dissolved when she was 2 years old. She lived with her mother, who remarried some years later. However, she never felt particularly wanted by any of her caregivers, nor did she have a positive, supportive relationship with her stepfather. Her father remarried when she was 5 and adopted another family, becoming absent both emotionally and physically from Hilary's life. She was sent to boarding school when she was 8. Although she knew other children who were sent to boarding school, Hilary felt strongly that her caretakers wanted to get rid of her. Hilary was diagnosed with major depression on Axis I; no diagnosis on Axes II and III; and problems with family of origin on Axis IV. She had a Global Assessment of Functioning score of 62 on Axis V, indicating moderate to mild difficulties in occupational functioning.

CASE FORMULATION

In Sessions 1 and 2, the therapist focused on forming a therapeutic relationship and building an alliance. By Session 3 the therapist had identified a number of markers for tasks to begin to address Hilary's problems. The major themes that emerged were unfinished business with Hilary's father, unresolved issues with her mother, and a lack of a sense of self-worth.

With respect to the first theme of Hilary's unfinished business with her father, it became clear very early in therapy that Hilary felt very rejected and wounded that she had not been included in her father's will. She had counted on inheriting money from her father and being able to retire comfortably. Instead, she was strapped financially and barely able to make ends meet. She had never been very close to her father when he was alive and had not tried to close the gap between them, assuming that her father did not wish much contact with her. In many ways, being conspicuously left out of the will was a painful but constant reminder that she had been a deep disappointment and source of shame for her father.

This feeling of rejection and despair had persisted for 13 years, since her father had died. Hilary had not been able to put this feeling behind her. In many ways, she felt resigned and hopeless about the possibility of changing her feelings. She felt stuck and powerless, which was a major source of her depression. In Session 1, she discussed her emotional response to the issue with her therapist and stated explicitly how it related to her depression.

In terms of Hilary's unresolved issues with her mother, Hilary recalled a very troubled relationship with her mother. Her contact with her as an adult had been very limited. For most of her life, she had felt rejected and punished by her mother. In Session 1 she described her relationship with her mother as one in which she was paid to stay away. She recalled how she was always being sent away to aunts and cousins during the school holidays. She said her mother was on a "different wavelength" and would not understand her feelings of depression and frustration. Hilary was also reluctant to talk to her because her mother was elderly and quite ill.

She explained how she not only felt unwanted by her mother throughout her life but at times maligned by her. She recounted a situation in her early adult life in which she was trying to make a career for herself within the family business and her mother sabotaged it. As a single young woman living in a foreign city with a child on the way, she had been forced to move and find work elsewhere, even though her parents could have helped and supported her.

In terms of Hilary's sense of self-worth, she had internalized a strong sense of failure, powerlessness, and shame that had been inherited from the way in which both parents had treated her. She definitely felt a lack of self-worth in their eyes. She felt like a failure and that both her parents discounted her and felt that "she had not amounted to much." She was aware that her first pregnancy and her broken engagement had disappointed them, with the result that she remained afraid of their censure and disapproval. Hilary's negative self-evaluations emerged early in therapy within the context of an unfinished business dialogue with her mother when she interrupted her emotional expression about her current predicament for fear of her mother's disapproval.

Early in therapy Hilary expressed a great deal of hopelessness and despair regarding the possibility of change. She had felt depressed for quite some time with little hope for improvement. It seemed clear that despite feeling bereft and defeated, partly as a result of the trauma she had experienced in her life, Hilary felt it was dangerous to explore her pain. She did not feel strong enough to cope with further rejection. In terms of her mother, she felt that as little hope as there was, she must preserve whatever relationship they had. At this point her therapist began to have a sense of the impact that Hilary's traumatic past had had on her, including her history of feeling unwanted and rejected and the heavy cost that she anticipated that she would feel by exploring painful emotions.

Hilary's core emotion scheme was that she was unloved and despicable, and she harbored a deep sense of shame. She was very self-critical and defensive about her behavior and would stifle her feelings and needs in the hope of winning others' attention and approval. She was distant from her emotional experience, speaking with an externalizing vocal quality that gave what she said a somewhat rehearsed quality. She was very analytical and intellectual in the way she presented her story and was reluctant to talk about her feelings, although she complained about the treatment she had received from her parents. Her nonverbal behavior was restrained, and she strove to remain in control of her emotions even when discussing very painful subjects.

BONDING AND AWARENESS

The formation of the alliance involved a process of Hilary and her therapist establishing mutually agreed on goals and related tasks early in therapy and continuing to monitor these throughout therapy to ensure that both parties felt they were on the right track. The therapeutic bond was an important component that was formed out of the experience of Hilary and her therapist working together to meet Hilary's goals and also through the establishment of an atmosphere of safety and trust so that Hillary felt secure enough to explore vulnerable emotions. The development of a mutually agreed on working alliance proved challenging and difficult in this case. At the end of Session 1, Hilary's therapist presented a rationale and plan for the focus of their therapeutic work as well as a perspective on Hilary's emotions and how best to work with them. With respect to Hilary's feelings of rejection by her mother, her therapist began to frame the possibility of doing some empty-chair work early on.

Therapist: I'd like to, in a way, respond to "What's the point?" or how there are ways. I think, while, you know, you, for example, said, "You know, there's my mother, but I don't know what to say to her, and I don't know how." It's like there's this, you know, the bridge is out.

Hilary:	Uh-huh.
Therapist:	My sense is that there is a lot of feeling, I would imagine and perhaps this is more me than you, but I would think from a, from the, uh, the historical sketch that you've given me, there, her, in a sense, kind of chucking you out of the family, I gather, although it's vague, that there are a number of things about which you feel mistreated, and I imagine there would be some strong feelings of anger and resentment and . . .
Hilary:	Yes.
Therapist:	And I would imagine, you know, with, if you're walking around with those kinds of feelings and they've not been conveyed, I will be becoming more active with you in making some suggestions and ways of, I think, you know, jettisoning that. That baggage requires to some degree a reexperiencing, of getting in touch with what it, you know, what it felt like for you, what it meant to you, and in that process, there's relief.
Hilary:	Uh-huh.
Therapist:	It's coming to terms, making peace.
Hilary:	Yes.

With respect to Hilary's self-critical process, the therapist suggested that it might be contributing to her depression and an important area for the two of them to focus on during the therapy.

Therapist:	I hear a kind of critical or punishing attitude towards yourself.
Hilary:	Uh-huh.
Therapist:	And I think, you know, that can also make you feel quite depressed.
Hilary:	Yes.
Therapist:	And I think somewhere you've got to come to terms with that, and I'll have some suggestions too about how to dismantle that cycle.

Hilary agreed that she wanted to make peace with her past and somehow move on. She also agreed with the therapist's view of the factors that were contributing to her depression. However, she was somewhat reserved, which suggested that she might not be in total agreement.

EVOKING AND EXPLORING

In Session 4, Hilary talked about her feelings toward her father. Her therapist suggested an empty-chair exercise to see if this would create mutual agreement about the goals of therapy and to heighten Hilary's experience of her father. After asking Hilary to imagine her father in the empty chair, her therapist encouraged her to express how she felt.

> *Hilary:* Um. You achieved the highest pinnacle at school, and it was all very well for you to want me to follow in your footsteps, but you did absolutely nothing to tell me about what to expect either in school or in the company—uh, with the result that I basically didn't do well in either of them, and that was a great disappointment for you. I believe that the final responsibility rested with you because you knew better. Your relationship with my stepbrother was very hurtful when you cut me out and accepted him in my place.

> *Therapist:* Well, I guess you're saying that "I felt that I, it's like I, wasn't good enough, and I was replaced."

> *Hilary:* That's right.

> *Therapist:* Yeah, tell him, that's what it felt like.

> *Hilary:* I, I didn't measure up to whatever you expected of me, and you threw me over for this other person, who was very nice, but nevertheless it hurt, and it hurt real hard. And then to find after you were gone that your power to hurt continued in the will was the final straw.

> *Therapist:* Uh-huh.

> *Hilary:* And beyond that even, that to appoint two such silly idiots as those cousins to manage your estate, and if you knew how much damage they have done through their incompetence. I hope you are somewhere writhing in remorse for your actions because you deserve it.

Hilary was clearly able to get in touch with some strong feelings of anger toward her father; however, hopelessness set in, and she found it difficult to express her needs to her father.

> *Therapist:* Switch here for a moment [*pointing to her father's chair*].

> *Hilary:* I couldn't respond from his point of view.

> *Therapist:* Are you sure?

> *Hilary:* I'm sure I couldn't. I could not put myself in that chair under these conditions.

> *Therapist:* Do you have a sense of what that's about? How are you stopping yourself? What goes through your mind? I assume you're telling yourself not to, you know, "Don't . . . I shouldn't because . . ."

> *Hilary:* I think it's just a—there's a level of futility in it that—the devil's reason, quite honestly.

Therapist:	Uh-huh. You know, as I listen to you and watch you, I mean, I had this sense of, it was almost like, no way. It's like it's a hot seat or something, do you know what I mean?
Hilary:	Yeah, but not only that, it's something that he has to account for and nobody can.
Therapist:	I see, so part of this is, is saying, when you're saying no to the chair, you're saying, "No, I don't want any part of it."
Hilary:	I hope, and I've done some stupid things in my life too, but the damage was slight enough that it was reparable. I'm referring to my relationship with my children. I made some mistakes, and it not, at no time did I, were these actions deliberate, but they were, they were not on the basis of not caring but . . .

Here Hilary defended her poor performance at school and work because she did not receive adequate guidance from her father (SASB [Structural Analysis of Social Behavior] 2-6) and hoped that he was being punished (SASB 1-6). In terms of the alliance, Hilary blocked her therapist's suggestion (SASB 2-1) to speak from her father's point of view. She said that she did not know what the point would be. This refusal might be seen as an expression of confusion about the tasks and goals and the objectives that they might be expected to facilitate as well as a desire to hold her father accountable for his actions and not let him off the hook. It might have been useful at this point to try to renegotiate the goals and tasks and to see what Hilary's views were about how to solve her current situation. Hilary was using external rules and standards to judge her father's behavior (EXP [The Experiencing Scale] Stage 2; LCPP [Levels of Client Perceptual Processing] Level 2) but was not yet able to articulate her own feelings and needs as a result of his behavior. Rather she shifted to judging her own behavior and defending herself as a parent (SASB 3-6).

At this point in the dialogue, Hilary began to discuss her relationships with other family members. Later in the session, she began to talk about how she had felt trapped between her parents as a child. She felt that she had been used as a pawn between her father and mother, and she sensed that she had disappointed them with her broken engagement and pregnancy. They did not return to the empty-chair task for the rest of the session. This might have been an indicator of disagreement about the tasks and goals of therapy as well as of Hilary's reluctance to experience powerful and overwhelming emotions. In the next few sessions, Hilary continued to explore her feelings of loss and resentment at her parents' behavior and to provide a sense of how her life had evolved to the present time.

In Session 8 Hilary's feelings toward her mother emerged in the form of resignation as she realized that her relationship with her mother might never be different. Hilary began the session as follows:

Hilary:	I was struggling with that questionnaire because basically I think without realizing it as a conscious, uh, effort I've sort of come to the, perhaps, realization that it really doesn't matter what I do. I don't think anything is going to change my mother's opinion.
Therapist:	Do you have a sense for what that shift represents or how you came to that realization?
Hilary:	Well, it's a little like that Roman expression "trying to placate the gods." There's a bit of self-preservation in there, but I just thought, why am I really putting myself through these gyrations because it really is quite pointless.
Therapist:	I would imagine there is some relief in that notion?
Hilary:	It's, uh, uh, it's a little new, uh, maybe too soon to say that there's relief, to be honest not very much relief.
Therapist:	More like resignation, kind of unresolved?
Hilary:	Sort of recognizing the pointlessness. But it almost destroys the urgency to bare my soul and apologize and say that I'm ashamed.

Hilary realized that she had been trying to appease her mother (SASB 2-5) but that her mother did not seem to care (SASB 1-8). This echoed the sense of abandonment that Hilary felt as a child and continued to feel as an adult. Her therapist mistakenly assumed that there might be some relief in realizing that things might not change as opposed to recognizing Hilary's deep sense of sadness and loss (SASB 1-2, 1-8). Hilary's observation of her mother's behavior was potentially a marker for empathic affirmation as Hilary entered a vulnerable space. Thereafter, once Hilary had processed her feelings of shame, disappointment, and sorrow, empty-chair work might have been indicated. In the preceding passage Hilary began to touch on her inner experience of being neglected and abandoned. This marked an important shift (EXP Stage 6; LCPP Level 6) as she began to realize that she might not have any control of how the other responds and as she moved into symbolizing her own experience but at the same time shied away from confronting the painful feelings (SASB 1-1, 3-8). Over the next few sessions Hilary continued to explore her sense of being neglected and ignored.

In Session 10 Hilary explored her feelings around a visit her father had made to see her 6 months before he died.

Hilary:	The thing I remember most about the visit was that he asked me to drive him over to see some old acquaintances in a very opulent house in the suburbs, and it was one of the hardest things I'd ever done. While he reminisced with this man and his wife about their time at school, I sat there like a lump on a log, unable to participate and not being invited to.
Therapist:	So you felt totally excluded?

> *Hilary:* Totally excluded, out of place, at a loss, really. I wish I had walked out and waited in the car.

> *Therapist:* So that was very painful for you?

> *Hilary:* Yeah, he was never like that with me, but to see it and really not to, not to experience it.

We see that Hilary felt she had been neglected and ignored by her father and his friends (SASB 1-8). She wished she had walked away (EXP Stage 4; LCPP Level 5; SASB 2-8, 3-5, 3-8), but she stayed in spite of the pain. Hilary neglected her own needs as she tried to minister to those of her father. In Session 11 Hilary revisited the issue of her father. This time, she was able to imagine her father in the empty chair while her therapist encouraged her to express her feelings about her father's visit to see her before he died.

> *Hilary:* Because I basically have—I was sent away. And you jumped at the chance to get me out of the way so that you would not have to face me on . . . And basically I stayed away for that reason. I stayed away for 25 years because I was not welcome.

> *Therapist:* Say it again.

> *Hilary:* I was not welcome in your life, and that's how I felt. And everything that you had put together in your home, you never invited to me to stay in. You never invited us as a family to come to visit you. Who were we?

> *Therapist:* So you're saying you felt like . . .

> *Hilary:* I was your big mistake, no question about it.

> *Therapist:* What would you want from him right now?

> *Hilary:* I wouldn't want anything from him, nothing at, at all.

> *Therapist:* So there's anger there somewhere?

> *Hilary:* I don't want anything else any more. It's, it's too late.

> *Therapist:* Too late, too painful. Take another deep breath; this is hard. There are all these words and feelings that want to be heard. I imagine you're sitting there kind of frozen, holding back that bitterness?

> *Hilary:* I just recognize the futility of saying more. It's,-it's [*sighs*], it sums up my feelings pretty well.

Hilary once again expressed how her parents failed to nurture, protect, and love her; instead she felt that she was rejected and sent away to fend for herself (EXP Stage 4; LCPP Level 5; SASB 1-7, 1-8). She expressed anger at their neglect and a sense of resignation that things would never be different (SASB 1-2, 2-5, 2-7, 2-8). She expressed her experience of her parents' behavior in behavioral terms (EXP Stage 3). Her therapist observed that she was not expressing her feelings but rather was holding back. However, Hilary gave up, feeling that it was futile to express herself further. In this way she too neglected herself (SASB 3-8) and was unable to respond to her needs in a caring, accepting way. A little later, with her therapist's encouragement, Hilary was able to express her need for more support and care when she was growing up (SASB 2-4, 3-4). However, when her therapist asked her to switch chairs and speak from her father's chair, she refused. Hilary was still having difficulty engaging in the task or seeing its relevance to her goals and objectives.

> Hilary: Instead of constantly you telling me how I'd failed and how I'd, mistakes I'd made, I needed help. Rather than that, and you couldn't give it to me, you didn't understand what was needed.

> Therapist: I'd like you to switch now.

> Hilary: [laughs] I'm not going to sit in his place.

> Therapist: Tell him; tell him what that would be like for you.

> Hilary: I wouldn't, I wouldn't want to be in your place because I dislike you so much. I wouldn't want to sit in your chair.

> Therapist: "Right now, I'm so disgusted with you."

> Hilary: Yes, that's an understatement.

> Therapist: Is it? So there's a whole lot of feeling that you're holding back?

> Hilary: I don't think I'm holding it back. I think I understand.

> Therapist: I guess I'm thinking that this anger that you have and this disgust, this charged feeling, is all a reflection of how hurt you were by him. And I'm thinking that his ability to hurt you was partly tied up in the fact that you did want his respect and his love and his understanding. He was your father; you wanted these things, and somehow, in spite of your attempts, the door was closed, and you've been carrying that pain around for a long time.

> Hilary: But I actually think it's gone further. It's affected the relationship with both my parents. I think in their way they both had a very selfish, self-seeking attitude of not wanting to be bothered with me.

Hilary was very angry with her parents. She seemed reluctant to admit how hurt and pained she was by their behavior, perhaps because she feared being overwhelmed by painful emotions. She continued to judge her parents' behavior (EXP Stage 2; LCPP Level 3) but had trouble allowing her own feelings of grief and sorrow to emerge fully in the session. More time and greater safety may have been necessary for Hilary to let go her anger and allow the feelings of intense sadness and pain at her parents' treatment of her to emerge. This session brought her back to the pain she felt about not getting what she needed from either parent. From her history it appeared that in her early years Hilary did not have a single person who made her feel that she was fundamentally acceptable. This had left a gaping wound so that she saw herself as essentially unlovable.

In Session 12 Hilary once again confronted her sense of failure. She was able to acknowledge how inadequate and incompetent she felt.

Hilary: I guess so. I, I, well, I think the biggest problem there was again the feeling of inadequacy.

Therapist: Between you and yourself?

Hilary: Yes, between me and myself there is this real problem.

Therapist: This feeling of . . .?

Hilary: Guilt, uh . . .

Therapist: "I'm a failure."

Hilary: Failure, shame, shame or whatever . . .

Therapist: OK, do you want to explore that a little?

Hilary: Yes, by all means.

Therapist: Let's see if we can . . . if you'd come and sit over here please. You really want to make her feel like she's a failure. How would you go about doing that? What would you say to her?

Hilary: [*referring to her cousin*] It's just the quality of her personal success and his inheritance. He has a richly furnished house on large grounds and two or three cars, and what do I have? Nothing, absolutely nothing, compared to this measure of success.

Therapist: What is that feeling, Hilary?

Hilary: Oh, frustration, you know, just . . .

Therapist: Right, switch please. Now what's it like to hear that? Can you tell yourself over here what that feels like?

Hilary: Oh it's nothing new; she's absolutely right.

Therapist: So you're agreeing with her. You're saying, "Yeah, you're right. Compared to them, I'm a failure." Is that it?

Hilary: Yes, yes.

Therapist: What's that like for you? What's it like to feel like a failure? What's that like?

Hilary: I don't know; it's just nothing new.

Therapist:	Any new sensations in your body or tightness?
Hilary:	Yeah, you know, you're just harping on the same subject time after time.
Therapist:	Yeah, now what do you want from her? Tell her.
Hilary:	Well half of me is saying get off my case.
Therapist:	OK. I would imagine, but don't let me put words in your mouth, but it sounds like half of you wants this?
Hilary:	Or maybe more, maybe all of me is saying, you know, just shut up, I'm tired of hearing the same song.
Therapist:	Say that again.
Hilary:	I'm absolutely sick to death of hearing that same song.
Therapist:	OK, switch. Do you see her sitting over there feeling, saying, "Why don't you leave me alone? Get off my case." Can you respond to her? What are you experiencing?
Hilary:	I mean, that's what it is. You're a useless failure.
Therapist:	Switch.
Hilary:	Incapable of looking after yourself and your children.
Therapist:	What's it like to hear that?
Hilary:	It hurts. It's all very well, but it hurts.
Therapist:	"It hurts when you say that to me; it's an awful feeling."
Hilary:	Yeah and I hurt down in this whole, this whole area [*pointing to stomach*].
Therapist:	What are you in touch with?
Hilary:	I'd just like the thing to end, Just stop it.
Therapist:	So make a case why she should stop. Tell her.
Hilary:	I don't know. Basically I can't make a case because she's right. But the best reason to stop is that it's so hurtful.
Therapist:	Tell her.
Hilary:	It just hurts and hurts and hurts. Just leave me alone.
Therapist:	All right, switch. Can you see her over there? What's she feeling? She's asking you to "leave me alone"?
Hilary:	I tell you I'm not going to leave you alone until you come to your senses.
Therapist:	What do you want from her? What do you want her to do?

172 CASES WITH POOR OUTCOME

Hilary:	Just stop hiding; you have to stand up for yourself.
Therapist:	OK. Can you be specific about what she should do, how should she do that?
Hilary:	She needs to stand up and make decisions about everything.
Therapist:	Be concrete that, you know, for example "here are some things that you can do to make me see you are looking after yourself."
Hilary:	Stop letting other people rule your life. Just stand up and do what is needed and do what is right.
Therapist:	Good. Again, is there a specific situation that you see her in that you can make reference to that this is what she should do?
Hilary:	Take care of the house; stop procrastinating; pay your bills on time; stop delaying things; and for God's sake, clear out the rubbish that's left. You're the one in charge of the house for goodness sake. At least take part in the household and stop hiding behind things.
Therapist:	So she's saying to you to take charge. "I want you to come out from behind your parents and take on your responsibilities, you know, taking care of the house." And your response is? Can you share with her just what it's like trying to do that, the business of taking care of yourself, what that's really like for you inside?
Hilary:	It's almost as if I'm afraid to do it or afraid that I'm not able to do it [throwing up hands in despair].
Therapist:	Do that again with your hands. "I'm incapable."
Hilary:	Almost incapable of doing it.
Therapist:	Ah, so, you're saying, "I want to do it, but I just can't."
Hilary:	That's right!
Therapist:	OK. Come over here for just a moment. How can you make Hilary feel there's no way she can do this? She can't clean up; she can't sort out that stuff; convince her.
Hilary:	Well, how many times have you started and tried to do it? You just can't do it. You just move things around from there to there and from there. If you don't need it here and now, get rid of it.
Therapist:	Switch. What's that feel like inside? Can you respond to it?
Hilary:	It's a lot clearer. Then I was sort of like in a fog before, but now the course of action is a lot clearer.
Therapist:	Uh-huh. Is that OK? How do you feel about that?
Hilary:	Yeah, I'll give it a go. I feel accepting of the direction as a positive statement, and I'm not sure but I think that's what it is.

This session seemed to have been helpful for Hilary. She partially resolved her self-critical dialogue to the extent that she was able to identify with her internalized critic who took on the voice of her father, saying "stand up and be responsible." She responded by voicing her fears, which allowed her to confront them (EXP Stage 4; LCPP Level 5). She felt helped by her critic, who pointed her in the right direction. However, she did not fully resolve her split because she was not able to access or express vulnerability or ask for help from this position. Her critic did not soften or express underlying fear nor were core feelings of inadequacy and shame replaced by pride or self-confidence. She did, however, feel supported by the tough love approach of her critic and more capable of acting in the future. Hilary reported prior to the next session that she had begun "clearing out the rubbish at home" and was feeling very good about it. Hilary moved from neglecting herself and blaming herself (SASB 3-6, 3-8) to trying to do what was in her best interest and trying to take care of herself (SASB 3-4). This was the extent of resolution that Hilary attained during therapy with respect to her issues of failure. She moved from applying harsh external standards to trying to articulate her own inner sense of direction and solve her dilemma (EXP Stages 4, 5; LCPP Level 4) about how to care for herself in a manner that was not punitive.

This was as much as Hilary was able to achieve in a brief therapy. She was not able to be more accepting, nurturing, and kind toward herself. More time would have been necessary for Hilary to develop a more loving and positive introject. It is likely that this could have been developed in a supportive, accepting therapeutic environment in which Hilary could have been taught to value herself, listen to her feelings, and use them as a guide to her needs and behavior. It would also have been important for her to forgive herself and overcome her deep sense of shame for disappointing her parents and to recognize that their standards were excessively high. She needed to feel worthwhile and valuable as a person in spite of her parents' rejection of her. These changes might also have been possible in a loving, supportive relationship outside of therapy; however, she did not have access to such a relationship at the time of seeking therapy.

Prior to Session 13, Hilary expressed strong feelings of resentment toward her father and some accompanying pain in an empty-chair dialogue, although the full extent of her pain regarding her father had not been expressed. She had not been able to hold her parents fully accountable for their behavior toward her and to commit to protecting and loving herself in spite of their neglect. Moreover, she was unable to take on the role of her father in the other chair and thus was not able to shift her view of him. She was not able to view herself or the other with forgiveness or understanding, and she was not able to provide self-acceptance just as her parents had not accepted her. Further work in therapy would have been needed to support her in holding her parents accountable for their behavior toward her and in processing her deep grief and sorrow at not having had the love and support that she needed as a child.

In Session 12 Hilary showed some movement with respect to her internalized sense of failure and shame that had its roots in her unfinished business with her father. This occurred when her critic supported her. In Session 13 she reported a dream in which she felt that she symbolically let go of her father.

Hilary: Sunday night I had a most unusual dream, which I would like to share with you. Out of the blue, uh, somebody comes crashing into the room and says, Where the hell have you been? We've been trying to reach you for a long, long time, and I'm sorry to have to tell you your father is dead. But the strange thing about it was he kept reiterating how desperately hard they'd been trying to find me, and I said, well, I'm so sorry, I've not been anywhere unusual. I've been here all the time, and I do not see why you've had so much trouble in finding me.

Therapist: So it's almost as though they were angry with you or somehow you'd not made yourself available.

Hilary: Well, uh, angry was maybe too strong a word, but certainly very frustrated because he, um, and I recall that it was a male person wanting to communicate my father's death to me. And it occurred to me when I sort of dwelt on it the following day that maybe finally I have laid down my wreath. The problem with my father is, perhaps, over. Maybe this particular issue does not exist for me anymore, the anger at father. And there was actually a great clarity the following morning, which, you know, in itself is quite remarkable, and maybe you want to comment on that.

Therapist: Uh-huh. That somehow in the dream that you've put your father to rest?

Hilary: I guess that's, yeah. I mean, there was no burial service or anything like that, but just the fact that he had died.

The therapist suggested putting Hilary's imaginary father in the chair one last time, in part to express her newfound feelings but also to understand just how resolved she was with respect to this issue.

Therapist: How do you feel?

Hilary: I got it off my chest. I've said it, and that's it, good-bye.

Therapist: So you're saying your good-byes. Say it again to him.

Hilary: You know, you know, that's it, good-bye. I've, I've come to, um, resolve it doesn't really matter a very great deal anymore.

In spite of never having received the approval and acceptance that she needed from her father, she felt she could lay the issue to rest. There was a sense of resignation, a letting go (SASB 1-1, 2-1) as Hilary tried to move on. This represented a shift in Hilary's emotional processing (EXP Stage 6; LCPP Level 6). The issue of Hilary's mother reemerged in Session 14, at which time she was able to make some progress.

Hilary: I would like things to be on an even keel and have, a just, a normal parent-to-child relationship, but it's too late for that because I don't think you want that anymore than I think father wanted it. There was a time when I wanted her to say that she cared for me. It doesn't bother me anymore, and there was equally a time when I took your monetary gifts as an expression of affection. I don't think I do anymore because you withhold the money part just the same way as you withhold the affection part. So, that's exactly how I feel.

Therapist: How are you feeling just now?

Hilary: I guess it's a bit of a relief to be able to say that.

Therapist: Could you summarize for yourself, in a sense, whatever it is that you feel that was important for you to say. She's saying, "I wish you'd write more often."

Hilary: I don't think it matters. I don't. I've just hit countless demonstrations throughout my life that I don't matter to you anymore than I mattered to my father, and it just hurt. It left a great big, uh, gap in my life, which basically I plastered over. I learned to live with it, and I think it meant because I was basically not shown affection by either you or my father, I really didn't learn how to express affection outward from myself. And I think that was the big damage and that was the great horror of the whole situation.

Therapist: What are you feeling just now?

Hilary: Well, I think it's probably just one more will that I've been cut out of, and my partner or somebody can turn around and say, well look, you're an absolute idiot because all you had to do was play your cards right and you could have . . .

Therapist: What does that mean, play your cards right?

Hilary: Well, I should have sucked up to her just for the sake of getting what you can out of her in the form of an inheritance or . . .

Therapist: So she wants cheery little letters, send them to her; she wants to hear you on the phone, . . . Is that what you mean?

Hilary: Yeah, but I'm dry when it comes to emotional connections with you.

Therapist: Can you tell her what that dryness is like?

Hilary: It's awful having nothing inside, a great big void that could have love and feeling and all sorts of beautiful things in a relationship between mother and daughter. It's made a pretty big dent in my reality.

Therapist: So I guess in a way you're saying to her, "look here, you want some emotional affection from me, I have always wanted it from you, and I've never felt that I've gotten it. I feel like there's a big hole because of it, and it's painful." What are you in touch with just now?

Hilary: I'm sort of done.

Therapist: Could you take a deep breath?

Hilary: Well, this is a bottom that needs to be scraped. I'll tell you, there's the residue—it can actually be quite poisonous to the whole system. It's proven that in many ways.

Hilary clearly expressed how she felt unloved and rejected by her mother and felt her only recourse was to withdraw her own affections from her (EXP Stage 4; LCPP Level 5; SASB 2-1, 2-2). Although this may have given her a sense of control in the relationship, she had not fully resolved her grief and sorrow at not receiving the love she wanted from her mother. This segment revealed a significant shift for Hilary, who up to now had harbored a hope that her parents, particularly her mother, would respond in a loving, caring way. She was in the process of relinquishing that hope and beginning to come to terms with its absence both in the past and in the future. Hilary was no longer looking to her mother to alleviate her financial distress. Hilary shifted her attention from anger and attempts to placate the other to recognizing the implications of her parents' behavior for her (EXP Stage 6; LCPP Level 6). Her parents' behavior had left her with an emotional void. She recognized that she had never been able to provide herself with the empathy and soothing that she so sorely missed as a child. Hilary needed to develop these skills in the context of an accepting, validating, and respectful relationship.

In Session 19, the final session, Hilary came in and reported that she had finally been able to write a letter to her mother.

Hilary: Well, I maintained my promise and indeed wrote to my mother. It was quite fortuitous, the, when I got back to the house that evening after our last session, um, I was greeted with, uh, a remark from my partner that my mother was very angry with me because I had not written to her. And in less than 2 days a letter was on its way to her. I was able to capitalize on our conversation here, and I went over a whole raft of things—how I've had difficulty with work and that's something of which I'm not particularly proud, and I wanted her to be proud of me, and it's just not possible under these circumstances, and for that I'm truly sorry. Lots of love.

Therapist: How'd you feel after you'd written it?

Hilary: I had it, it was strange actually, I had a lot of mixed feelings. Um, I was, one side of me drove me to do the, the deed, and the other side was saying you are rather silly because you might just live to regret it. But the deed is done and that feeling has been overcome, and I'm not sitting here or there on tenterhooks about the outcome and what will happen. One side is not necessarily feeling good but feeling satisfied that I have accomplished it.

Hilary moved on and let go her hope that her mother would assist and protect her. She openly disclosed her own position (SASB 2-2) and was prepared to go her separate way (SASB 2-1). To begin to repair herself from the loss of not receiving the love and support that she received as a child, Hilary needed time to process her painful, sad, and vulnerable emotions. However, she was still scared of being overwhelmed by these feelings and continued to try to stifle and ignore them (SASB 3-6, 3-8). It was likely that she would require a longer term of therapy to begin to develop positive ways of treating herself and to learn to process her emotional experience productively. Consequently, she was unable to reorganize her experience and continued to access dominant maladaptive emotions such as hopelessness and pain instead of more adaptive emotions such as sadness, acceptance, and pride, necessary for long-term change.

SUMMARY AND ANALYSIS

Although Hilary made some progress in therapy and was able to express some strong feelings of resentment and remorse, posttherapy change measures indicated that she did not leave therapy feeling less depressed, nor did she feel resolved with respect to the issues that brought her to therapy. This is reflected in her posttherapy change scores that indicated very little change. There are a number of factors that might have accounted for Hilary's lack of change. As mentioned earlier, the alliance is an essential component for change in emotion-focused therapy. Although the therapeutic bond at most points was reasonably strong, there was some indication that the client and her therapist had disparate goals and objectives for how to improve or remedy Hilary's depression. Hilary was most concerned about financial matters, and her therapist was more focused on her psychological state. In Session 10 Hilary expressed her concerns about money, which she saw as very important to her feelings of depression, and the therapist tried to focus on Hilary's feelings of low self-esteem.

There seemed to be a breakdown in the alliance as there was a disagreement about the source of Hilary's problems. Hilary attributed them to external factors, whereas the therapist attributed them to internal problems. Consequently, the therapist and Hilary were working at cross-purposes. Later in Session 10, Hilary indicated her uncertainty that therapy could help her to resolve her current situation.

At the end of Session 10 on the Barrett-Lennard Relationship Inventory, in response to the item "I felt criticized by my therapist during the session," Hilary endorsed "occasionally." There was some suggestion that Hilary did not feel fully accepted by her therapist and, more important, was questioning whether therapy would be able to help her with her problems. However, this was an isolated event because Hilary did not typically endorse relationship items on the postsession forms in a negative manner across therapy.

Another important component of the alliance was mutual agreement on the tasks of therapy. In this regard it is possible that although Hilary wanted to participate, she was not always comfortable with the method of exploring emotions. One part of her wanted to be a "good client" and participate, and another part found it too overwhelming and wished to return to her more avoidant style of emotional processing. The conflict between the part of her that wanted to "get better" and make progress and the part that found it too emotionally overwhelming was pervasive from the beginning of therapy and continued throughout.

At termination Hilary had not changed much in terms of her scores on the Beck Depression Inventory (BDI), which moved from 15 to 13, showing that she was still mildly depressed. The absence of change on the BDI was consistent with Hilary's report of small-to-moderate changes at four points, during Sessions 4, 7, 16, and 19. There was also no change in her self-esteem, which remained low from the beginning to the end of therapy. However, she did show some improvement in the amount of distress she reported in terms of her interpersonal problems and the number of symptomatic complaints she had at the end of therapy as indicated by her scores on the Inventory of Interpersonal Problems and the Symptom Checklist—90—Revised, respectively. Of all the clients, Hilary's ratings of the working alliance were in the low range, 4.50 to 5.67. Although she did not note any major ruptures with her therapist, she indicated only moderate agreement on the goals and tasks of therapy.

It was difficult for Hilary to make significant progress in this short-term therapy. She did make some progress in terms of accessing and expressing some difficult emotions and gained some internal strength and clarity by letting go of some long-standing, difficult feelings toward her father. It seemed that Hilary's traumatic and wounding history had left her quite hopeless and depressed. Throughout her life she had felt rejected, worthless, and unwanted. At the age of 63, she was quite disappointed with herself and her accomplishments. Perhaps in response to feeling so hopeless and bereft, she had typically adopted an avoidant style of approaching her emotions and struggled with this throughout therapy. Indeed, this was evident in many of the imaginary dialogues with her parents in which she would "hit a wall," particularly when she tried to adopt the role of her parents. It seemed that adopting the role of her parents was too painful and overwhelming. As a result, Hilary was unable to transform her emotional experience and narrative of "I am worthless and unlovable" to "I am worthwhile and lovable." Hilary might have benefited from a longer term therapy that would have afforded the opportunity to build a stronger alliance and a mutually agreed on framework for her problems and ways of tackling them. She might also have benefited from time to explore more difficult emotions to get underneath them to the more positive, affirming, adaptive emotions necessary to produce long-standing change and to develop alternative ways of treating herself and interacting with others.

IV

IMPLICATIONS FOR PRACTICE

8

COMPARING AND CONTRASTING: IDENTIFYING FACTORS THAT CONTRIBUTE TO POSITIVE AND NEGATIVE OUTCOMES

As stated in chapter 1, our objectives in reviewing good and poor outcome cases of clients who participated in emotion-focused therapy (EFT) for depression were threefold: first, to provide clinicians who wish to master EFT for depression with an inside view of what EFT looks like so as to provide a better sense of the process and structure of such treatments; second, to begin to search for specific factors that might improve treatment delivery; and third, to identify those people who will benefit from a brief treatment, those who might require a longer term of therapy, those who might benefit from some pretherapy preparation, or those who might benefit from a different treatment altogether. In this chapter we identify some factors that we see as contributing to the success and failure of the good and poor outcome cases.

An examination of the cases reviewed in this book supports the observations of a number of psychotherapy researchers (Lambert & Bergin, 1994; Orlinsky, Grawe, & Parks, 1994; Prochaska, DiClemente, & Norcross, 1992) that effective treatment is not just a function of delivering a particular type of therapy well but is also very much contingent on specific client factors as well as factors external to therapy that either support or thwart clients' progress in therapy. First we focus on the factors that seemed to differentiate between good and poor outcome clients, and then we address specific therapeutic strategies that can be implemented to assist therapists using an emotionally focused approach to intervene when clients are experiencing difficulties that are associated with poor outcome (see chap. 9, this volume).

CLIENT FACTORS

An examination of all the clients presented in this book reveals a number of factors that they share, including difficult early environments and problems with affect regulation and depression as well as characteristics that differentiate the two groups.

Early Environments

The difficulties that the clients reviewed in this book encountered in their early childhood environments are consistent with the observations in our earlier book, *Emotion-Focused Therapy for Depression* (Greenberg & Watson, 2005), that people with depression have negative emotion schemes that have their origin in traumatic and difficult early life events. Research has shown that people with depression have an elevated proportion of negative emotion memories of the distant past (Smith, 1996). With respect to their early childhood environments and relationships with caretakers, both good and poor outcome clients reported that they had experienced either neglect or physical, sexual, or verbal abuse, or had caretakers who were unpredictable, invalidating, and critical. Their early home lives lacked adequate warmth, safety, and nurturing that would have allowed them to flourish and realize their potential.

Among the good outcome clients, Gayle (see chap. 3, this volume) experienced her parents as unsupportive and her mother as critical and disapproving. She felt abandoned by her parents at an early age because they seemed to value her brother more than her and did not protect her from her brother's physical assaults. Anna's mother (see chap. 4, this volume) was unpredictable and moody, turning on her without cause. Consequently, Anna never felt safe with her mother and silenced her responses as she tried to placate her mother and avoid her wrath. David's (see chap. 2, this volume) parents were emotionally unavailable. His mother was cold and taciturn, leaving David feeling scared and unlovable. His father was unable to provide support and guidance because he was very dependent on his wife and unable to adequately care for his children after her death.

An examination of the poor outcome clients reveals that Hilary (see chap. 7, this volume) was an unwanted child born to parents who divorced when she was very young. As a child she did not feel that she was welcome at home because she spent her life being shipped out to boarding schools and sundry friends and relatives. Later she moved away after she was actively pushed out of the family business by her mother. Whereas Hilary felt neglected and unclaimed, Sean (see chap. 6, this volume) described his mother as a "shark." He felt victimized by her and unable to stand up to her verbal and emotional assaults. Although Richard (see chap. 5, this volume) said that his childhood had been good, he recalled he had experienced depression at a very young age and had assumed the care of his ailing mother after his father's death. He was also aware that he was more sensitive than his brothers. He gave the impression that no one had attended to his emotional needs when he was young, though this was not confirmed in therapy. As an adult he continued to take care of others' needs, putting their needs ahead of his own to his detriment.

The poor outcome clients were unable to activate and realize their potential, as was evident in their career paths. When they entered therapy, the poor outcome clients were floundering in their careers and were uncertain of their direction or value to others. Richard (see chap. 5, this volume) left home early and was having difficulties in his career because he was unable to write. He felt uncertain of his life course when he came to therapy. Sean (see chap. 6, this volume) was so scarred by his mother's treatment that he was unable to assert himself with other people, especially at work, and expressed great difficulty with making his way in the world. Hilary (see chap. 7, this volume) had been unable to recover after a successful career was terminated prematurely. The difference between the good and poor outcome cases was that the clients in the good outcome cases had had someone in their early childhoods who provided them with some form of care and support. In contrast, the early childhoods of the clients in the poor outcome cases seemed barren of any support from another person in their environments. Richard, Hilary, and Sean did not mention a single figure who stood out as kind and caring; whereas Anna, Gayle, and David identified neighbors, teachers, siblings, and friends who provided care, support, and kindness. In addition, two of the three good outcome clients had had a previous experience of therapy, which they had found helpful.

Affect Regulation

In terms of their difficulties with affect regulation and depressed mood, all six clients were depressed when they entered treatment and had difficulties with affect regulation. As noted in chapter 1, five essential components of affect regulation are awareness of emotion and bodily sensations, labeling, modulation of arousal, reflection on emotion, and expression of emotion.

These emotion-processing skills are emphasized and developed in EFT for both individuals and couples. One important difference that emerges between the good outcome clients and the poor outcome clients reviewed in this book is their affect regulation.

The good outcome clients were aware of their feelings and were in touch with their emotions and bodily sensations. They were able to identify their feelings and represent them symbolically. Although they did not have difficulty labeling their feelings, they had difficulty modulating their levels of arousal effectively and expressing their feelings, needs, and wants appropriately to others. The good outcome clients needed to learn how to access more adaptive feelings and reflect on their feelings to solve difficulties as opposed to silencing themselves or overreacting.

David (see chap. 2, this volume) was aware of his sadness and regret at the loss of his mother. He was aware that he was scared of authority figures and enjoyed interacting with people. He also used his more adaptive feelings as a guide to make choices and steer his life course. Gayle (see chap. 3, this volume) too was aware when she was sad or angry. She accessed and transformed her shame by grieving her losses and accessing more adaptive, empowering anger. She was able to stand back and observe her behavior and how she expressed herself and wanted to be different. She especially wanted to be gentler and less critical and irritable with her children and to improve her sexual relationship with her husband. Anna (see chap. 4, this volume) had spent many years seeking to improve herself and overcome the difficulties she had experienced as a child. Like David, she tended to use her adaptive feelings as a guide to her behavior, listening to her feelings of discomfort with her housemate to decide whether she wanted to change the nature of their friendship and using her own sense of excitement to find direction in terms of her career. All these clients not only were aware of their feelings so that they processed their feelings at Stage 4 and higher on The Experiencing Scale (EXP) but they also were able to reflect on them and on their behavior to develop alternative ways of being.

In contrast, the clients in the poor outcome cases had difficulty becoming aware of their feelings and labeling them in conscious awareness. They spoke of actively avoiding feeling or experiencing numbness in relation to their feelings. The poor outcome clients shied away from knowledge of their feelings because they were scared that exploring them would be too painful. Moreover, when their therapists suggested that it might be useful to explore their feelings to get a better sense of what was happening in their lives and to try to change their behavior, they expressed doubt that identifying and working with feelings would be useful.

Richard (see chap. 5, this volume) spoke about encountering a "black hole" when he tried to identify his feelings. He was terrified of being lost in them and felt a deep sense of shame about himself that made it difficult to disclose his feelings. Hilary (see chap. 7, this volume) was quite distant from her emotions and was very analytical and intellectual in how she approached her problems. She saw the exploration of feelings as an attempt to make her feel worse and saw no point in "raking over old coals." Sean (see chap. 6, this volume) was more aware of his feelings than Richard or Hilary; however, at the beginning of therapy he was quite hesitant and skeptical that exploring feelings would be useful in helping him overcome his depression. He was also scared of being overwhelmed by his feelings and drowning in them. However, as therapy progressed he came to see the value of exploring his feelings.

In chapter 1 we discussed a model of emotional processing that comprises the following continuum: bodily sensation and arousal, awareness of arousal, access to feelings, labeling, reflection, modulation, and expression of feelings. For emotional processing to be effective, it is important first to be aware; second to identify and label the experience accurately; third to modulate one's level of arousal; fourth to reflect on emotional experience to integrate it into other aspects of one's environment, current situation, and future goals; and fifth to express emotions in a way that will enhance one's functioning to meet one's needs and goals and either promote contact with others or protect the self. If one conceives of emotional processing on a developmental scale that starts with awareness and labeling and ends with reflection and expression, then the poor outcome clients were at a lower level on the scale of emotional processing than the good outcome clients to the extent that the poor outcome clients were less aware of what they were feeling.

Both Richard (see chap. 5, this volume) and Sean (see chap. 6, this volume) had learned to silence their adaptive feelings and their needs. They did not attend to their bodies nor were they aware of the flow of their emotional experiences; they preferred to distance themselves from their feelings because they viewed their experiences as shameful and repugnant to others. However, Sean was more able to connect with his feelings than either Richard or Hilary (see chap. 7, this volume); consequently, he was able to resolve some of the experiential tasks and experience a significant shift in how he treated himself and regarded his experience by the end of therapy.

The poor outcome clients all expressed great difficulty becoming aware of and naming their feelings. Two of them said that trying to access their feelings was like "looking into a black hole." The process of attending to and becoming aware of their feelings to know and understand them was extremely difficult and uncomfortable. They tended to ignore their feelings and subjective awareness either by invalidating them, saying that they did not count, or by thinking that they should feel differently, or they avoided their feelings altogether, trying to pretend they did not have them. The awareness and labeling of feelings is the most basic level of emotional processing and affect regulation. The inability to know and name their feelings meant that these clients were somewhat oblivious to the impact of events on themselves, unaware of what they needed and how to act, and unable to communicate effectively with others. Not having access to their feelings in conscious awareness meant that they were unable to reflect on them to problem solve effectively and express them appropriately to meet their needs satisfactorily. These clients needed to acquire the skills to attend to and name their inner experiences to reflect on them. These skills take time to acquire and master.

All three clients came from backgrounds in which their feelings did not receive attention, were disrespected, and were dismissed. Nor were the early developmental deficits that may have occurred in terms of their emotional processing compensated for or moderated by relationships with other caretakers in childhood or significant others in the clients' adult lives. Had they received alternative models of care that provided them with the opportunity to explore their feelings and pay them more attention, they might have been readier to engage in a brief EFT for depression.

At the beginning of therapy, none of the poor outcome clients saw the immediate value of focusing on their emotional experience. To work successfully in an emotion-focused treatment, they needed time to develop a sense of the relevance of exploring emotions and how it might be helpful to do so. Clients' willingness to explore and share their feelings is important to the development of a productive working alliance in EFT. Often it is the first task that clients and therapists negotiate when clients enter an emotion-focused treatment. Although emotion-focused therapists may work with clients who are reluctant to explore their feelings in a longer term treatment, it is likely that reluctance to explore feelings is a poor prognostic indicator that short-term EFT will be effective.

To help clients become aware of and label their experiences, emotion-focused therapists need to assume an empathic, exploratory stance as clients begin to unpack and represent their inner and outer experiences and develop a narrative in which they can then locate their reactions and the emotional propositions or schemes that they have developed from that experience. This requires that therapists be patient and take time to develop clients' emotional processing skills before clients can begin to be more self-focused and define specific areas of change. During this phase it is usually difficult for clients and therapists to engage in two-chair or empty-chair work because clients lack the necessary emotional processing skills that these tasks require, including the awareness and labeling of feelings as well as ways of modulating those feelings through nurturing and accepting behaviors. Once clients start to become aware of their emotions and begin to process them in conscious awareness, then both clients and therapists are in a position to become aware of clients' emotion schemes. Once clients' emotion schemes have been identified, clients are in a position to modify and change these schemes and their ways of reacting to the world and themselves.

Another area of emotional processing that was difficult for the poor outcome clients was their capacity to modulate their affective reactions. None of them were able to soothe themselves effectively. Although they were able to distract themselves with work, television, or physical activity, their pain flowed beneath, and they felt unable to deal with it effectively. All three clients had difficulty expressing their emotions and talking about their difficulties with others and, to the degree that their feelings were unknown, were unable to reflect on them to solve their current difficulties. For example, Richard (see chap. 5, this volume) did not speak of his feelings to anyone, including his wife. Hilary (see chap. 7, this volume) was able to distract herself and kept busy but continued to feel depressed. The poor outcome clients needed to learn the skills of emotional awareness and labeling before they could engage in reflection and modulation of their emotional experiences and begin to develop alternative and new ways of expressing themselves.

In contrast, the good outcome clients valued their emotional experiences. They saw them as important. For example, Anna (see chap. 4, this volume) was upset that she silenced herself with her mother and actively worked to be more self-disclosing. Gayle (see chap. 3, this volume) too wanted to share her feelings with others, as did David (see chap. 2, this volume). This capacity and willingness to engage with emotional experience is very important to the successful delivery of a short-term emotion-focused treatment because it allows for the smooth and quick development of a working alliance. In the absence of such agreement on how to work in therapy, therapists and clients need to step back to help clients overcome their shame and fear about exploring emotions and inner experiences before they can engage in the work of changing clients' emotion schemes to overcome their depression.

GOOD OUTCOME CLIENTS

Although the good and poor outcome clients shared some experiences, a number of factors distinguished between the good and poor outcome clients. A review of the good outcome cases reveals a number of factors that are common to all three that distinguish them from the poor outcome cases. These include both intrapersonal and interpersonal factors. The intrapersonal factors include a willingness to self-disclose; a clear specification of a problem with a focus on the self and the clients' emotional functioning; an ability to act on newly acquired insights and behavioral options that emerged in the session; a capacity to access adaptive feelings and self-care and compassion for the self; and an ability to shift perspective, and have aspirations and dreams. In terms of the interpersonal factors that were helpful, the good outcome cases all had access to social support.

Many of these capacities were revealed by clients' scores on the various process measures. Clients' scores on the EXP indicated the type of emotional processing that they were engaged in as well as their capacity to reflect on their experiences and pose questions about them to come up with different perspectives or ways of viewing their experiences or of feeling so as to resolve issues. Clients' scores on the Structural Analysis of Social Behavior (SASB) reflected their capacity to treat themselves in positive or negative ways that allowed them to accept, value, and nurture themselves and their emotional experiences as opposed to controlling, annihilating, or neglecting themselves and their emotional experiences. Cognitive and emotional shifts were apparent in clients' scores on the Levels of Client Perceptual Processing (LCPP) and EXP as they identified moments when they resolved specific problems, came up with new ways of looking at problems, or devised new ways of acting. As noted earlier, the other distinguishing feature of the good outcome clients was that they all experienced problems with emotional expression but did not have difficulty being aware of or labeling their feelings.

Intrapersonal Factors

The good outcome clients seemed to benefit enormously from treatment. They were able to use what was offered and make the changes they required almost without their therapists seeming to try very hard. Changes occurred very quickly, often within the first four sessions, and continued with the same momentum for the rest of the treatment. It was as if these clients came to therapy already primed to respond positively. They formed easy alliances with their therapists and were cooperative. There was a good fit between their objectives and their therapists' interventions early on. It is clear from the SASB ratings that these clients were open to their therapists' suggestions and were willing to trust and rely on their therapists for guidance and support.

Action Orientation

The good outcome clients can be described as agentic. Not only did they state a problem in terms of their own functioning but they also set about purposefully to understand and change it in therapy. This type of behavior in therapy would be rated as Stage 5 on the EXP. These clients' agentic behaviors were notable outside of therapy too, as the clients tried to implement new behaviors and respond differently to the people and events that they encountered. Using the Prochaska et al. (1992) stages of change model, the good outcome clients could be considered to be in the action phase of change when they entered therapy.

Gayle (see chap. 3, this volume) was able to access empowering anger, became more assertive and was able to express her needs and wants to others. She decided not to see her parents and changed her appearance even though she realized her mother might disapprove. She began setting limits with others and felt better doing so. Anna (see chap. 4, this volume) was able to stand up to her critic after Session 7. Subsequently, she stopped procrastinating, developed a business plan, and clarified her feelings about her housemate. David (see chap. 2, this volume) changed his interaction with employers and installed a music system for himself that he had delayed completing for a number of years. In addition, he actively challenged his self-criticisms outside of therapy and tried to change his interactions with his wife and other family members. All these clients were eager to implement changes and improve the quality of their lives. Being in the action stage of change is very important in short-term therapy. If clients come in ready and able to implement changes, then there is no need for their therapists to work with them to consider whether change is useful or valuable or something that they have the inclination or stamina to do. Thus clients and therapists can quickly forge a positive working alliance and work to resolve clients' issues instead of exploring the possible benefits of therapy and how these might be achieved.

Self-Disclosure

As evidenced by their SASB ratings, all the clients were expressive and freely self-disclosed to their therapists. They seemed to trust their therapists and wanted to share what was happening in their worlds. There was an easy flow to the dialogue in the session with the clients openly sharing their concerns and emotions. The clients were able to recall and were willing to share their memories of their parents and the events that caused them pain. Their conversation was not stilted, and they readily responded to their therapists' empathic responses, requests for clarification, or ways of structuring the session.

Gayle (see chap. 3, this volume) recalled how mistreated she had been by her brother, her parents' response to his behavior, her early marriage, and current interactions with her parents. Anna (see chap. 4, this volume) shared information about her early marriage, current relationship, and life events to give her therapist a clear sense of how she functioned and what the important events in her life were. David (see chap. 2, this volume) recalled memories from his childhood and adolescence that were meaningful to him, including his mother's death and its consequences for him. He was also able to describe his current situation in a colorful and detailed way that easily gave his therapist access to his world.

It is very helpful if clients are able to freely self-disclose in a short-term emotionally focused treatment and allow their therapists quick access to the important aspects of their lives. This enables clients and therapists to identify the factors that might be contributing to the clients' current problems and life difficulties and clients' predominant emotion schemes. Clients' capacity to share and inform their therapists about emotionally salient events allows emotion-focused therapists to enter into their clients' worlds more easily, thus making it easier to empathize and resonate to their clients' pain.

Self-Focus

The good outcome clients came to therapy with a problem that was clearly specified in terms of something that they wanted to change about themselves. Early in treatment they were able to pose questions about their experiences that were rated at Stage 5 on the EXP. In addition, these clients were able to focus on and explore problematic aspects of their experiences to achieve problem resolutions and shifts in their experiences as evidenced not only by their scores on the postsession change measures and outcome measures but also by the number of Stage 6 ratings on the EXP. The good outcome clients had a sense of what they needed to change to alleviate their depression. Thus, therapists and clients did not need to engage in extensive exploration at the beginning of therapy to ascertain what was contributing to clients' feelings of depression. Therapists were more easily able to formulate with their clients a focus of inquiry and an understanding of how their clients functioned as opposed to having to shift them from a focus on the world and their intense feelings of depression.

Gayle (see chap. 3, this volume) did not want to perpetuate her family's cycle of abuse and wanted to stop looking for her mother's approval. Anna (see chap. 4, this volume) was aware that she had difficulty setting limits and assumed too much responsibility for others. She wanted to be more attentive to herself and to stop invalidating her feelings. David (see chap. 2, this volume) wanted to work on self-criticism and his difficulties in his marriage. These clients possessed considerable self-knowledge so that they were able to observe themselves, talk about themselves, and describe themselves to their therapists and relate their actions and feelings to the events in their lives. This made it easy for their therapists to formulate ways of working with their clients' difficulties in an emotion-focused way and to develop agreement about the goals and tasks of therapy.

Positive Introjects and Adaptive Emotions

Early in therapy the good outcome clients found it easy to access more adaptive feelings and show concern and care for themselves as evidenced by how they were able to access compassionate and caring behaviors and resolve specific two-chair and empty-chair tasks. The presence of these behaviors was supported by the SASB ratings in the good outcome clients' dialogues that were scored in Quadrants 1 and 2, indicating self-acceptance, assertion, nurturance, and guidance. When engaged in two-chair or empty-chair tasks, the good outcome clients were able to disclose feelings and show compassion toward themselves and others and expressed a desire to be more self-protective. Along with concern and care for themselves, these clients were able to be assertive with others and toward the critical part of themselves very early in therapy. Although these clients were self-critical and demanding of themselves and tended to invalidate what they felt, they nonetheless were also capable of nurturing and guiding themselves using their emotional experiences as guides. They seemed to possess both positive and negative introjects.

Gayle (see chap. 3, this volume) came to accept her anger as well as her feelings of sadness and disappointment and to appreciate the care and concern that she experienced from the people around her instead of trying to make her mother more loving and kind. She realized that she was lovable and that people cared about her, and she in turn was able to extend love to her children and husband. At midtherapy she asked her husband to stand up for her to her parents, but by the end of therapy she was appropriately assertive on her own behalf. By the fifth session, Anna's (see chap. 4, this volume) critic had softened, and Anna recognized that she did not want to treat herself so harshly. Anna was also able to assert that she did not deserve to be invalidated and began to treat herself with more respect. As early as the second session, David (see chap. 2, this volume) recognized that people had supported him throughout his life. Later he was able to accept that his mother had loved him as best she could but had never received proper nurturing herself so did not know how to express her feelings or nurture her own children. By the end of therapy he accepted that he was loved and lovable. It is noteworthy that all the good outcome clients were able to access and implement accepting, caring, nurturing, and self-assertive behaviors after being in therapy for only a few sessions.

Cognitive Flexibility or Capacity to Shift Perceptions

All three good outcome clients were able to come to alternative views about themselves or others. This was evidenced by their scores on the LCPP and the EXP. They were able to look at experiences in new and fresh ways and to integrate these new views to generate new ways of behaving and relating to others. This capacity to shift gestalts or see alternative perspectives allowed them to come to new insights and ways of looking at the world. These clients seemed to show greater cognitive flexibility than the poor outcome clients. The latter seemed to be constrained by a specific worldview and had difficulty considering alternatives. It is unclear whether the capacity to shift perspective is trait or situation specific. The shifts may be partly a function of the good outcome clients' easier access to positive introjects or, alternatively, changes in their depressed mood. The good outcome clients may have had access to a wider range of behaviors than the poor outcome clients and may have been able to see themselves as worthy of different treatment early in therapy.

They were capable of compassion toward themselves and others and able to throw a gestalt switch. All three clients were able to take another person's perspective and empathize with another's suffering in spite of having been injured or wounded by that person. They were able to show empathy toward themselves. This capacity was very important in helping them engage productively in two-chair and empty-chair work. The good outcome clients seemed to have the infrastructure necessary to enable them to resolve self-criticism or interpersonal difficulties because they could see others' perspectives and were capable of nurturing and self-protective behaviors.

Gayle (see chap. 3, this volume) changed her view of herself as needing her mother's support to being able to validate herself independently of her mother. She was also able to recognize that others whom she had viewed as unsupportive were indeed supportive. Anna (see chap. 4, this volume) was able to reassure herself and to see herself as competent. She learned how to reach out to people for support to achieve her goals instead of trying to do everything herself. She expressed concern for her mother's well-being even though she felt invalidated by her. David (see chap. 2, this volume) came to recognize that his mother and father had loved him in their own way. He realized how impoverished his parents' childhoods and emotional lives had been and that they had probably done their best to love and support him. He was also able to see his daughter-in-law's brusqueness in a new light so that he no longer felt uncomfortable around her. All these clients had to form new gestalts of their experience to view themselves and others differently and thereby open new options in terms of how they treated themselves and others.

Aspirations and Goals

All three clients had aspirations and goals for their lives outside of therapy. They had the capacity to dream and imagine goals and lives different from those they were pursuing. Anna (see chap. 4, this volume) and Gayle (see chap. 3, this volume) were focused on self-improvement both physically and in terms of their careers and work goals. Anna returned to school to improve her qualifications and find more satisfying and remunerative work. She felt positive about the experience of returning to school, which gave her feelings of mastery and competence. Gayle changed her occupation and felt proud of herself for being able to successfully compete for a new position and privileged to have acquired it. David (see chap. 2, this volume) became clearer about what he enjoyed doing and made plans to steer his career in a more satisfying direction. These clients' sense of agency was highlighted as they acted on their aspirations and tried to realize their dreams. Their capacity to dream and imagine a different world was important in guiding them in new, more satisfying directions. Their dreams gave them hope and a sense of direction that was useful in countering the sense of exhaustion and futility that they experienced when depressed. Their dreams showed them a way out and provided both them and their therapists with a compass for what they were trying to achieve.

Interpersonal Factors

The good outcome clients were all able to establish good interpersonal relationships. They established good alliances with their therapists and had strong social support networks which provided comfort and support in times of stress.

Working Alliance

The importance of the working alliance in facilitating positive outcomes in psychotherapy is well documented (Horvath & Symonds, 1991; Lambert & Barley, 2002; Norcross, 2002), and in emotion-focused therapy particularly, the therapeutic relationship is seen as a fundamental agent of change. Emotion-focused therapists focus much of their efforts on ensuring that their clients feel understood, accepted, and prized. It has been suggested that the successful implementation of tasks provides a good indicator that the relationship conditions have been met (Watson & Greenberg, 1994). The successful implementation of tasks demonstrates that clients feel heard and understood, and that clients and therapists are working toward joint goals in ways that are mutually compatible. In addition, the provision of therapist empathy is seen as an active ingredient that effects major changes in how clients treat themselves and others (Bohart, Elliott, Greenberg, & Watson, 2002; Steckley & Watson, 2005).

The good outcome clients came into therapy better able to negotiate their needs with those of their therapists (Safran, Muran, Samstag, & Stevens, 2002). As we saw earlier, the good outcome clients were able to trust their therapists right from the beginning of therapy. They entered therapy with the belief that their therapists could help them and continued throughout to rely on their therapists' interventions and support. They experienced their therapists as understanding and felt that they shared the same objectives. They responded quickly to their therapists' suggestions of how the two of them could work together on the client's problems. David (in chap. 2, this volume) readily agreed that he was too self-critical and thought that it would be helpful to work on changing this way of treating himself even though as the therapy progressed it became clear that his unresolved grief over his childhood also contributed to his depression, as did his marital difficulties. In a similar fashion, Gayle (see chap. 3, this volume) responded to her therapist's suggestions and began to work to differentiate herself from her mother so that she could become more self-accepting and less self-critical.

The good outcome clients readily engaged in the therapeutic tasks. The tasks seemed to make sense to them, and they were able to become aware of their feelings and freely express these to their therapists, allowing their therapists to tailor their interventions even more to their clients' needs and focus on aspects of their clients' experiences that became more salient over the course of therapy, such as Anna's relationship with her mother and her housemate (see chap. 4, this volume) and Gayle's distress with an ex-boyfriend (see chap. 3, this volume). The good outcome clients' capacity to forge positive alliances allowed their therapists to be more adaptive and responsive to their needs so that change was more likely to occur.

Social Support

In addition to establishing positive therapeutic relationships, the good outcome clients had strong social support networks. Two of the three good outcome clients were married, and all of them had children. They all enjoyed being with people and recognized and accepted the support and care that they received from others. None of the good outcome clients saw themselves as loners. They sought interactions with others and enjoyed social activities even though they were depressed. In fact, it was often the support that they received from others that helped them shift their perspectives and provided encouragement and validation when caretakers or significant others failed them.

Gayle (see chap. 3, this volume) received support from colleagues at work and experienced her husband as very supportive. She was also very concerned about her children and actively tried to be a good mother. Over the course of therapy, she chose to seek additional support from friends instead of her mother to diminish her dependence on her critical parent. Anna (see chap. 4, this volume) was a very concerned mother who enjoyed spending time with her children. She missed contact with her sisters and wanted to establish a close, loving relationship with a man. David (see chap. 2, this volume) enjoyed outings with friends and teaching his students. He was focused on improving his interpersonal relationships at work and with family members. Overall, the good outcome clients were able to integrate their own capacities with the scaffolding of therapy to make productive changes in their lives. This was not the case for the poor outcome clients.

POOR OUTCOME CLIENTS

The poor outcome clients did not show the same type of engagement in the therapeutic process as did the good outcome clients. Although histories of neglect and abuse were not specific to the three poor outcome cases because all six clients entered therapy with some history of abuse and neglect, the sense of neglect seemed more extreme in at least two of the poor outcome cases than in the good outcome cases. There was a sense of barrenness and emptiness that was conveyed in the narratives of two of the poor outcome clients' early childhoods and by their lack of vivid, specific memories. Two of the three poor outcome clients appeared to have had little guidance and conveyed a sense of being left to drift with the current; the third experienced very high expectations in an uncaring environment. All three had become resigned to their fates and did not believe things could improve.

To better understand these clients' difficulties, one needs to look at the factors that may have impeded the poor outcome clients from responding to a 16-week treatment. An examination of the poor outcome clients reveals a number of intrapersonal and interpersonal factors that are different from the good outcome clients in the ways that they engaged in therapy. The intrapersonal factors include impoverished narratives, the absence of a self-focus, shame, harsh negative introjects and an absence of positive introjects and ways of treating the self that are soothing and nurturing, lack of awareness of and difficulty labeling feelings, hopelessness and resignation, being in the contemplation stage of change, difficulties with the working alliance, and diminished social support.

Intrapersonal Factors

Impoverished Narratives

Two of the poor outcome clients were unable to supply detailed and clear descriptions of memories or events in their lives that would have allowed their therapists an inside view. Richard (see chap. 5, this volume) did not have a clear narrative of his life story that would have helped him and his therapist to contextualize his pain and current life difficulties. In spite of his therapist's attempts to get a better sense of his history, Richard was unable to supply much detail about his early childhood memories or his current life situation. His description of his life history was sparse so it was difficult to get a sense of how he had been treated or what it felt like to grow up in his particular environment. Both Richard and Hilary's (see chap. 7, this volume) descriptions lacked immediacy and color, qualities that would have allowed a therapist entrée into their worlds and provided them with the opportunity to apprehend better the impact of events on their clients so that they could empathize appropriately. Sean (see chap. 6, this volume) was the only one of the three who was able to describe his home environment and to provide a very clear sense of how he had experienced it.

In the absence of more concrete, specific, and vivid details, it was difficult for therapists to identify clients' core emotion schemes and to conceptualize their difficulties or to see how they were experiencing life and what might be contributing to their current problems. Also it was more difficult to process painful experiences that were the source of emotion schemes in the absence of clients' having coherent narratives, vivid episodic memories, or a clear sense of direction. A clear sense of clients' histories and memories of important life events can help emotion-focused therapists see the emotional triggers as well as the ways in which clients have learned to respond and cope with early environments. Early memories of specific events, even in the absence of intense emotion, can provide a compass to direct therapists to the salient events and possible emotion schemes that may be causing difficulty for their clients. The narratives and recollections of early experiences also inform therapists about clients' vulnerabilities and help guide them in how to respond empathically. The absence of descriptions of external events in the lives of these clients made it more difficult for their therapists to feel or intuit the inner worlds that their clients found difficult to share and represent in therapy.

Absence of a Self-Focus

Along with impoverished narratives, the poor outcome clients did not have a clear focus in terms of what they needed to change about themselves. These clients were consumed and overwhelmed by their negative feelings of depression or focused on outside events, for example, a parent's behavior or other people's judgments about their work or performance. They had yet to clarify for themselves what they were doing that was contributing to their problems and identify what they could change about themselves to feel better. Only Sean (see chap. 6, this volume) was able to formulate his rage as a problem as indicated by ratings of Stage 5 on the EXP. There were few if any Stage 5 ratings on the EXP in the transcripts of the other two poor outcome clients. To develop a self-focus in their clients, therapists needed to help their clients expand their narratives and talk about themselves so that they could describe and observe themselves and their behavior. This would have helped clients to increase their self-knowledge and to understand their reactions to troubling external events and people who caused them distress.

Shame

As a result of their impoverished childhoods and the treatment they had received at the hands of caregivers, the three poor outcome clients were deeply ashamed of themselves and their experiences. They had extreme difficulty sharing their experiences with others, and although they were able to open up somewhat with their therapists and valued the opportunity to do so, they were unable to explore their experiences in an easy and unguarded way that might have opened up new ways of looking at their experiences or increased their self-understanding.

Richard (see chap. 5, this volume) was unable to share with his wife, let alone his therapist. In fact, he was more open with his therapist than he had been with anyone else in his life to that point. Hilary (see chap. 7, this volume) felt like an outcast and was ashamed of her lifestyle in comparison to that of her extended family. She had great difficulty sharing her thoughts and feelings, seeing herself as despicable. Sean (see chap. 6, this volume) had been deeply shamed by his mother as a way of controlling and managing his behavior. Shame was one of the chronic and enduring emotion schemes that these clients needed to change in therapy before each of them could begin to explore the experiences that were contributing to their depression so as to effect changes in their lives. The deep chronic nature of their shame made it intractable to reversal in a short-term treatment.

Lack of Positive Introjects and Adaptive Emotions

As a result of their early childhood environments and the emotional neglect they had experienced, two of the poor outcome clients lacked positive ways of experiencing and relating to themselves. Only one poor outcome client was able to become more self-accepting and compassionate over the course of therapy; however, these were very new behaviors that needed more time and therapeutic support to take hold more deeply. As indicated by the ratings on the SASB and LCPP, the poor outcome clients were critical, rejecting, and controlling of themselves and found it difficult or were unable to be aware of, attend to, and listen to their experiences with empathy, respect, and tolerance. They were not able to cherish and enjoy themselves in ways that would have been nourishing and would have helped them to replenish themselves, nor were they able to be self-protective and direct and guide themselves in ways that would have been in their best interests. At best they were oppressive and coercive as they tried to monitor and control their behavior without heeding the impact of these behaviors on themselves or attending to what they might have needed more urgently.

Richard (see chap. 5, this volume) was especially cruel and harsh as he tried to negate his needs and wants. He recognized that he bullied himself so much that it was like being in an abusive relationship. Hilary (see chap. 7, this volume) was able to access some of the things that she required. She danced and participated in social events; however, she too was extremely critical of herself and expected herself to be stoical and tended to invalidate her feelings, needs, and wants. Although Sean (see chap. 6, this volume) too was very critical of and controlling with himself, he was able to feel compassion for and pride in his son and was then able to think of applying these feelings to himself. Of the three, Sean had access to more positive introjects than did Richard and Hilary, who were very critical and punishing of themselves. The poor outcome clients were unable to access adaptive feelings and/or soothe themselves in times of distress. They lacked the ability to organize resiliently in response to stress or to modulate and moderate their affective states so that they could manage their feelings without being overwhelmed and swamped by them.

A review of the poor outcome clients' SASB ratings shows that they all had ratings in Quadrants 2 and 3 with scores of 6, 7, and 8, indicating that significant others had treated them in harsh, punitive ways and that they too were neglectful, harshly attacking, and critical of themselves. The presence of these harsh, negative introjects without the presence of more positive, loving, and affirming ones made it difficult for the poor outcome clients to engage in positive, self-affirming behaviors to overcome their depression. Of the three, Sean (see chap. 6, this volume) was able to access positive introjects during the course of his therapy and draw on the compassion he felt for his son to provide himself with empathy and support.

Hopelessness and Resignation

All three poor outcome clients seemed quite hopeless and resigned to their fates. Although they expressed anger and disappointment, they seemed unable to access and share their feelings and assert themselves with the people who had hurt them or disempowered them in some way. Sean (see chap. 6, this volume) was beginning to change over the course of therapy, but these changes had not become entrenched, and as a result, he relapsed after therapy terminated. Richard (see chap. 5, this volume) and Hilary (see chap. 7, this volume) were not able to shift their sense of hopelessness sufficiently in the 16-week treatment to effect changes in their moods and behaviors. A sense of agency and a clear sense that they could actively change themselves and alter their moods were lacking and served as an impediment to their being able to improve in a short-term treatment. Building a belief in their agency and capacity to alter their life stories was very challenging to their therapists, who were constrained by time in a short-term treatment. All three clients required time to develop a sense of themselves as active agents who could make an impact on their worlds and change how they were feeling and acting.

Stage of Change

The poor outcome clients may be characterized as being in the contemplation stage of change. They were only beginning to consider that therapy might be an option; however, they were not yet clear how it might be useful or even whether they had the energy and will to engage in what they all saw as a painful exercise. Their sense of hopelessness left them feeling defeated and their focus on the outside world made it hard for them to see the relevance or utility of focusing on themselves to change how they were construing, perceiving, or behaving in the world. Their therapists remarked that it felt as if they were trying to convince their clients of the benefits of therapy. All three of them were skeptical that therapy could be useful. They were resigned to their situations and did not expect that they could change.

Hilary (see chap. 7, this volume) expressed skepticism about the value of dealing with her feelings about her parents' actions toward her. She felt that others needed to change and did not see how effecting changes within herself would improve matters. In a similar fashion, Richard (see chap. 5, this volume) felt that he lacked any control or power to alter his life substantially and did not believe that he could do things that would improve his deep sense of depression. Sean (see chap. 6, this volume) was initially skeptical, but as therapy progressed he began to see the possibilities of change and made some important shifts. Over the course of therapy he began to move into an action stage of change; however, as this process occurred during therapy, he needed more time to work on resolving the issues that contributed to his depression.

Interpersonal Factors

Two aspects of interpersonal relatedness were highlighted in the poor outcome cases: the working alliance and clients' social support.

The Working Alliance

The importance of the working alliance is well recognized in therapy in general and in emotionally focused therapies specifically. It is of note that none of the poor outcome clients reported poor alliances with their therapists. Clients' scores hovered around 4 to 6 on a 7-point scale. In terms of the SASB ratings, however, clients were reluctant to rely on their therapists and trust their therapists' guidance and support. These clients did not have a history of people who were supportive, understanding, and caring and had had to rely on themselves from very early on; consequently, it did not come easily to them to trust and rely on their therapists. There were no significant ruptures in the three poor outcome cases; rather, the clients' and therapists' formulations of the formers' difficulties did not mesh completely. One client reported uncertainty about how much his therapist liked and appreciated him but did not express disagreement about what they were doing in therapy. However, a review of the transcripts showed that the client made some comments that indicated that he was uncertain about engaging in certain tasks and even questioned whether he was depressed. All three clients were very analytical and rational and had difficulty exploring and expressing their emotions, a fundamental objective in EFT.

When therapy is going well there is a sense of fluidity and synchronization that participants and especially therapists experience as a flow. As with professional ballroom dancers, there is an ease and coordination of movement that seems effortless. In contrast, in the poor outcome cases the dancing was jerky with many missteps as the participants tried to work together like amateurs beginning to learn the steps of a new dance or coordinate with the style of a new dance partner. A review of the poor outcome cases conveys a sense of struggle as therapists tried to dance in step with their clients. The therapists had a sense that they had not been able to align themselves with their clients' objectives or persuade them of the efficacy of their formulations. As a result, they felt helpless and often uncertain as to how to remedy the situation in the short term. The three therapists were all aware that things were not meshing with their clients. For their part, clients appeared hesitant to follow their therapists' lead at certain times. When this happened some therapists pulled back and tried to refocus their interventions to get back in step with their clients.

Both Hilary (see chap. 7, this volume) and Sean (see chap. 6, this volume) were reluctant to follow their therapists' suggestions. Hilary was angry and felt at the mercy of other people. She wanted other people to be different and worried that she would not be able to control the future or her mother's actions. She did not want to explore her emotional experience and had difficulty with chair work when she was asked to voice her critical thoughts because she felt that this would make her feel worse. Richard (see chap. 5, this volume) too questioned whether he was depressed as he expressed uncertainty about his therapist's formulation of his difficulties. The poor outcome clients' sense of hopelessness and resignation made it difficult for them to accept their therapists' formulations that getting in touch with their inner experiences and changing the ways in which they treated themselves would make any difference. Two of the therapists spoke about feeling that they cared more about their clients' pain than their clients did at times. One therapist said that she felt that it was like trying to convince a drowning man of the advantages of swimming to shore.

In the case of Hilary (see chap. 7, this volume), it seemed that at times she felt that her therapist did not understand how hard her current job situation was and how demeaned she felt in her current occupation. She expressed skepticism about the value of dealing with her feelings about her parents' actions toward her. Although, at the end of therapy she did express relief that she had managed to write a letter to her mother in which she was able to express her feelings to her. Richard (see chap. 5, this volume) too thought that he had to live with his feelings of depression. He could not imagine that he could be different, nor did he feel he deserved to be. Sean (see chap. 6, this volume) too initially expressed skepticism with therapy; however, as he began to see things differently and became more compassionate toward himself, he became more trusting and accepting. Each person's resignation made it difficult for him or her to agree to engage fully in the tasks of emotionally focused therapy. Although they said that they trusted their therapists to help them, they needed to be convinced that they could in fact overcome their depression without changing what had happened in the past or transforming other people in the past and present.

Social Support

Early in therapy it was clear that the poor outcome clients lacked adequate social support. Richard (see chap. 5, this volume) had casual acquaintances with whom he played tennis. He was able to engage with people intellectually; however, he too was emotionally withdrawn and did not reveal himself to anyone, not even his wife. Of the three, Hilary (see chap. 7, this volume) had the most social support because she belonged to a number of organizations and pursued several hobbies with enthusiasm, giving her an outlet from work and family conflict. However, it did not seem that she was able to call on these contacts for emotional support. Although she had a partner, she experienced him as disengaged, and she was estranged from her extended family, feeling that they had disowned her and left her to fend for herself while they enjoyed the benefits of money and status. Sean (see chap. 6, this volume) felt criticized and put down by his wife and betrayed by colleagues at work. However, he did have a good relationship with his son, who helped him see what he needed and how it could be provided.

CONCLUSION

A comparison of the six cases reveals a number of factors that contribute to positive and negative outcomes in brief emotion-focused therapy for depression. Some of these factors reflect different stages of development in clients with respect to their level of affect regulation, their stage of change, the formulation of their narratives, and their capacity to reflect on themselves. Clients who are aware of their feelings and able to label them are more able to respond quickly in an emotion-focused therapy in contrast to those clients who still need to develop the skills of attending to their inner experience and labeling it in words. On a similar note, those clients who are at the action stage of change enter therapy willing and able to respond to their therapists' suggestions, whereas those clients who are not fully convinced that therapy can be useful, or who are unsure of what is required of them, have a more difficult time using the tools that their therapists offer. These clients need more time to acquaint themselves with the nature of therapy and to determine its usefulness to their current life circumstances and difficulties.

In terms of clients' narratives, some clients are more readily able to focus on themselves and have developed coherent narratives of their life histories, whereas others have yet to engage in this task in a way that is useful in a therapeutic context and that will enable them to make good use of their therapists' interventions and suggestions. Given the important differences between clients with positive outcomes and those with negative outcomes, it seems important to think of ways of intervening that might be more useful to those clients who experience difficulty in achieving positive outcomes in brief emotion-focused therapy. In chapter 9 we will explore how emotion-focused therapists might work more effectively with clients experiencing some of the difficulties we have identified.

9

THERAPEUTIC STRATEGIES: GENERATING ALTERNATIVES

In keeping with the objectives of emotion-focused therapy (EFT) to identify markers that can guide therapeutic practice and lead to the successful resolution of specific client problems, the examination of the good and poor outcome cases provides a preliminary guide to how emotion-focused therapists might work with different clients at different stages in therapy. It is clear that not every client can benefit from a short-term treatment and, more important, that not every client enters therapy at the same stage of change or with the same emotional processing capacities or quality of narrative. In this chapter, we suggest some ways that emotion-focused therapists might work with clients who are having difficulty establishing goals; providing vivid, detailed narratives; or engaging in exploration of their feelings.

Moment-by-moment responding has been emphasized in EFT to develop formulations and guide therapeutic interventions (Elliott, Watson, Goldman, & Greenberg, 2003; Greenberg, Rice, & Elliott, 1993; Greenberg & Watson, 2005). However, a review of the unsuccessful cases suggests that in addition to attending to their clients' moment-by-moment experiencing in the sessions, emotion-focused therapists may need to assess a number of other factors at the beginning of therapy and during treatment if their clients are experiencing difficulties engaging in the tasks of therapy. To respond to their clients' difficulties, emotion-focused therapists can assess the quality of clients' narratives, clients' manner of processing emotions, clients' capacity to focus on themselves, clients' access to positive introjects and adaptive emotions, and clients' sense of hopelessness and shame. Some clients may have deficits with all these tasks; others may have difficulty with only one or two.

DEVELOPING CLIENTS' NARRATIVES

A precondition of EFT is that clients present an overview or story of their lives to provide both themselves and their therapists with a context for their current difficulties. Narratives afford a sense of continuity and a framework for understanding events and experiences. Although emotion-focused therapists focus primarily on current difficulties, knowledge of a client's history provides a compass and guide to emotionally salient events and the possible sources of the client's emotion schemes. Narratives also give therapists a window into their clients' lives and inner worlds, enabling them to enter into their clients' experiences more empathically as they try to imagine the different scenarios that their clients have encountered. The capacity to generate pictures of a scene is an essential component of the experience of feeling empathic toward another (Greenberg & Ruchanski-Rosenberg, 2002).

Some clients come with clear and coherent narratives and are able to highlight the salient events to furnish their therapists with immediate entrée into their inner worlds. However, other clients may not yet have generated a story that provides themselves or their therapists with a clear sense of the significant events in their lives and the sources of relevant emotion schemes. In the absence of vivid, concrete, and clear narratives, emotion-focused therapists need to help clients generate a life story. This requires a safe relationship and the opportunity for clients to explore and share their memories of the events in their lives. To facilitate this, therapists need to be empathic and open to their clients' experiences so that they can formulate their life stories in a safe, unthreatening environment. An empathic, nonjudgmental, and congruent stance on the part of therapists communicates acceptance and valuing of clients and their experiences that therapists hope clients will internalize to facilitate changes in their behavior.

As they work with their clients, emotion-focused therapists can assess the quality of clients' narratives by asking themselves whether they have a sense of their clients' lives both past and present. They can consider whether they have adequate histories and whether their clients have shared lively, vivid anecdotes that give an inside view of their experiences at different times in emotionally salient ways. Another way therapists can assess this is to ask themselves whether they could play a movie of a client's life.

In the absence of clear narratives or events that help to illuminate clients' current difficulties, emotion-focused therapists may need to be especially active. At these times they may need to imagine themselves into the sparse details of their clients' lives to try to help the process unfold. This requires extreme sensitivity on the part of emotion-focused therapists as they tentatively try to conjecture what it might have been like for their clients on the basis of the minimal information they have. For example, in chapter 5 it might have been useful if Richard's therapist had taken more time to explore Richard's early memories before trying to engage in two-chair work and to focus on Richard's self-critical process. Getting a good overview of David's history over three sessions was very useful to David's therapist in chapter 2 and seemed important to him. In contrast, Richard did not share information voluntarily; moreover, when his therapist asked him what it was like growing up, he replied that it had been fine and that he did not know why he was so depressed. His therapist did not probe further at that point, respecting Richard's reluctance. However, it might have been helpful to explain to Richard that sharing some of the details would be useful to provide a picture and give his therapist a sense of his experiences prior to his entering therapy. It can often take time to convince clients that it will be useful to them to explain the details of their lives, especially if they are wary of confronting the pain, but it may be essential to facilitate a good outcome.

It was difficult to gain access to Richard's history because of his deep sense of shame. His therapist needed to pay more attention to these feelings to try to help him overcome them. However, it may have taken more time than was available in a short-term treatment for Richard to overcome his feelings of shame, to come to trust his therapist, and to be more accepting of his inner world. It is likely that in a relationship in which he felt respected, valued, and heard, he would have gained confidence and begun to trust that he was acceptable and that his experiences would not be dismissed or judged negatively. In this case his therapist would have had to work patiently with him to recall and describe his life prior to entering therapy. It would have been very important to explain the benefits of disclosing his experiences and to assure him that his therapist would respect his pace. On a similar note, Hilary and Sean might have benefited more from treatment if their therapists had paid more attention to their senses of shame.

As emotion-focused therapists work to build trust and establish a feeling of safety as well as communicate respect and empathy for clients' experiences, they can continue to gently probe for the details of their clients' lives to begin to build narratives. These narratives will provide a context and begin to assist clients to view their experiences from the outside so that they can reflect on them. To facilitate access to their clients' narratives and the details of their lives, emotion-focused therapists can ask clients when they began to feel a certain way or when they recalled feeling a certain way for the first time and then ask clients to describe what was going on for them at that time. Emotion-focused therapists can ask clients to describe the significant people in their lives, such as parents, spouses, siblings, friends, or partners. For example, it would have been useful to know what Richard's parents and siblings were like or to have Hilary describe her parents. In Hilary's case, the therapist had some sense of how she was treated by her parents, and this was true for Sean as well. However, with Richard it was a lot less clear. Emotion-focused therapists can also ask clients to provide details of their current lives, especially those connected to certain feelings, so that they can begin to intuit what life might be like for their clients. For example, Anna's therapist, trying to help Anna come to terms with her sisters' attitudes toward her, said, "So they sound quite judgmental in their attitudes, a little snobbish. Am I right?" After Anna agreed, her therapist was able to say, "I imagine you feel quite excluded and somehow overlooked by them." Anna agreed, saying that was exactly how she felt. This allowed her to express her feelings more clearly in an empty-chair task, and she was able to ask her sisters to accept her and not judge her so negatively because she had less money than they did.

To imagine themselves into their clients' worlds, emotion-focused therapists can also ask themselves what it might be like to be their clients or experience certain events. They can try to imagine living under various circumstances and ask themselves what might have led clients to treat themselves or deal with their emotional experiences in particular ways. These conjectures can then be offered to clients to determine whether they resonate with clients' current difficulties and ways of being in the world. For example, Hilary's therapist might have focused on her sense of being rejected and tried to conjecture what it was like to be passed around from person to person and school to school. Her therapist might have said, "It sounds as if there was nowhere warm and safe for you as you were continually bundled from one place to another. Is that what it felt like?" Here the therapist needs to ask the client to check with his or her bodily sense to determine whether this sense is accurate or not. If the client agrees, the therapist can ask the client what contributed to this sense. The therapist can then ask the client to describe what that was like for her. Once therapists and clients have built an understanding of those aspects of the clients' earlier experiences that have contributed to their current difficulties, they are in a better position to identify the triggers as well as the potential tasks that need to be worked on in therapy.

If clients have not yet had the opportunity to construct their life stories, it may be unrealistic to think that they can complete this task and resolve their depressions in 16 weeks. Often clients need time to develop a sense of safety, to feel a greater sense of entitlement to their own story, and to overcome any shame they may have about the events in their lives and their responses to those events. Another factor that can hinder clients from sharing their stories can be a fear about betraying significant others and breaking a family code "not to wash your dirty laundry in public." It is possible that Richard felt constrained not to betray his family. He seemed protective of his family, or alternatively, he may have been unaware of the events that were difficult for him and contributed to his sense that he should not burden others.

Emotion-focused therapists need to be aware when their clients are experiencing conflicts about self-disclosing because these may need to be resolved before clients can focus on their feelings of depression or other reasons that brought them to therapy. Therapists can suggest two-chair exercises to try to resolve the conflicts that clients might be experiencing about subjecting their own and other family members' experiences to scrutiny. All these tasks require that emotion-focused therapists be patient and sensitive as they work to build strong relationships with their clients from which clients can then draw support to develop the strength to help them change fundamental ways of being in the world.

DEVELOPING CLIENTS' EMOTIONAL PROCESSING SKILLS

Once clients and therapists have developed a story of the clients' past and current experience, they can begin to focus on the impact that various experiences have had on clients. If clients have access to their feelings, they will pepper their descriptions of their memories and the stories about their lives with their reactions to and feelings about those events (Klein, Mathieu-Coughlan, & Kiesler, 1986). They may talk about events and their functioning from an inner perspective, revealing their subjective perceptions, judgments, value frameworks, and feelings about their inner and outer worlds. When clients are in touch with their experiences in a session, often their voices break or change. Their voices become softer; the contours are more ragged (Rice & Kerr, 1986); and there may be signs of emotion in their faces that they do not verbalize explicitly. For example, their eyes may tear up; alternately, they may become overtly emotional in the session (Kennedy-Moore & Watson, 1999). Clients often provide information about their affective experience in tandem with exploring the events in their lives; however sometimes, as with the poor outcome clients in this book, clients may need to learn how to focus and attend to their bodily sensations and inner experiences and label them in words (Gendlin, 1996; Leijssen, 1998).

To assess clients' emotional processing, emotion-focused therapists can ask themselves whether clients refer to their feelings when they recount events. Therapists can attend to clients' vocal quality to determine whether they are in touch with their feelings. If clients are not in touch with their feelings, their voices will be rhythmical, chatty, and have the sense of telling a story with little sign of emotion or suggestion that they are actively turned inward searching for fresh ways to articulate their experiences (Rice & Kerr, 1986). Hilary, Richard, and Sean seldom betrayed signs of emotion. Their therapists had difficulty helping them to turn inward to explore their pain. All three clients would have benefited from their therapists' spending more time reflecting their feelings to help them become more aware of their inner experiences and label them in words. Helping their clients articulate their inner experiences would also have facilitated the clients' ability to see their experiences in new ways, to reflect on their feelings, and to develop a stronger sense of self. Richard and Hilary occasionally expressed sadness, but they quickly pulled away and became distant from their inner experiences.

To help clients become more aware of their feelings, emotion-focused therapists can ask their clients what they are feeling at various points to determine how easy it is for clients to report on their inner states. They can observe whether their clients are analytical and distant from their affective experiences (Leijssen, 1998; Toukmanian, 1986). When they are distant from their experiences, clients may make few references to their feelings and are likely to be more focused on their own and other people's behavior. They may also be adept at presenting other people's points of view but have great difficulty articulating or becoming aware of their own inner experiences. These clients often look to their therapists for direction and express difficulty knowing what they want. Therapists can assess whether their clients are aware of their feelings by asking themselves the following questions: Do clients show signs of incongruent emotion, such as smiling and laughing, while recounting painful events; do they invalidate and criticize themselves for feeling; and do they express fear and anxiety around their own and other people's expression of feeling? If the answers are affirmative, therapists may need to pay special attention to helping their clients become more aware of their inner experiences and develop a tolerance and an acceptance of those experiences. To better understand how clients treat their emotional experiences, therapists can also ask how emotion was expressed at home when clients were children, how it was received or responded to, and how their parents handled their own emotions. The answers to these questions will provide therapists with clues as to how their clients might be treating their own feelings and guides to where to focus their interventions.

Emotion-focused therapists can use empathic response modes and focusing predominantly if clients are having difficulty becoming aware of and labeling their experiences (Bohart, Elliott, Greenberg, & Watson, 2002; Elliott et al., 2003; Greenberg, Rice, & Elliott, 1993). Hilary's experience, in chapter 7, suggests that it would have been helpful to spend more time exploring and learning about her childhood and how she had experienced the events in her life. In retrospect, Hilary needed to grieve her losses and to hold her parents accountable for having failed her before she could move on to develop ways of treating herself that were more self-enhancing. Hilary was also grieving the loss of her career. It might have been useful for her therapist to help her process her sense of defeat and despair at being rejected and pushed out once again. Instead, following the research protocol, her therapist tried to focus on overcoming her depression using two-chair and empty-chair work. However, Hilary was not quite ready to engage in those tasks because she did not have access to positive introjects and was not yet able to see how changing herself would be beneficial. Hilary may have benefited from a longer period of empathic listening and exploration as well as empty-chair work around her parents' neglect of her and the loss of her career.

In addition to assisting clients to become more aware of their inner experiences, therapists who are empathic can use clients' life histories to imagine how clients might respond in different situations and to understand what triggers certain reactions. Therapists can acquire a sense of their clients' goals and objectives in therapy specifically and in their lives more generally. Emotion-focused therapists can use their background knowledge derived from clients' histories and the anecdotes they have shared about their lives to formulate conjectural empathic responses about clients' emotion schemes regarding current situations that they are having difficulty articulating or expressing. For example, Hilary's therapist might have said,

> From what you have told me about your mother, it seems she was so angry and trapped after you were born that I imagine it might have been hard for her to respond to you in the way that you needed her to do. So you became very independent and tried to meet your own needs. Does this fit for you?

This is a highly conjectural response, but it is an attempt to frame Hilary's experience and to provide a view and framework to understand how she might be behaving in the present. For example, Hilary might have been experiencing a lot of shame around her needs, given they made her mother so angry. Thus she would need support to be able to see her needs as valid and natural in spite of her mother's reaction. It is very important with conjectural responses to have clients check with their bodily responses to determine whether the view fits. If there is any doubt, the emotion-focused therapist should let the conjecture go and try to help the client represent his or her experience in a manner that fits better or move on to representing other aspects of the client's experience.

BUILDING POSITIVE INTROJECTS AND ADAPTIVE EMOTIONAL EXPERIENCE

A lack of positive ways of treating the self is a significant deficit that needs to be addressed before clients can successfully resolve some of the tasks of EFT. An underlying presumption in two-chair and empty-chair work is that clients are sufficiently resilient, have a sufficiently well-developed sense of self, and have access to positive emotions and ways of treating themselves. However, this is not always the case. Some clients do not have access to positive introjects or ways of treating themselves because either they never experienced validation, nurturing, caring, and protection of significant care-takers or they do not see themselves as deserving of validation or compassion. In some cases clients may need to develop a stronger sense of self or develop accepting and nurturing ways of treating themselves before they can challenge the critic, assert their needs and wants, and reassure and soothe themselves in times of distress. For example, to set boundaries with internalized critics or significant others, clients may need to be self-assertive and able to stand up for themselves; they also need to be able to experience compassion for themselves and feel that they deserve it. All three of the poor outcome clients needed help to acquire more positive introjects.

Emotion-focused therapists need to assess whether clients have access to resilient self-responses and positive introjects and, if so, whether they are able to access their adaptive emotions and be self-caring and supportive. Two-chair and empty-chair tasks can be used as diagnostic indicators of whether clients have resilient self-responses and positive introjects and are able to treat themselves in accepting, loving, and protective ways. If clients are unable to access adaptive emotions and respond to themselves in positive ways during these tasks, this is a good indicator to therapists that more empathic relational work and self-compassion and self-soothing work are needed to help clients acquire or strengthen their positive introjects and develop more adaptive behaviors.

Emotion-focused therapists can use empathic responses and provide an accepting, prizing, and nonjudgmental relationship for their clients to help them build internal working models of how to treat themselves in more positive ways. Therapists' acceptance of their clients' experiences teaches clients to be more accepting of their inner experiences and their emotions. This allows clients to explore their emotional experiences and understand them so that they can see their needs and transform their emotion schemes so as to overcome their feelings of depression. Positive therapeutic relationships also provide an antidote to clients' feelings of shame and can engender hope as clients begin to feel valued and supported. Therapeutic empathy, acceptance, and concern are essential to strengthen clients' positive introjects or lay the groundwork to develop them if they have not formed as a result of clients' relationships with others outside of therapy (Elliott et al., 2003; Greenberg et al., 1993; Rogers, 1965; Steckley & Watson, 2005; Watson, 2001).

In chapter 5 Richard did not feel he deserved to treat himself kindly or with compassion so was unable to stop bullying and oppressing himself. His therapist needed to provide him with a supportive, accepting, empathic, and prizing relationship to help him build a positive introject and develop alternative ways of treating himself. Some clients may need to learn to value themselves and see themselves as deserving before they can be more compassionate, less self-critical, and less oppressive in their treatment of themselves. In the absence of positive introjects it is unlikely that clients will be able to make use of a short-term treatment. Clients usually need a longer term of therapy to build positive introjects that they can then use to counteract negative behaviors.

Clients can develop more resilient and stronger senses of self by building a larger repertoire of positive behaviors or more positive introjects. With more positive introjects they will be more able to protect themselves and engage in nurturing and benevolent behaviors to enhance their well-being, instead of neglecting and oppressing themselves. Self-soothing dialogues in two chairs in which the client is encouraged in different ways to develop compassion for the self are also helpful (Greenberg & Malcolm, 2002; Greenberg & Watson, 2005). Once clients have developed more resilient and stronger senses of self, they can then begin to engage in two-chair tasks and unfinished-business work to help increase awareness of what they are doing to themselves. They can then work with their therapists to develop alternative behaviors and ways of treating themselves.

DEVELOPING A SELF-FOCUS

Emotion-focused therapists need to assess whether their clients are self-focused and reflecting on their experiences to explore them in purposeful ways that will likely facilitate a shift in perception, mood, or behavior. Therapists can ask themselves whether their clients are posing questions about their behavior and trying to understand its origins and their own specific ways of behaving. If clients do not naturally engage in reflection and do not assume an agentic stance in therapy (Bohart & Tallman, 1999), emotion-focused therapists can work to encourage and develop these behaviors. Systematic evocative unfolding and the identification of problematic reaction points can help clients develop a self-focus (Rice & Saperia, 1984; Watson & Greenberg, 1996). By helping clients become aware of and identify reactions that they experience and see as problematic, therapists can enhance clients' awareness of how they behave and stimulate them to reflect on their ways of reacting and being in the present to identify personal styles of being that may be ineffective or inappropriate in their current context. Emotion-focused therapists can encourage a self-focus by suggesting homework exercises that ask clients to observe their behavior over the week between therapy appointments and watch for times when they consider their reactions to be puzzling in some way (Rice & Saperia, 1984; Watson & Rennie, 1994). Perhaps the reaction may seem incommensurate with a situation, for example, feeling rage at someone pushing in line at the grocery store or perhaps a client may regard a reaction as silly or bizarre.

Therapists can encourage their clients to adopt a questioning stance toward their experiences and to observe themselves and judge whether their own behavior is problematic in some way. The identification of problematic reactions facilitates clients' becoming more distant from their experiences and looking at themselves from the outside instead of being overwhelmed by intense emotion or being overly rational and disengaged. By having clients attend to their behavior, emotion-focused therapists are encouraging them to question their behavior and to focus on themselves and not what others are doing. This is a radical shift that can help clients move into an action phase of therapy, which is important if EFT is to be successful. Both Hilary and Richard might have benefited from their therapists' suggesting a homework exercise to observe their behavior to see if that might have helped them to reflect on and view their behavior differently.

Another way that emotion-focused therapists can help clients develop a self-focus is to attend to the moment-by-moment markers and to try to help clients formulate their experiences in terms of specific cognitive–affective problems such as conflict splits and unfinished business (Elliott et al., 2003; Greenberg & Watson, 2005; Paivio & Greenberg, 1995). These tasks can focus clients and make them more aware of how they are processing their experiences and treating themselves and can stimulate them to be more aware of and search for alternatives.

OVERCOMING SHAME AND HOPELESSNESS

If clients are to overcome their feelings of depression, it is important that emotion-focused therapists help their clients overcome their negative feelings of shame and hopelessness and instill hope that things can be different and a belief that they are deserving and worthwhile. Some of this remoralization will occur with the support of an empathic, healing relationship. One of the important features of empathy is that it contributes to helping clients feel stronger and more in control. The shift from a focus on others to a focus on self is also an important aspect of getting clients to become more agentic. As clients begin to focus on their own behavior, there is a greater sense of control and less of a sense that they are at the mercy of other people's whims. The support that clients receive from their therapists also helps to moderate clients' moods, which can contribute to their feeling less hopeless and more able to act in the world in a way that will be more satisfying. As they begin to observe their behavior and the events in their lives, clients also acquire new perspectives and greater distance from what is happening so that they may feel less overwhelmed by their problems (Rime, Finkenhauer, Luminet, Zech, & Philipott, 1998; Rogers, 1965; Watson & Rennie, 1994). In addition, experiencing the other as empathic, accepting, and nonjudgmental can help clients reveal themselves and overcome their sense of shame (Rogers, 1965).

Other ways that therapists can help clients overcome their sense of hopelessness and shame is by encouraging them to access their unacknowledged adaptive feelings of anger or sadness. Helping clients to access adaptive emotions is a key to overcoming hopelessness, as is encouraging them to become aware of their problems and how they are dealing with things. They can observe that clients seem ambivalent about change and explore this with them. Often the ambivalence may reflect feelings of hopelessness or shame that need to be overcome before clients can deal effectively with the issues for which they sought therapy. Changing these negative feelings requires relational and exploratory work with therapists actively and deliberately working to build therapeutic relationships using primarily empathic response modes as well as some didactic teaching (Elliott et al., 2003). For example, Hilary's therapist might have reflected Hilary's ambivalence and observed that she tended to silence herself and was having difficulty opening up. Therapists can ask their clients how come they are silencing themselves and try to explore what is going on with their client to see if it can be resolved. Two-chair work can be used to help clients explore the internal conflict between the side that wants to be in therapy and the side that is reluctant to help resolve ambivalence about the therapeutic process.

The poor outcome clients were only beginning to trust their therapists and see how therapy might be useful, though they still felt quite ashamed of their feelings and reactions. In chapter 6 Sean's depression remitted, but he relapsed soon after the end of treatment. It is likely that he needed more time to consolidate his changes so that he would be able to maintain them in the face of setbacks. Richard, in chapter 5, was beginning to think that therapy might be useful and expressed a desire to continue in treatment. His therapist, thinking that he might respond to a different treatment, referred him to another treatment program. Like the others, Hilary, in chapter 7, was beginning to make changes but these were just sprouting and needed more time to take root and flourish in order that she might overcome her sense of depression. She was beginning to overcome her sense of shame and was able to write a letter to her mother expressing how she felt. Both Hilary and Richard were just beginning to formulate their problems in a self-focused manner and move from trying to change others to adopting a more internal perspective that would have helped them change the ways in which they treated themselves.

ASSESSING CLIENTS' STAGE OF CHANGE

When clients are having difficulty resolving issues in therapy, emotion-focused therapists can assess their clients' stage of change. It is important to remember that the clients reviewed in this book all reported positive alliances. However, a review of the transcripts revealed that therapists and clients were not in step. At these times emotion-focused therapists may need to assess their clients' stage of change (Prochaska, DiClemente, & Norcross,

1992; Prochaska & Norcross, 2002). Two of the poor outcome clients, Richard and Hilary, were moving from a precontemplation stage to a stage of contemplating therapy, and Sean was in the contemplation stage of change. Clients who are at the early stages of change are unlikely to benefit from short-term therapy. Clients in the precontemplation and contemplation stages of therapy might benefit from some preparation or introduction to the nature of therapy so that they can get a sense of what they need to do to use the experience optimally.

CONCLUSION

In the future it will be important to assess whether clients are ready and have the capacity to engage in a brief treatment. On the basis of the differences that have been identified in this book, it will be important to try to develop measures that will be able to identify clients who will benefit from short-term treatments and those who will require longer term therapy or alternative interventions to successfully overcome their depression. All three poor outcome clients needed time to develop a commitment to and belief in the therapeutic process; work through their shame; develop a coherent narrative to contextualize their pain; develop a self-focus; learn to attend to and label their feelings; develop more positive introjects and access adaptive feelings so that they could respond to themselves in accepting, loving, and self-enhancing ways; and learn to reflect on their emotional experiences to solve their problems in living and create more satisfying interpersonal relationships. These tasks are essential ingredients for the successful resolution of clients' depressions in an emotion-focused treatment and may be difficult to develop sufficiently to ensure positive, long-term change in short-term therapy protocols such as these clients received. They are tasks that require time, patience, and commitment on the part of both clients and therapists as they both learn to dance together to help clients develop new ways of relating to themselves and others.

REFERENCES

Bachman, J., & O'Malley, P. (1977). Self-esteem in young men: A longitudinal analysis of the impact of educational and occupational attainment. *Journal of Personality and Social Psychology, 35,* 365–380.

Beck, A. T., Rush, A. J., Shaw, B. F., & Emery, G. (1979). *Cognitive therapy of depression.* New York: Guilford Press.

Beck, A. T., Steer, R. A., & Garbin, M. G. (1988). Psychometric properties of the Beck Depression Inventory: Twenty-five years of evaluation. *Clinical Psychology Review, 8,* 77–100.

Beck, A. T., Ward, C. H., Mendelson, M., Mock, J., & Erbaugh, J. (1961). An inventory for measuring depression. *Archives of General Psychiatry, 4,* 561–571.

Benjamin, L. S. (1974). Structural analysis of social behavior. *Psychological Review, 81,* 392–425.

Benjamin, L. S., Foster, S. W., Roberto, L. G., & Estroff, S. E. (1986). Breaking the family code: Analysis of videotapes of family interactions by Structural Analysis of Social Behaviour (SASB). In L. S. Greenberg & W. Pinsof (Eds.), *The psychotherapeutic process: A research handbook* (pp. 391–438). New York: Guilford Press.

Bohart, A. C., Elliott, R., Greenberg, L. S., & Watson, J. C. (2002). Empathy. In J. C. Norcross (Ed.), *Psychotherapy relationships that work: Therapist contributions and responsiveness to patients* (pp. 89–108). New York: Oxford University Press.

Bohart, A. C., & Tallman, K. (1999). *How clients make therapy work: The process of active self-healing.* Washington, DC: American Psychological Association.

Derogatis, D. L. (1983). *SCL–90–R administration, scoring, and procedures manual—II.* Boston: Psychometrics Research.

Derogatis, L. R., Rickels, K., & Roch, A. F. (1976). The SCL–90 and the MMPI: A step in the validation of a new self-report scale. *British Journal of Psychiatry, 128,* 280–289.

Elliott, R., Watson, J. C., Goldman, R., & Greenberg, L. (2003). *Learning emotion-focused psychotherapy: The process-experiential approach to change.* Washington, DC: American Psychological Association.

Foa, E. B., & Kozak, M. J. (1986). Emotional processing of fear: Exposure to corrective information. *Psychological Bulletin, 99,* 20–35.

Freud, S. (1977). *Case histories: Dora and little Hans* (A. Richards, Ed.). Harmondsworth, England: Penguin Books. (Original work published 1901)

Gendlin, E. T. (1996). *Focusing-oriented psychotherapy: A manual of the experiential method.* New York: Guilford Press.

Goldman, R. N., Greenberg, L. S., & Angus, L. (2005). The effects of adding specific emotion-focused interventions to the therapeutic relationship in the treatment of depression. *Psychotherapy Research, 15,* 248–260.

Greenberg, L. S., Elliott, R. K., & Foerster, F. S. (1990). Experiential processes in the psychotherapeutic treatment of depression. In C. D. McCann & N. S. Endler (Eds.), *Depression: New directions in theory, research and practice* (pp. 157–185). Toronto, Ontario, Canada: Wall & Emerson.

Greenberg, L. S., & Foerster, F. S. (1996). Resolving unfinished business: The process of change. *Journal of Consulting and Clinical Psychology, 64*, 439–446.

Greenberg, L. S., & Malcolm, W. (2002). Resolving unfinished business: Relating process to outcome. *Journal of Consulting and Clinical Psychology, 70*, 406–416.

Greenberg, L. S., & Paivio, S. C. (1997). *Working with emotions in psychotherapy.* New York: Guilford Press.

Greenberg, L. S., & Pascual-Leone, J. (1995). A dialectical constructivist approach to experiential change. In R. A. Neimeyer & M. J. Mahoney (Eds.), *Constructivism in psychotherapy* (pp. 169–191). Washington, DC: American Psychological Association.

Greenberg, L. S., & Pascual-Leone, J. (2001). A dialectical constructivist view of the construction of personal meaning. *Journal of Constructivist Psychology, 14,* 165–186.

Greenberg, L. S., & Pedersen, R. (2001, November). *Relating the degree of resolution of in-session self-criticism and dependence to outcome and follow-up in the treatment of depression.* Paper presented at the meeting of the North American Chapter of the International Society for Psychotherapy Research, Puerta Vallarta, Mexico.

Greenberg, L. S., Rice, L. N., & Elliott, R. (1993). *Facilitating emotional change: The moment-by-moment process.* New York: Guilford Press.

Greenberg, L. S., & Ruchanski-Rosenberg, R. (2002). Therapists' experience of empathy. In J. C. Watson, R. N. Goldman, & M. S. Warner (Eds.), *Client-centered and experiential psychotherapy in the 21st century: Advances in theory, research and practice* (pp. 204–220). Ross-on-Wye, England: PCCS Books.

Greenberg, L. S., & Watson, J. C. (1998). Experiential therapy of depression: Differential effects of client-centered relationship conditions and process-experiential interventions. *Psychotherapy Research, 8,* 210–224.

Greenberg, L. S., & Watson, J. C. (2005). *Emotion-focused therapy for depression.* Washington, DC: American Psychological Association.

Horowitz, L. M., Rosenberg, S. E., Baer, B. A., Ureno, G., & Villasenor, V. S. (1988). Inventory of interpersonal problems: Psychometric properties and clinical application. *Journal of Consulting and Clinical Psychology, 56,* 885–892.

Horvath, A. O., & Greenberg, L. S. (1989). Development and validation of the Working Alliance Inventory. *Journal of Counseling Psychology, 36,* 223–233.

Horvath, A. O., & Symonds, B. D. (1991). Relation between working alliance and outcome in psychotherapy: A meta-analysis. *Journal of Couseling Psychology, 38,* 139–149.

Kennedy-Moore, E., & Watson, J. C. (1999). *Expressing emotion: Myths, realities, and therapeutic strategies.* New York: Guilford Press.

Klein, M. H., Mathieu, P. L., Gendlin, E. T., & Kiesler, D. J. (1969). *The Experiencing Scale: A research and training manual.* Madison: Wisconsin Psychiatric Institute.

Klein, M. H., Mathieu-Coughlan, P., & Kiesler, D. J. (1986). The Experiencing Scales. In L. S. Greenberg & W. Pinsof (Eds.), *The psychotherapeutic process: A research handbook* (pp. 21–71). New York: Guilford Press.

Kuiper, N. A., & Olinger, L. J. (1989). Stress and cognitive vulnerability for depression: A self-worth contingency model. In R. W. J. Neufeld (Ed.), *Advances in the investigation of psychological stress* (pp. 367–391). New York: Wiley.

Lambert, M. J., Barley, D. E. (2002). Research summary on the therapeutic relationship and psychotherapy outcome. In J. C. Norcross (Ed.), *Psychotherapy relationships that work: Therapist contributions and responsiveness to patients* (pp. 17–37). New York: Oxford University Press.

Lambert, M. J., & Bergin, A. E. (1994). The effectiveness of psychotherapy. In A. E. Bergin & S. L. Garfield (Eds.), *The handbook of psychotherapy and behavior change* (pp. 143–189). New York: Wiley.

Lane, R. D., & Schwartz, G. E. (1992). Levels of emotional awareness: Implications for psychotherapy integration. *Journal of Psychotherapy Integration, 2*, 1–18.

Leijssen, M. (1998). Focusing microprocesses. In L. Greenberg, J. Watson, & G. Lietaer (Eds.), *Handbook of experiential psychotherapy* (pp. 121–154). New York: Guilford Press.

McGough, J., & Curry, J. F. (1992). Utility of the SCL–90–R with depressed and conduct-disordered adolescent inpatients. *Journal of Personality Assessment, 59*, 552–563.

Norcross, J. C. (2002). Empirically supported therapy relationships. In J. C. Norcross (Ed.), *Psychotherapy relationships that work: Therapist contributions and responsiveness to patients* (pp. 3–16). New York: Oxford University Press.

Orlinsky, D., Grawe, K., & Parks, B. K. (1994). Process and outcome in psychotherapy. In A. Bergin & S. Garfield (Eds.), *Handbook of psychotherapy and behavior change*. New York: Wiley.

Paivio, S. C., & Greenberg, L. S. (1995). Resolving "unfinished business": Efficacy of experiential therapy using empty-chair dialogue. *Journal of Consulting and Clinical Psychology, 63*, 419–425.

Pos, A. E., Greenberg, L. S., Goldman, R., & Korman, L. (2003). Emotional processing during experiential treatment of depression. *Journal of Consulting and Clinical Psychology, 71*, 1007–1016.

Prochaska, J. O., DiClemente, C. C., & Norcross, J. C. (1992). In search of how people change: Application to addictive behavior. *American Psychologist, 47*, 1102–1114.

Prochaska, J. O., & Norcross, J. C. (2002). Stages of change. In J. C. Norcross (Ed.), *Psychotherapy relationships that work: Therapist contributions and responsiveness to patients* (pp. 303–314). New York: Oxford University Press.

Rice, L. N., & Greenberg, L. S. (1984). *Patterns of change.* New York: Guilford Press.

Rice, L. N., & Kerr, G. P. (1986). Measures of client and therapist vocal quality. In L. S. Greenberg & W. Pinsof (Eds.), *The psychotherapeutic process: A research handbook* (pp. 73–105). New York: Guilford Press.

Rice, L. N., & Saperia, E. P. (1984). Task analysis and the resolution of problematic reactions. In L. N. Rice & L. S. Greenberg (Eds.), *Patterns of change* (pp. 29–66). New York: Guilford Press.

Rime, B., Finkenhauer, C., Luminet, O., Zech, E., & Philipott, P. (1998). Social sharing of emotion: New evidence and new questions. In W. Stroebe & M. Hewstone (Eds.), *European review of social psychology* (Vol. 9, pp. 225–258). Chichester, England: Wiley.

Rogers, C. R. (1965). *Client-centered therapy: Its current practice, implications and theory.* Boston: Houghton Mifflin.

Rosenberg, M. (1965). *Society and the adolescent self-image.* Princeton, NJ: Princeton University Press.

Safran, J. D., Muran, C. J., Samstag, L. W., & Stevens, C. (2002). Repairing alliance ruptures. In J. C. Norcross (Ed.), *Psychotherapy relationships that work: Therapist contributions and responsiveness to patients* (pp. 235–254). New York: Oxford University Press.

Salovey, P., Hsee, C. K., & Mayer, J. D. (1993). Emotional intelligence and the self-regulation of affect. In D. M. Wegnerr & J. W. Pennebaker (Eds.), *Handbook of mental control* (pp. 258–277). Englewood Cliffs, NJ: Prentice Hall.

Samilov, A., & Goldfried, M. R. (2000). Role of emotion in cognitive–behavior therapy. *Clinical Psychology: Science & Practice, 7,* 373–385.

Schmitz, N., Kruse, J., Heckrath, C., Alberti, L., & Tress, W. (1999). Diagnosing mental disorders in primary care: The General Health Questionnaire (GHQ) and the Symptom Check List (SCL–90–R) as screening instruments. *Social Psychiatry and Psychiatric Epidemiology, 34,* 360–366.

Smith, T. (1996, July). *Severe life stress: Major depression and emotion-related negative memory.* Paper presented at the meeting of the International Society for Research on Emotions, Toronto, Ontario, Canada.

Steckley, P., & Watson, J. C. (June, 2005). *An examination of the relationship between clients' attachment experiences, their internal working models of self and others, and therapists' empathy in the outcome of process-experiential and cognitive–behaviour therapies.* Paper presented at the 35th Annual Meeting of the International Society for Psychotherapy Research, Montreal, Quebec, Canada.

Stricker, G., & Gold, J. (Eds.). (2006). *A casebook of psychotherapy integration.* Washington, DC: American Psychological Association.

Toukmanian, S. G. (1986). A measure of client perceptual processing. In L. S. Greenberg & W. M. Pinsof (Eds.), *The psychotherapeutic process: A research handbook* (pp. 107–130). New York: Guilford Press.

Watson, J. C. (2001). Revisioning empathy: Theory, research, and practice. In D. Cain & J. Seeman (Eds.), *Handbook of research and practice in humanistic psychotherapies* (pp. 445–473). Washington, DC: American Psychological Association.

Watson, J. C. (2006). Resolving trauma in process-experiential therapy. In G. Stricker & J. Gold (Eds.), *A casebook of psychotherapy integration* (pp. 89–106). Washington, DC: American Psychological Association.

Watson, J. C., & Bedard, D. (2006). Clients' emotional processing in psychotherapy: A comparison between cognitive–behavioral and process-experiential psychotherapy. *Journal of Consulting and Clinical Psychology, 74*, 152–159.

Watson, J. C., Gordon, L. B., Stermac, L., Kalogerakos, F., & Steckley, P. (2003). Comparing the effectiveness of process-experiential with cognitive–behavioral psychotherapy in the treatment of depression. *Journal of Consulting and Clinical Psychology, 71*, 773–781.

Watson, J. C., & Greenberg, L. S. (1994). The working alliance in experiential therapy: Exacting the relationship conditions. In A. Horvath & L. S. Greenberg (Eds.), *The working alliance: Theory, research and practice* (pp. 153–172). New York: Wiley.

Watson, J. C., & Greenberg, L. S. (1996). Emotion and cognition in experiential therapy: A dialectical-constructivist position. In H. Rosen & K. Kuelwein (Eds.), *Constructing realities: Meaning-making perspectives for psychotherapists* (pp. 253–276). San Francisco: Jossey-Bass

Watson, J. C., Greenberg, L. S., Rice, L. N., & Gordon, L. B. (1996). *Client task specific change measure—Revised.* Unpublished self-report measure of postsession change, Department of Adult Education and Counselling Psychology, Ontario Institute for Studies in Education, University of Toronto, Toronto, Ontario, Canada.

Watson, J. C., & Rennie, D. (1994). A qualitative analysis of clients' reports of their subjective experience while exploring problematic reactions in therapy. *Journal of Counseling Psychology, 41*, 500–509.

Weissman, A. N., & Beck, A. T. (1978). *Development and validation of the Dysfunctional Attitudes Scale: A preliminary investigation.* Paper presented at the 86th Annual Convention of the American Psychological Association, Toronto, Ontario, Canada.

Yalom, I. (1989). *Love's executioner and other tales of psychotherapy.* New York: Basic Books.

INDEX

Dysfunctional Attitude Scale, 20

Early environment. *See* Environment, early
Emotional processing, 6, 187
    accessing through empathic responses, 210–211
    assessment of, 209–210
    development of skills for, 209–211
    of good outcome clients, 54–55, 187, 189
    in Hilary case, 210–211
    of poor outcome clients, 134, 138, 179, 180, 186–189
Emotion-focused therapy
    bodily felt experience in awareness and processing of, 6
    brief vs. need for longer time, 215
    case formulation in, 11–15
    case studies protocol, 15–24
    client factors in successful treatment, 5
    client markers in, 12–13
    effectiveness of, 3
    emotion schemes in, 5
    empathic responses in, 10
    examination of unsuccessful cases, 4–5
    objectives of case history presentations, 4–5
    overview of tasks–client objectives match, 4
    phases of treatment in, 11, 13–15
    principles of, 6–11
    regulation of emotional arousal in, 5
    relationship components in, 7–8
    steps in processing emotional experience in, 6, 187
    task components in, 8–11
Emotion schemes, defined, 5
Empathic relationship
    collaboration on tasks and goals of therapy in, 7–8
    creation of safe environment in, 7
    moment-to-moment attunement to client in, 7
Empty-chair work
    indication for, 8
    purpose of, 8
Environment, early
    common factors in good and poor outcomes, 184
    good outcome clients, 184, 185
    poor outcome clients, 185
Evocation, empathic, 10

Evoking and exploring
    in case formulation, 11, 14
Experiencing Scale
    stages of, 16–17
    use of, 17
Exploration, empathic, 10

Fear
    anger and, 138, 143
    of change, 78
    as core emotion, 140
    of emotion, 140
    as enemy, 80
    of failure, 152–154
        focus on bodily feeling of, 152–154
    of loss, 108
    of mother, 46, 47–49
    realization of mother's, 49
    of sadness, 156
Focusing
    indication for, 9

Gayle: generating new emotional responses
    bad mother concern in, 55, 56
    bonding and awareness in, 55–56
    case formulation
        anger toward parents, 54
        emotional processing in, 54–55
        maladaptive emotion scheme, 55
        negative self-image in, 54
        negative view of others in, 54
    core emotion scheme, loneliness and sense of not belonging, 61, 62–63
    diagnosis in, 54
    early environment, 53–54, 184
    empty-chair work
        to release anger and disappointment with parents, 79–80
    evoking and exploring feelings in, 56–69
        anger toward father, 59–60
        anger toward mother, 57–58
        boundary with mother, 62
        core sense of invalidation, 68
        empty-chair dialogues with mother, 56–59, 61–62
        empty-chair dialogue with father, 59–60
        focus on sexual abuse and effect on relationships, 64–65
        impact of mother's behavior, 58–69

movement from anger to assertion
of needs, 63, 65
need for acceptance for who she is,
69
need for approval from others, 66,
67–68
relationship with brother, 65
role play of mother, 58–59
self-judgment by external standards,
58, 59
generation of new emotional responses
in, 70–81
anger toward inner critic, 78
assertion of needs and limit setting
with self-critic, 72–73
emotion in relation to family relationships, 79
fear of trusting change, 78
freedom from fear, 81
guilt for being victim of sexual abuse,
73
limitation on self-abusive behavior,
75
recognition of fear as biggest enemy,
80
seeking and getting support from
others than her mother, 80
self-assertion following liposuction,
78
two-chair dialogue with internal
critic and reaction to it, 70–72
work with critical inner voice, 80
maladaptive eating in, 54, 56
mother in
anger toward, 57–58
boundary setting with, 62–63, 80
differentiation from, 63
disapproval of, and awareness of impact, 66–67
holding accountable for failure to
protect, 75–77
need for forgiveness of sexual abuse,
73–75
role play of, 58–59
unfinished business with, 56
need for approval, 54, 56
sexual abuse as child, 55
stressors in, 53
summary of relationship problems and
expression of feelings, 22
Good outcome clients. *See also* Poor outcome
clients

affect regulation in, 187, 189
early environments of, 184, 185
factors in, 189–190
interpersonal factors, 194–195
social support, 196
working alliance, 195
intrapersonal factors in
ability to shift perspective, 193–194
action orientation, 190–191
adaptive emotions, 192–193
aspirations and goals, 194
cognitive flexibility, 193–194
positive introjects, 192–193
self-disclosure, 191
self-focus, 191–192

Hilary: disparate therapeutic goals
analysis
avoidant style of emotional processing, 179, 180
internal vs. external factors as source
of problems, 179
money vs. feelings of low self-esteem,
178
no change in self-esteem, 179
participation in tasks of therapy, 179
bonding and awareness in, 164
empty chair work for rejection by
mother, 164–165
focus on self-critical process, 165
goal to make peace with past, 165
case formulation
core emotion, feeling unloved and
shame, 164
negative sense of self-worth, 163
unfinished business with father,
162–163
unresolved issues with mother, 162,
163
diagnosis, 162
early environment, 162, 185
evoking and exploring in
anger toward father, 165–166
anger toward parents, 170–171
father's visit before he died, 168–169
inability to be forgiving or understanding of self or others, 174–
175
movement from external standards,
174
neglect and rejection by parents,
169–170

neglect of herself and her needs, 170
recognition of emotional implications of parents' behavior toward her, 176–177
rejection by mother and letting go of hope for change, 177–178
relationships with other family members, 167
resentment toward father, 174
resignation about relationship with mother, 167–168
sense of failure and inadequacy in self-critical dialogue, 171–173
speaking from father's perspective in, 167, 168
father in
anger toward, 165–166
letting go of, 175–176
resentment toward, 174
taking his perspective, 167–168
unfinished business with, 162–163
visit before he died, 168–169
financial concerns and, 162
mother in
letting go of hope for change, 177–178
rejection by, empty chair work for, 164–165, 177–178
resignation about relationship with, 167–168
unresolved issues with, 162, 163
summary of resolving parental rejection and neglect, 23
Hopelessness
Anna's, 84
Hilary's, 169–170
overcoming through adaptive emotions, 215

Introjects. *See* Positive introjects
Inventory of Interpersonal Problems, 20

Levels of Client Perceptual Processing (LCPP)
levels in, 17–18
utility of, 17

Narratives
assessment of, 206
betrayal of family and significant others and, 208–209
as context, 206, 207

development of, 206–209
lack of, Richard, 133–134
of poor outcome clients, 133–134, 197
shame and, 207, 208
therapist imagining into, 207, 208

Outcome measures, 19–20

Poor outcome clients, 196–197
affect regulation in
capacity to modulate arousal, 188
inability to reflect on feelings, 189
lack of awareness and labeling of feelings in, 186–188
reluctance to explore and share feelings, 188
early environments of, 185
interpersonal factors in, 200
social support, 202
working alliance, 201–202
intrapersonal factors in
absence of self-focus, 198
hopelessness and resignation, 199–200
impoverished narratives, 133–134, 197
lack of adaptive emotions, 198–199
lack of positive introjects, 198–199
shame, 198
stage of change, 200
Positive introjects
assessment of client access to, 211–212
building, 211–213
empathic responses in building of, 212
in good outcome clients, 192–193
lack of, in poor outcome clients, 198–199
Richard and, 212
self-soothing dialogues for, 213
Postsession measures, 19
Process measures
Experiencing Scale, 16–17
Levels of Client Perceptual Processing, 17–18
Structural Analysis of Social Behavior, 18

Refocusing, empathic, 10
Resignation
Hilary's, 167–168
in poor outcome clients, 199–200
Richard: bonding inhibited

ABOUT THE AUTHORS

Jeanne C. Watson, PhD, is an associate professor in the Department of Adult Education and Counselling Psychology at the University of Toronto, Ontario, Canada. She did her graduate training in client-centered therapy and studied psychotherapy processes and outcomes with Laura Rice at Toronto's York University. Her experience with Dr. Rice impressed on her the power of being attuned to clients' moment-to-moment experiencing and the need to understand each client's unique perspective. Subsequently, she worked with Leslie S. Greenberg to integrate gestalt approaches and began to develop more fully as an emotion-focused therapist in her work with both individuals and couples. Dr. Watson continues to do research on the processes and outcomes in emotion-focused therapy and has written extensively on empathy, the working alliance, emotional expression, depression, and the theory and practice of emotion-focused therapy.

Rhonda N. Goldman, PhD, is an associate professor at the Illinois School of Professional Psychology at Argosy University in Chicago and a staff therapist at the Family Institute at Northwestern University in Evanston, Illinois. She became interested in process-experiential therapy in graduate school, where she worked with her mentor, Leslie S. Greenberg. Process-experiential therapy combined her various interests in existential philosophy, client-centered therapy, Zen Buddhism, and gestalt therapy. Currently, she practices, conducts research, and writes about emotion-focused therapy, including empathy, vulnerability, depression, and case formulation. She is interested in the applicability of the process-experiential approach for work with a variety of populations.

Leslie S. Greenberg, PhD, is a professor of psychology at York University in Toronto, Ontario, Canada. After completing a master's degree in engineering in 1970, he changed paths and trained in client-centered therapy with Laura Rice. He trained for 3 years at the Gestalt Institute of Toronto. He graduated in 1975 and then began a 15-year odyssey to integrate gestalt and client-centered therapy and to embed them in emotion theory. After training in more directive systemic approaches, he integrated these approaches into the development of an emotionally focused approach to couples. The style of integrating, leading, and following that is at the heart of process-experiential therapy grew from these influences. Dr. Greenberg has written extensively on the theory and practice of emotion-focused therapy with couples and individuals.